Religion in a
Changing World

Recent Titles in
Religion in the Age of Transformation

Religion in a Changing World

Comparative Studies in Sociology

Edited by
Madeleine Cousineau

Religion in the Age of Transformation
Anson Shupe, Series Adviser

Westport, Connecticut
London

Library of Congress Cataloging-in-Publication Data

Religion in a changing world : comparative studies in sociology /
   edited by Madeleine Cousineau.
      p.   cm.—(Religion in the age of transformation, ISSN
   1087–2388)
      Includes bibliographical references and index.
      ISBN 0–275–96078–1 (alk. paper).—ISBN 0–275–96079–X (pbk. :
   alk. paper)
      1. Religion and sociology.   I. Cousineau, Madeleine.   II. Series.
   BL60.R4216   1998
   306.6—dc21   98–15658

British Library Cataloguing in Publication Data is available.

Library of Congress Catalog Card Number: 98–15658
ISBN: 0–275–96078–1
         0–275–96079–X (pbk.)
ISSN: 1087–2388

First published in 1998

Praeger Publishers, 88 Post Road West, Westport, CT 06881
An imprint of Greenwood Publishing Group, Inc.

Printed in the United States of America

The paper used in this book complies with the
Permanent Paper Standard issued by the National
Information Standards Organization (Z39.48–1984).

10 9 8 7 6 5 4 3 2 1

3-4-99

Copyright Acknowledgments

The editor and the publisher gratefully acknowledge permission to use the following materials:

To Sister Marie Augusta Neal, S.N.D. de Namur,
Past President of the Association for the Sociology of Religion
and of the Society for the Scientific Study of Religion,

who inspired me not only with a love of sociology
but also with her example of how to teach it,

this book is gratefully dedicated.

Contents

Contents   ix

Acknowledgments

I would like to begin by expressing my deepest gratitude to the twenty-seven colleagues who responded to the invitation to contribute their efforts to this book and who cooperated with my demands for revisions, as well as all the cuts needed to fit twenty-three chapters into one volume. It has been a pleasure to work with you.

Special thanks go to Anson Shupe, our series adviser, and to James T. Sabin, Director, Academic Research and Development, of the Greenwood Publishing Group, for believing in this project and giving me encouragement to carry it out. I would also like to thank Helen Rose Ebaugh for her encouragement and for helpful comments on the content.

Thanks are also due to the people who taught me the sociology of religion and inspired me as a teacher and scholar: Sister Marie Augusta Neal, Paule Verdet, Sally Cassidy, and the late T. Scott Miyakawa. Scott was especially helpful in keeping me aware of the importance of integrating non-Western perspectives into the study of religion. I am also grateful to my colleagues in the Association for the Sociology of Religion, the Society for the Scientific Study of Religion, and the Religion Section of the American Sociological Association, whose ideas and research have deepened my understanding of our subfield and whose friendship has enriched my life.

Finally, my students at the University of Massachusetts Boston and at Mount Ida College by their enthusiasm for this field of study provided me with the motive for organizing this book. I am especially grateful to the international students who helped to contribute a global perspective to our discussions.

Introduction

Madeleine Cousineau

The impact of religion on society has become impossible to disregard. In recent years the mass media have been carrying accounts of the variety of ways in which a supposedly secularized world keeps interacting with religion. These situations have included religiously inspired revolutions in Latin America and the Middle East; the growing influence of the New Christian Right in the United States; religious conflicts in Ireland, Israel, and Islamic nations; the emergence of religious pluralism in post-Soviet Russia; and the links of religious groups to a variety of social issues, including ecology, feminism, and economic justice.

The transnational nature of many of these developments calls our attention not only to the globalization of societies but also to the globalization of religion itself. We cannot understand contemporary societies without looking at their interrelatedness. Neither can we understand the religions existing today without examining their place in the world system. Although the importance of studying religion and society comparatively was emphasized by early social theorists, such as Emile Durkheim and Max Weber, this type of study became even more important in the last few decades of the twentieth century. Rapid transportation and instant communication have effectively shrunk the world. While this "smaller" world may not have the intimacy of a global village, the present context in which people live is definitely a global metropolis, with all of the hazards and advantages that this term implies. For example, not only are formerly isolated indigenous and peasant societies being invaded and often destroyed by the forces of the world market, but when people in some of these societies become organized and fight back, their middle-class supporters send appeals for solidarity and action by fax and computer networks all over the world.[1]

Religion itself has been described as an agent of globalization (Beyer 1994; Robertson 1987, 1992). Throughout human history, missionaries, conquerors, and other migrants helped to diffuse both their own social and cultural practices and those which they discovered in the places to which they traveled. At the same time, religion was shaped by the societies to which it was carried, as is evident in some of the chapters in this book. Today with communication among societies all over the world occurring at a faster pace than ever before, the mutual influence of religion and the global order is even more evident. The chapters in this volume show a variety of cases in which religion interacts with this changing world, both on a large scale and in the behavior of individuals.

This book is intended primarily for use in courses in the sociology of religion, although the substantive topics covered also make it a valuable resource for scholars, and the clarity of language makes it accessible to general readers as well. The range and arrangement of chapters have been determined by pedagogical goals. The book is divided into the three main categories of individual religion, religious organization, and the relationship of religion to larger social forces. This follows an approach sometimes taken by textbooks, for which this volume may provide supplementary readings. The chapters themselves are related to the range of topics usually covered in an undergraduate or graduate course in the sociology of religion: religious identity, community, conversion, congregational structures, religious roles, church and sect, the religious division of labor, race, ethnicity, gender, religious pluralism, secularization, religion and politics, religion and social issues, and new religious movements.

There is also an attempt to cover as wide a range as possible in terms of religious traditions and geographic settings, although this attempt has been subordinated to the priority of covering the previously mentioned list of topics. The reader may notice a predominance of articles based on research conducted in North America. Since the book is being published in the United States, it is assumed that the majority of readers will be from this country and Canada. Our aim is to provide material from settings with which the readers will likely be familiar, then to bring in comparative cases that will enable them to expand their knowledge by learning about other societies.

Students taking a course in the sociology of religion often expect to learn about a variety of different traditions. The inclusion of a number of religions represents an attempt to satisfy this interest. Thus the chapters contain information related to Christianity (mainline Protestants, evangelicals, pentecostals, Roman Catholics, and Eastern Orthodox), Judaism, Islam, Hinduism, traditional Chinese religion, Yoruba religion, Wicca, a UFO religion, and other new religious movements.

Some of the chapters are clearly transnational in their analysis, while others focus on a single country. Some of the writers examine the relationship of religion to large-scale social processes, while others look at the meaning of religion to individuals. Nevertheless, all of the cases presented are explicitly or implicitly related to religion as it comes to terms with social realities that are being played out at the dawn of the new millennium and that are related to a process of transformation influenced by forces that are both local and international. This is the environment in which people are living their daily lives. It is the context in which many are seeking religious experiences—by means of beliefs, organizational structures, everyday practices, and rituals—that they hope will help them to make sense of this ever-changing world.

NOTE

1. For example, the Institute for Global Communication, based in San Francisco, is part of an international association of computer networks that is accessible via the Internet and that provides both e-mail and electronic bulletin boards for individuals and nongovernmental organizations (NGOs) promoting social justice, democracy, ecological concerns, and the rights of women, indigenous peoples, rubber tappers, organized labor, peasant farmers, and other groups that may find themselves at a disadvantage in the world system. Some of these NGOs have ties to churches and other religiously affiliated organizations.

REFERENCES

Beyer, Peter. 1994. *Religion and Globalization.* Newbury Park, CA: Sage Publications.
Robertson, Roland. 1987. "Globalization and Societal Modernization: A Note on Japan and Japanese Religion." *Sociological Analysis* 47 (Supplement):35–42.
———. 1992. *Globalization: Social Theory and Global Culture.* London: Sage Publications.

Religion in a Changing World

PART I

INDIVIDUAL RELIGION, CHOICE, AND IDENTITY

Religion is a system of meanings. It is a way that people have of making sense of their lives, although it is not the only way. Many people have personal philosophies that are not linked to religion. Those who do choose to be religious have a set of values that they connect to something beyond the here and now. These values may shape the great and small decisions that they make. For example, prayer may be a means of discerning appropriate courses of action in various situations and a way of relieving anxiety during times of personal difficulties, such as when one faces the problem of family violence. Religious customs are used to mark the important events of a person's life—the birth of a child, the death of a loved one, marriage, and rituals to celebrate entry into adulthood, such as bar mitzvah or confirmation.

The mention of *choice* in religion suggests an orientation that is relatively new, historically speaking. Ancient peoples did not think of religion as a choice. Their spiritual beliefs were totally integrated into their cultures, into their ideas about nature. People did not usually question the absolute truth of those beliefs. In later times, people who did question prevailing religious beliefs suffered serious persecution and even death. This was the fate not only of Christians in ancient Rome. In the Middle Ages, when Christians were themselves in control of the political system, they persecuted those who held on to pre-Christian beliefs, including both Jews and pagans, and labeled those who came up with newer ideas as "heretics." It is interesting to note that the word "heretic" comes from the Greek *hairēaikos*, which means "able to choose." It is only in modern societies that people have been able to take for granted that there is a choice, that one may switch between different denominations, seek a religion that affirms one's cultural or racial identity, or renew the commitment to one's original belief system.

Choices exist because modern societies are pluralistic, that is, they offer a variety of possibilities, including religious possibilities. This is a consequence of secularization. Although people often think of secularization as the end of religion, that is not really the case. Secularization has come to mean that modern societies are no longer dominated by any *particular* belief system. A secular society has no official state religion that is financially supported by the government and that gives legitimacy to government leaders and their policies. Other social institutions, such as education, health care, and the mass media, are also outside the control of religion. The absence of a dominant belief system also frees up the institution of religion itself, since a variety of religions are now able to develop. This gives greater freedom both to nonreligious people and to believers. Since there is no one religion influencing the state, people are not likely to be put to death for their choices, or "heresies."

The range of religious options characteristic of modern societies allows people to choose the religion that makes the most sense to them in relation to their life experiences or to choose no religion at all. A person's choice of religion may be an important aspect of that person's identity, because religion has the capacity to define who he or she is. It provides a person with a sense of belonging in relation both to the relatively small unit of a congregation and to the larger unit of a religion that may be located in many different parts of the world. Religious identity may also tie in with ethnic or cultural identity and with the history of a people.

The chapters in Part I explore various dimensions of individual religion, choice, and identity. The first chapter, by N. J. Demerath and Yonghe Yang, discusses the meaning of denominational switching among Protestant churches in the United States. This is followed by two chapters that examine people's attempts to recapture an ancestral religion as part of their cultural identity, M. Herbert Danzger's study of nonreligious Jews who make the choice to become religious, even orthodox, and Mary Curry's study of African Americans who seek out the pre-Christian religion of the Yoruba people. Helen Ralston describes the role of religion in the identity of South Asian women who immigrate to other countries. The religious views of middle-class Americans are described by Dean Hoge, Benton Johnson, and Donald Luidens in their chapter on Presbyterian baby boomers and by Debra Kaufman in her chapter about young Jewish women and men. The final contribution in this section, by Nancy Nason-Clark, examines the role of religion in helping evangelical Christian women to deal with domestic violence.

The religiosity of individuals, their personal choices, and their ways of dealing with life's difficulties are sociologically important. For it is in the lives of individual persons that the link is made between religion and social structure. Religion provides the beliefs on which people act, and their actions help to shape the groups, communities, and societies in which they live.

1

Switching in American Religion: Denominations, Markets, and Paradigms?

N. J. Demerath III and Yonghe Yang

Only a few decades ago, one's religious affiliation was considered as unchanging as one's gender, race, or ethnic group. Once a Protestant, Catholic, or Jew, always a Protestant, Catholic, or Jew. Even within Protestantism itself, once a Baptist, Presbyterian, or Adventist, always a Baptist, Presbyterian, or Adventist. Beginning in the 1960s, however, these perceptions began to change. Now some people see switching religions as almost on the same level as switching any other consumer product. In fact, sociologists often speak of a religious "marketplace."

But such changes are easily exaggerated. Recent headlines and media stories sometimes give the impression that religious switchers are now a majority of the population and that as a result the country has turned sharply to the religious right. Because religion is in keen demand among potential consumers in an increasingly active marketplace, this is seen as one more disconfirmation of the hypothesis of "secularization." Far from becoming secular or nonreligious, the country is undergoing "sacralization" and becoming more religious. In fact, there is a good deal of loose interpretation in all of this. Let us take a look at recent social scientific evidence on the subject to see what is really going on and why.

FACT AND FICTION ON CHANGING RELIGION

To begin, it is by no means clear that religious switching is actually increasing. It is true that Wade Clark Roof and William McKinney (1987) have heralded a new age of "religious voluntarism"—by which they mean increasing individual religious choices without the old constraints of denominational loyalties and customs, and which may include staying in one's parents' religion, changing to another religion, or abandoning religion altogether. However, Paul Sullins (1993) has recently argued that there has been a statistically significant *decline* in religious switching over time. But then C. Kirk Hadaway and Penny Marler (1993) show that matters are a little more complicated. They find that switching *within* large denominational families has increased, but not switching *between* such denominational clusters. For example, there may be a good deal of switching among the "liberal" or more secularized denominations, such as the Presbyterians and the Congregationalists, and a good deal of switching among "conservative" or more religiously traditional denominations, such as Southern Baptists and Jehovah's Witnesses. However, there is much less switching between Presbyterians and Jehovah's Witnesses or between Southern Baptists and Congregationalists.

As for the proportion of religious adherents who report switches in their religious preference, affiliation, or membership—all slightly different—this too has been variously estimated. No study of the population at large reports an actual majority of switchers. Some 40 percent have changed at least their religious preferences, if not their formal memberships, over time. However, this would drop to less than 30 percent if we looked only at major switches in denominational families, such as liberal, conservative, and moderate (such as Methodist or Lutheran) Protestants. It would drop even further if one counted only switches between Protestantism, Catholicism, and Judaism.

Put another way, almost two thirds of Americans remain loyal to the religions of their youth. However, the retention rates vary among religious groups, from a low of 55 percent among Presbyterians to some 80 percent among Southern Baptists and a high of 85 percent among Mormons (Yang 1996). Moderate Protestant denominations like the Methodists and Lutherans average some 70 percent retentions, while Catholics and Jews are each slightly higher—in large part because their social communities are more tightly bonded and have stricter norms against intermarriage.

To what extent is the overall picture of American religion changing as a result of this switching process? Again, not nearly as much as some headlines would suggest. According to some newspaper and television stories, liberal churches are plummeting downward while conservative churches are surging upward, largely because liberal church adherents are leaving in droves for conservative alternatives. While there is some truth to the liberal decline (cf. Demerath 1997), there is also a good deal of inaccuracy concerning the reasons why.

In general, liberal denominations have indeed lost members as conservatives have gained. But note some important qualifications. First, not all liberal churches are declining, just as by no means every conservative church is growing. Thus, few churches have grown more spectacularly than the nondenominational (and sometimes almost nonreligious) "mega-churches" that emphasize a sense of community and a wide range of social, athletic, and therapeutic activities rather than conventional Christian doctrine and ritual. The expanding numbers of the very liberal Unitarian-Universalists would make almost any conservative denomination proud. And even within many of the liberal denominations that are losing members overall, about a third of the congregations are growing, about a third are experiencing losses, and about a third are staying the same.

Meanwhile, many conservative churches are newer and smaller, and they have an entrepreneurial quality that makes their numbers change very quickly and gives them higher turnover rates. Not only do members come and go within these new churches, but the churches themselves sometimes disappear, to be replaced by new ones. Moreover, those conservative congregations that endure often undergo some of the same transitions that more liberal churches have already experienced—that is, a tendency to soften (or to secularize) the demands they make on their members. Nor are the people who leave the liberal churches the same people who account for the growth of the conservative churches by joining there. Most switchers out of liberal religion move into the ranks of the nonreligious—though this is temporary for at least half of them, who ultimately find their way back to some form of religious affiliation. In fact, a higher proportion of conservative dropouts find their way to liberal churches than vice versa.

A major reason for conservative church growth is not their ability to pick off liberal strays, but rather their greater success in retaining their own members from one generation to the next through the special attention they give to Sunday school, youth groups, and recreational activities for children and teenagers. Whereas liberal congregations sometimes seem havens for the elderly, conservative congregations have remained young by keeping their children and the children of their children.

SWITCHING MOTIVES

Now that we have learned something about the amount of switching, let us turn to the reasons for it and ask why people switch in the first place. Before we introduce some data, it is important to note that there is a larger issue at stake in the results. This involves two conflicting interpretations of religion as a marketable commodity. In his classic work *The Sacred Canopy*, Peter Berger (1967) discussed the way in which old religious boundaries are losing their urgency, leaving individuals increasingly free to choose new religious affiliations based often on nonreligious criteria. For Berger, such religious switching reflects a weakening of older religious communities and commitments and the rise of a new marketplace in which religions compete along increasingly secular lines—for example, the convenience of the location, the quality of the Monday-through-Friday day care centers, or the nature and variety of the adult recreational activities provided.

But recently another interpretation of marketed religion has emerged among several scholars who reject any secularization premise and insist that the choice of a religion is a "rational choice" that marks a resurgent quest for religion's most sacred qualities (cf. Finke and Stark 1992; Warner 1993; Iannaccone 1991, 1995; and for a critical response, Demerath 1995). From this perspective, switching is more likely to mark a religious gain than a loss—more sacralization than secularization—as individuals are involved in an active search for an affiliation that is religiously optimal.

At this point, it is useful to examine some evidence. As it happens, a study of a national sample of Americans actually asked people why they had changed religions. This was part of a special module on religion within the General Social Survey of the National Opinion Research Center at the University of Chicago. If the primary motives are tied to ordinary life course events like moving from one community to another or marrying into a different faith, this would seem to support

Berger's older notion of weakened religious bonds and choices prompted by increasingly secular factors. On the other hand, if the switching motivations are more religious in character, such as matters of doctrine or clergy preference, this would support the newer interpretation.

The basic findings are easily summarized. Of the 1,481 respondents in this sample, 536 or 36 percent report that they have had at least one other religious preference besides their present one. The inclusion of Catholics, who do not change religions as often as Protestants, no doubt accounts for a lower rate here than the 40 percent plus that is cited in some studies of Protestants alone. Overall, however, almost two-thirds of the sample have remained loyal to their original religious preference; and since not all of the one-third who have changed preferences may have actually changed formal memberships, this indicates a level of shopping behavior that is lower than the image of a highly dynamic religious market might predict.

Among those who have switched, one-third switched only once, more than a quarter switched twice, and nearly 10 percent switched three times or more. Approximately half switched before they were 22 years old, 82 percent of them did so before they were 30, and only some 10 percent of the switchers are over the age of 35 (cf. Yang 1996). Clearly, switching is more prevalent among young people.

Table 1.1
Switching Motives
Reasons were cited either singly or jointly for changing religious preferences since youth.

Secular Motives:	
Marriage	23%
Friends	16%
Family (excluding spouse)	14%
Location	11%
Just for a change	1%
Religious Motives:	
Dissatisfaction with previous theology	19%
Dissatisfaction with previous clergy	5%
Positive attraction of new beliefs	7%
Other positive aspects of new religion	3%

N = 412 total reasons cited by 536 switchers, with 185, or 35%, not answering the question.

Source: Data from 1988 Special Religious Module, General Social Survey, National Opinion Research Center, University of Chicago.

Turning to motives and the data in Table 1.1, respondents were asked to select from a list of possible motives the one or two reasons for their switch. First, it is worth noting that some 35 percent did not answer the question and cited no reason at all for switching. As for the reasons that were checked or provided (either alone or in tandem), 65 percent involved basically secular considerations involving marriage, friends, family, or location in that order, but also including 1 percent who were just plain looking for a change.

By contrast, 34 percent cited religious motives of one sort or another. For a combined 24 percent (19 percent + 5 percent), the religious motive involved dissatisfaction with their previous preference. This could mean dissatisfaction with too much religion or too little. In fact, it is more likely to involve too much, because we know that most switchers leave mainline denominations, and most take up at least temporary residence in the "no religious preference" category. Note that only a combined 10 percent (7 percent + 3 percent) cited a positive attraction of the beliefs or other religious characteristics of their new affiliation. But since some of these were coupled with nonreligious factors with no indication of priority, there may be even fewer instances in which a religious attraction is the decisive factor.

Of course, this same caution applies in reverse to the more secular motives, since the percentages reflect motives, not individuals, and some respondents cited both a secular and a religious motive jointly. On the other hand, while the table sets aside those who gave "No Answer" to the question, if one added these respondents to those who switched without citing a clear religious reason, the proportion of religious switchers would drop even further.

As with almost any data set, there is something here for both of the contending images of switching in the religious marketplace. There is no question that there are people who switched their religious affiliations for clearly religious reasons, ranging from deep-seated convictions about their beliefs to problems with the minister, priest, or rabbi. What is more striking, however, is the considerable majority of the switchers who report changing their religious preferences for nonreligious and nonideological reasons. For these people, switching is largely determined by life circumstances involving marriage, friends, location, family matters, and possibly social and geographical mobility.

In sum, there is little indication that switching is usually due to a religiously sensitive shopper's changing assessment of alternative religious products. Switching usually occurs in early stages of one's adult life as a response to the kind of nonreligious contingencies that affect young people, including marriage and career choice. These younger adults are the least religious group and the least likely to invoke strong religious criteria in the denominational marketplace.

In fact, these conclusions are supported by other studies that infer motives from characteristics that are statistically correlated with switching (cf. Newport 1979; Hadaway 1980; Van Rompaey and Suchman 1991; Suchman 1992; Sherkat 1991; and somewhat paradoxically, Sherkat and Wilson 1995). In addition to the youth factor, there are indications that switching is associated with social mobility and related geographical mobility. Except among some high-status groups such as Jews, liberal Protestants, and "nones," switchers tend to have higher occupational prestige than stayers. This supports the traditional explanations that denominational switching is related to upward status mobility. And while it is true that "switchers" tend to be slightly more religiously active overall than "stayers," the comparison is a bit misleading. After all, the switchers have at least taken some action regarding their religion, while the stayers include many whose faith and practice may have lapsed even if their memberships have not.

CONCLUSION

This chapter began with some questions concerning a recent tendency to portray American religion as tilting sharply to the right, partly as a result of an unparalleled rise in denominational switching, which some interpret as the result of a restored religious consciousness in a religious marketplace that offers exciting proof that the secularization hypothesis is false.

As so often happens in the world of social science, good stories are vulnerable to good information. There is some truth in all of the above, but there are also some badly misleading inaccuracies. Yes, liberal denominations are losing members overall while conservatives are gaining, but there are ebbs and flows within each, and the trends are not just a matter of new religious questing or of switching itself. Yes, switching does occur, but not at much higher rates than before and not necessarily in the direction suggested by the tilting thesis. Overall, switching motives seem to be tied more to secular contingencies than to deeply sacred choices, although both may be found not only in the population at large but also in many of the same individuals.

Meanwhile, several concluding comments on motives are in order. Today it is often assumed that conservative religious organizations are more "truly religious" than liberal churches. While there may be some truth to this as religion is conventionally regarded, there are also some important reasons to pause before passing an ultimate judgment. Just as the sacred is far from banished from liberal sanctums, the secular is no stranger to conservative settings. The "old-time religion" of yesterday rarely survives unchanged today, as even the most conservative pentecostal or fundamentalist groups must continually adapt to changing circumstances and constituencies. James Hunter's (1987) study of evangelicals shows how every generation is marked by an erosion of older practices and the development of new ones. Nancy Ammerman (1991) chronicles the conflict that can result from these changes in her gripping analysis of political in-fighting among the Southern Baptists. On the other hand, it is also possible for groups that have slid toward the secular to discover a new source of the sacred, as Stephen Warner (1988) points out in his study of a California Presbyterian church that has gone charismatic.

Even within the actual services of the most intense groups, there is some question whether religion is an end in itself or a means to the kind of deep bonding and emotional gratification that is also discernible at some political rallies, rock concerts, sporting events, and neighborhood gatherings. Many of the most dynamic conservative churches are extraordinarily adept in providing social services ranging from day care and recreational activities to twelve-step programs and relief assistance. At one level, the very distinction between religious ends and religious means is forced and contrived. But like the larger distinction between sacred and secular, it alerts us to some important aspects and interactions within the religious experience that are sometimes overlooked.

Finally, what about the secularization hypothesis itself? Actually it makes a difference whether the term is defined in terms of *product* or *process*. If secularization as product envisions a completely secular society marked by religious extinction, there is no question that the hypothesis is false. On the other hand, if secularization as process means only the tendency for every sacred commitment to undergo change, demystification, and a loss of saliency over time, there is no question that the hypothesis is true. But as so often happens, the two warring concepts here are more complementary than contradictory. Secularization and sacralization are two key processes in human history generally. Each responds to each other in a never-ending oscillation. The dynamic between them applies not only to religion but also to that wider range of sacred phenomena that make social life meaningful in its broadest sense.

REFERENCES

Ammerman, Nancy T. 1991. *Baptist Battles*. New Brunswick, NJ: Rutgers University Press.

Berger, Peter L. 1967. *The Sacred Canopy*. Garden City, NY: Doubleday Anchor.

Demerath, N. J. III. 1995. "Rational Paradigms, A-Rational Religion, and the Debate over Secularization." *Journal for the Scientific Study of Religion* 34:105–112.

———. 1997. "Snatching Defeat from Victory in the Decline of Liberal Protestantism: Culture versus Structure in Institutional Analysis." In N. J. Demerath, Peter D. Hall, Terry N. Schmitt, and Rhys H. Williams (eds.), *Sacred Companies: Organizational Aspects of Religion and Religious Aspects of Organizations*. New York: Oxford University Press.

Finke, Roger, and Rodney Stark. 1992. *The Churching of America, 1776–1990*. New Brunswick, NJ: Rutgers University Press.

Hadaway, C. Kirk. 1980. "Denominational Switching and Religiosity." *Review of Religious Research* 21 (Supplement):451–461.

Hadaway, C. Kirk, and Penny Long Marler. 1993. "All in the Family: Religious Mobility in America." *Review of Religious Research* 35:97–116.

Hunter, James D. 1987. *Evangelicalism: The Coming Generation*. Chicago: University of Chicago Press.

Iannaccone, Laurence R. 1991. "The Consequences of Religious Market Structure." *Rationality and Society* 33:156–177.

———. 1995. "Voodoo Economics? Reviewing the Rational Choice Approach to Religion." *Journal for the Scientific Study of Religion* 34:76–89.

Newport, Frank. 1979. "The Religious Switcher in the United States." *American Sociological Review* 44:528–552.

Roof, Wade Clark, and William McKinney. 1987. *American Mainline Religion*. New Brunswick, NJ: Rutgers University Press.

Sherkat, Darren E. 1991. "Leaving the Faith: Testing Theories of Religious Switching Using Survival Models." *Social Science Research* 20:171–187.

Sherkat, Darren E., and John Wilson. 1995. "Preferences, Constraints, and Choices in Religious Markets: An Examination of Religious Switching and Apostasy." *Social Forces* 73:993–1026.

Suchman, Mark C. 1992. "Analyzing the Determinants of Everyday Conversion." *Sociological Analysis* 53:15–33.

Sullins, D. Paul. 1993. "Switching Close to Home: Volatility or Coherence in Protestant
    Affiliation Patterns?" *Social Forces* 72:399–419.
Van Rompaey, Stephen E., and Mark C. Suchman. 1991. "Religion, Life-Cycle, and History:
    An Exploratory Temporal Analysis of Interfaith Conversion." Unpublished paper,
    Morrison Institute for Population and Resource Studies, Stanford University, Stanford,
    CA.
Warner, R. Stephen. 1988. *New Wine in Old Wineskins*. Berkeley: University of California
    Press.
————. 1993. "Work in Progress toward a New Paradigm for the Sociological Study of
    Religion in the United States." *American Journal of Sociology* 98:1044–1093.
Yang, Yonghe. 1996. *The Structure and Dynamics of Ideological Pluralism in American
    Religion*. Unpublished Ph.D. dissertation, Department of Sociology, University of
    Massachusetts, Amherst, MA.

2

The "Return" to Traditional Judaism in the United States, Russia, and Israel: The Impact of Minority and Majority Status on Religious Conversion Processes

M. Herbert Danzger

The process of religious conversion has been studied by many researchers (see, for example, Kilbourne and Richardson 1989; Lofland 1977; Lofland and Stark 1965; Snow and Machalek 1984). However, none has considered whether there is any difference between the process of choosing a religion that is part of the mainstream of one's society and choosing a minority religion. This chapter will show how these differ. It examines the impact of majority/minority status on the conversion process, focusing on Jews who choose the Orthodox tradition of their religion and who make that choice in three different countries. In two of these countries, the former Soviet Union and the United States, Judaism has a minority status. In the third, Israel, it is the majority religion.

Jewish identity involves components that are ethnic and religious. Ethnic Jews who are not religious are called "secular Jews." Religious Jews are grouped in three main denominations: Orthodox, Conservative, and Reform. In the United States, roughly 60 percent of Jews are not affiliated with any synagogue. Among those who are affiliated, about 35 percent are Reform, 41 percent Conservative, and 20 percent Orthodox (Kosmin et al. 1991). Reform Judaism is the least traditional of the three, Orthodox Judaism is the most traditional, and Conservative Judaism falls between the other two. This denominational structure is unique to the United States. In Israel, Reform and Conservative Jews constitute only a tiny portion of the Jewish population. The Dati (roughly equivalent to the U.S. Orthodox) constitute about 38 percent of the population. About 20 percent identifies as "secular." The rest consider themselves "somewhat observant" (*The Jewish Week*, December 5, 1997). In the former Soviet Union, Orthodox Jews constitute a small percentage of the Jewish population, and Reform and Conservative Jews are even fewer in number. The rest are secular. (There are no hard data.)

"Conversion" to Orthodox Judaism may be made from the Conservative or Reform traditions or from being a secular Jew. Conversion is often referred to as "return," since Orthodoxy represents the most traditional option.

METHOD

We provide here a threefold comparison. We compare Jews raised in secular or non-Orthodox homes who returned to Orthodox Judaism in the United States, in the former Soviet Union (FSU), and in Israel. To be secular or non-Orthodox is defined as not observing the rules of *kashrut* or Sabbath and to be Orthodox is defined as observing these rules in the manner required by Jewish religious law. Briefly, *kashrut* means that one may eat only kosher food and that this food is prepared in such a manner that dairy and meat, and even the pots in which they are prepared and the dishes on which they are served, are not mixed. Sabbath observance means that on the seventh day of each week one may not do any work, ride in a car, answer a phone, turn on or off a light, or cook anything.

In this chapter we compare the three groups in terms of the processes, stages, and steps by which they became Orthodox Jews. The people studied here are all Jews by birth. Thus their return to Orthodoxy is an intensification of identification with religion. While this process may produce strains on existing relations, it does not usually produce a sense of betrayal of relatives and friends, as might happen with a conversion to a totally different religion.

The data on which we draw are from two sets of in-depth interviews: (1) a study of Israeli and American Jewish returnees (Danzger 1989) and (2) a study presently underway of Soviet émigré returnees to traditional Judaism in the United States and Israel.

Among the American and Israeli returnees 204 interviews were conducted, forty-one with women. Of the 204 interviewees, fifty-four were rabbis, administrators, or religious outreach workers. Almost half of these fifty-four were also returnees who had been reared in a non-Orthodox home.

The study of Soviet émigrés included three research trips to Israel as well as a trip to three cities in the former Soviet Union: Kiev, Moscow, and St. Petersburg. For the second study 141 interviews have been conducted so far, including thirty-nine with women. Sixty-two of the 141 interviewed were administrators, rabbis, or teachers in outreach programs. Of these more than half were returnees.

THE DATA

Before introducing the interview material it may be helpful to offer a few observations on the place of Jews in the Soviet Union. During the period of the Tsars, Jews in Russia often suffered from pogroms,[1] blood libels,[2] and outright government discrimination. Later, under the Communist regime, Jews were defined as a nationality. A region, Birobidjan, was designated as their homeland, but in fact it was not their homeland. Nonetheless, their identity passes were stamped with the letter "J," for Jew. Given the history of hostility to Jews in the former Soviet republics, this "J" suggested official stigmatization and hostility. It undermined Jewish identity as a Soviet subgroup, and many Jews considered themselves tied to a larger Jewish nation. When Golda Meir (later prime minister of Israel) visited Moscow as Israel's first ambassador in 1948, she was mobbed by Soviet Jews. As a consequence, the U.S.S.R. forbade the dissemination and the teaching of Zionism as fostering dual loyalties. In spite of this, forty-one years later, when an Israeli basketball team played in Russia, the fans were wildly enthusiastic Jews (*New York Times*, October 14, 1989). One should also note that emigration to Israel was considered traitorous. Those who attempted to emigrate were jailed. Under these circumstances, it comes as no surprise that Jewishness in the Soviet Union came to be seen as ethnic national identity.

Group 1: Émigrés from the Former Soviet Union

The Soviet émigrés described below, although interviewed in Israel, began their conversion in the former Soviet Union. It becomes clear that they experienced a two-step process of conversion, identifying first with the Jewish people and only later with the religion of Judaism. Their conversion process also was typically a long one rather than a sudden change.

Of the fourteen Soviet émigrés who began their return to tradition in the former Soviet Union, not one experienced a sudden conversion. None of the men failed to go through an ethnic identity period before their religious return, but this process was less clear for the women, for reasons to be explained below. The relationship of ethnic identity to conversion is evident in the experiences of three specific people, who will be called Eli, Moshe, and Nora.

Eli first became intensely aware of ethnic identity at age twelve, during the Six Day War of 1967. His father had a shortwave radio on which they both listened to the Voice of America. His father, who had lived in Lithuania, had attempted to emigrate to Israel in 1939. But the conquest of the Baltic states by the Nazis forced his father instead to flee to the interior of Russia. Although his father was completely secular and hid his national identity, the Six Day War brought this interest to the foreground and with it a strong perception by Eli of his own Jewish identity. By the time he was seventeen he had taught himself enough Hebrew that he was able to listen to Kol Israel—the Voice of Israel—on the shortwave radio.

During his studies toward a doctorate in sciences, Eli began to acquire and read books on Judaism. At age twenty-three he married a young Jewish scientist with a mild interest in Zionism and Israel. His interest in things Jewish continued to intensify. In 1981 he applied for a visa to Israel and was refused. He and his wife had both anticipated this development as she was engaged in sensitive military work. They expected that after a few years, when her knowledge was outdated, she would be permitted to leave for Israel. In the meantime, as a means of asserting their Jewish identity they began to practice Judaism.

Both Eli and his wife were dismissed from their jobs. She found another job as a teacher. He began attending a yeshiva (a seminary offering studies in sacred Jewish texts and particularly in the Talmud). Within a short time, however, the yeshiva was informed of Eli's application for a visa to Israel, and he was dismissed from the school as well. He continued studying on his own, becoming in the process not only an Orthodox Jew but also a rabbi and teacher of others.

Moshe recounts a similar story. He too was brought up in a home devoid of religious practice. He was aware, through his parents' whispered accounts, that he was Jewish. On Passover his parents would eat matzo, the unleavened bread reminiscent of the exodus of Jews from Egypt. But it was simply taken with tea and had no more significance than a cracker. No rituals were observed. The Six Day War was something he recalled as important but not as a defining experience. For Moshe the defining moment came when his application to university was rejected. He appealed his rejection and on that occasion met several other rejected applicants. He believed that they were all Jewish and that they had been rejected for that reason. This distanced him from Russians, and he began to seek his own identity as a Jew.

After his appeal was rejected, Moshe sought out a synagogue. "I wasn't looking for a religious connection. I was looking for some tie to my people," he said. However, on his arrival at the synagogue, he found only a Swedish tourist, with whom he discussed ballet. After this unsatisfying experience Moshe went back to his scientific studies. He continued his quest for his Jewish identity. He sought works on Zionism, but he could not find any. Such work was banned as subversive. Finally, he came across a Bible. He considered it a primary source on the history of his people rather than a religious work.

His search led to his meeting Eli, who was already giving underground classes. At first Moshe was pleased to be exposed to other Jews discussing their Jewishness. He had no interest in religion or in religious observances. But slowly, under the influence of Eli and the group of students attending these underground classes, he began to see the essence of Jewish identity in Judaism rather than in national identity. Several other men had similar stories.

A woman's account introduces some variations. Nora grew up in a middle class family. Her father was a doctor who had been decorated for his heroism and contributions to medical science. She had been raised to be proud of her Jewishness, which was always defined in national and cultural terms. As a child she had been small for her age, but she had always been ready to take on other children who insulted Jews, no matter how big they were.

Following the Six Day War, Nora's father, who had by then retired, applied for a visa to Israel. This request was refused, and the family lost many of the privileges they had formerly enjoyed. In 1973 when the Soviet Union under pressure from the United States agreed to let some Jews out, her father left for Israel, and Nora decided to visit the United States. Asked by Jewish groups to lecture on the plight of Soviet Jews, she became involved in a speaking tour. While she was on tour, her father died. She immediately arranged to go to Israel for his funeral. When booking the flight she was asked whether she wanted a kosher dinner. Once the question was raised she began to consider it carefully and to consider what it meant to be Jewish. She decided to eat the kosher meal. She considers that choice her decisive moment. Although she did not become fully Orthodox, she nonetheless came to define her Jewishness in religious terms. Nora's story is different from that of other traditional women interviewed, who indicated that, in returning to traditional Judaism, they followed their husbands' lead.

Eli and his wife were interviewed separately. Both their accounts made clear that it was his initiative that propelled them into further involvement, first into Jewish ethnicity and later into religion. When I asked him how his wife felt about his increasing involvement in Jewish activities, which created risks for both of them, he answered that in Russia husbands tend to lead.

Almost all the other cases of return to tradition in the Soviet Union follow this pattern of starting with ethnic identification and later moving to religious identification. I have found only two partial exceptions to this two-step process, both of which involved some degree of ethnic identification. One of these was a that of a young woman drawn to the Russian Orthodox Church who turned to Jewish groups at the point where she was almost considering conversion. Another involved an old man who attributed his return to a moment when, working as a pilot on a river boat, he almost drowned.

The two-step pattern of involvement, first ethnic identity and afterward religious identity, is the same for American returnees.

Group 2: American Jews

Jewish identity in the United States has vacillated between an ethnic and a religious identity. The 1960s saw a rebirth in Jewish ethnic identity. In truth, this was a part of a larger pattern of ethnic reidentification for many Americans in the wake of the Black civil rights movement (Alba 1990). It was also a precursor to the movement of religious return for Judaism.

Following the Six Day War, many American tourists visiting Israel were recruited by the yeshiva seminaries for the newly Orthodox. These schools flourished as a result of the ethnic pull of Israel for Jews. In account after account, the students indicated they had no interest in religion but were instead visiting the land of their people. They were in Israel because the Israelis had won the Six Day War and as Jews they were proud of this.

The cases of Josh, Shmulie, and Hank illustrate the importance of ethnic identification in the movement of religious return. Josh came from a large city in Texas. As a child, Josh had close ties to his grandfather, who was Orthodox. After the death of the grandfather, the family joined a Reform synagogue. Meanwhile, the family of his future wife, Judy, lived in upstate New York. Although her family was affiliated with a Conservative synagogue, their religious commitment was weak. Josh and Judy each signed up for a volunteer social work program in Israel. Neither was interested in religion. They met and married in Israel and returned to the United States. In 1975 they returned to Israel. This time Josh wanted to learn more about Judaism. He entered a yeshiva and became increasingly more religiously involved. As a result Judy entered a religious program for women, and they both became Orthodox and fully observant.

Shmulie and the woman who would become his wife went to Israel for a year of study at the university. They met and began living together. Months later they decided to get married. In the course of adjustment they discovered that they both had deep religious feelings. They began attending religious schools and became Orthodox.

Hank, born in the Midwest to a Reform Jewish family, deepened his Zionist feelings and sense of Jewish identity at university. Seeking a greater sense of identity he went to Israel. There he began to feel the need to become religious in order to identify fully.[3]

There were also those American Jews who were a part of the hippie countercul-ture of the 1960s and 1970s. Here we see a new religious identity being developed that began with a rejection of mainstream cultural identity. This facilitated an openness to the affirmation of ethnic identity. There is a subtle, but nonetheless real difference between the mainstream and hippie patterns of return. Some of the first wave of newly Orthodox were hippies. While other hippies were getting involved in various Eastern religions, Jewish hippies thought they found many similarities between these religions and Orthodox Judaism. They perceived Orthodox Judaism as an antiestablishment, countercultural choice. Kosher food was seen as a parallel to macrobiotic food. The religious beard was identified with the hippie beard, and the Orthodox yeshiva with the Hindu ashram. For this group, a small but significant part of the movement of return to traditional religion first involved identification with the counterculture and then later identification with Jewish ethnicity and Judaism.

Group 3: Israeli Jews

In contrast to the pattern observed for both Soviet émigrés and Americans, conversion for Israelis was more typically a one-step process of religious iden-tification. In Israel Jewish ethnic-national identity is taken as a given. The national calendar celebrates Jewish holidays. The armed forces provide kosher food for all soldiers. The Bible is used for the study of history in the public non-religious schools. Judaism is the dominant religion. Although the one-step pattern is typical here, one finds differences between Jews of European origin and Jews from Arab lands.

At *yeshivot* (seminaries for the study of Torah) for returnees in Israel that cater to both Israelis and Americans, it is apparent that it is the Israelis who dress in the dark clothes typical of the traditionally Orthodox. Why does this style of clothing characterize the Israeli returnee rather than the American returnee? The Israeli already has Jewish ethnic identity. Ordinarily, in fact, he has a second ethnic identity—that of Ashkenazi (European) or Sephardi (Arabic) origin. Sephardic ethnic identity in Israel is ranked lower than Ashkenazic, and in Israel Sephardim seem to constitute the bulk of the returnees. For the Israeli school dropout or former drug user, becoming a returnee means leaving a low-ranking status and attaining a higher-ranking status. One is no longer a deviant or a delinquent. In contrast, Americans seem more interested in affirming an ethnic identity than in shedding an earlier identity. They continue to wear the clothing associated with their earlier identity.

Israelis of Ashkenazi origin tended not to change clothing styles as rapidly as did Sephardim. They generally were not only higher in ethnic status but also better off economically and were not eager to abandon their former identity completely. Nonetheless, their stories reflect a sudden commitment to religion.

The accounts of conversion provided by returnees suggests how this occurs. For example, Ika Israeli was a successful artist and discotheque owner. Ika was born to parents who were antireligious socialists. He was raised on a *kibbutz* (collective farm) and knew very little of Judaism. In his late twenties he spent two years in Paris studying art. By his late thirties he had achieved a measure of success and was well known in avant-garde circles in Israel. Following the Six Day War in 1967, Israel was carried into the era of hippies and flower children by the mass media and by visitors from abroad.

Ika opened a discotheque that soon become a success, but he found life empty of meaning. He left Jerusalem for the mountains of Sefad. Alone in his retreat, reading Martin Buber and works on Zen Buddhism, he began to consider the possibility of exploring a religious life. After a short period of withdrawal Ika joined a yeshiva. He threw himself into it completely, spending his days in study of the Talmud and the religious legal codes.

Uri Zohar, an Israeli TV personality, had a similar story. He had been born in Israel to a secular middle-class family. An outgoing, lively personality, he entered Israel's fledgling TV industry and became the host of a popular game show. Israel's near defeat in the Yom Kippur War of 1973 affected him deeply. Some of his friends in the arts and media had begun taking religion seriously. He entered a yeshiva to study and within a short time decided to become religious. His description of his experience with prayer is paradigmatic. "I tried to pray, but I couldn't. . . . I felt foolish. I just stood there and wished for a long time that I could experience the feeling of prayer. And then it came to me and I could pray in sincerity and not feel foolish." Uri Zohar eventually was ordained as a rabbi and went on to become a leading figure in the Israeli movement of return.

Several Israeli students at a yeshiva for returnees were pilots in the Israeli Air Force. For them too, the near defeat of Israel in 1973 was traumatic. Needless to say, as members of this most elite group of Israeli soldiers, there was no need for an earlier stage of ethnic identification. Their reasons for return were more traditionally religious. They sought courage and reassurance in a violent and terrifying world. I was struck by one of the songs they chose to sing at the late Sabbath afternoon meal. The words were, "The entire world is a narrow bridge, but the crucial point is never to be afraid."

In contrast to American and Russian Jews, Israelis returning to tradition did not follow a two-step pattern of ethnic identification followed by religious return. They tended to experience a more rapid process of conversion.

Generalizing from this data to other situations, one could sum up by saying that the structural situation of minority religions typically requires a different conversion path than that of dominant religions.

CONCLUSION

Data on Jewish "return" or conversion to traditional Judaism suggests that the societal context of return has a major impact on the process of conversion. In both the United States and the former Soviet Union this is a two-step process involving first ethnic identification and later religious identification. In Israel, where Jewish ethnic identity is a taken-for-granted aspect of Israeli identity the return to traditional religion does not require a deeper involvement in ethnic Jewishness prior to religious return.

The pattern for couples in the FSU is somewhat complicated by the fact that women follow the lead of men. For American couples, women seem less dependent on their men and articulate these stages more clearly. Furthermore, American men sometimes follow women into traditional Judaism.

In broader terms, the argument presented here suggests that the majority/ minority status of converts and of the religion to which they are converting affects the conversion process. The two types examined in this chapter are only a portion of the possible variations. Judaism is a religion in which ethnicity and religion are intertwined. Would Irish or Italian Catholicism or American Protestantism be similar? How much cultural affinity must exist before there is a sense of ethnic identity?

Moreover, there is also the case of moving from the religion of a majority group to that of a minority group. Would the new religious involvement in Judaism of a secular Jewish Israeli immigrant to America involve a *prior* renewed or heightened sense of ethnic identity? These questions suggest points that require further study.

NOTES

I am grateful for the support provided for this research by the Research Foundation of the City University of New York, the Memorial Foundation for Jewish Culture, and the Lucius N. Littaur Foundation. An earlier version of this chapter has appeared in Anson Shupe and Bronislaw Misztal (eds.), *Religion, Mobilization, and Social Action.* Copyright © 1998. The chapter has been included in this volume with permission of GREENWOOD PUBLISHING GROUP, INC., Westport, CT.

1. Russian pogroms were attacks by Christian mobs against Jews, generally involving destruction of property, looting, murder, and rape, while the civil and military authorities provided no protection and secretly or even openly supported the mobs.

2. Blood libel is the allegation that Jews murder non-Jewish children to use their blood for Passover and other rituals. These libels, which led to massacres of Jews, first emerged in Europe during the Middle Ages and continued into the twentieth century, most often in Russia and more recently in Nazi Germany.

3. For a full discussion of these cases and others see Danzger (1989).

REFERENCES

Alba, Richard. 1990. *Ethnic Identity: The Transformation of White America.* New Haven: Yale University Press.

Danzger, M. Herbert. 1989. *Returning to Tradition: The Contemporary Revival of Orthodox Judaism*. New Haven, CT: Yale University Press.

Kilbourne, Brock, and James T. Richardson. 1989. "Paradigm Conflict, Types of Conversion, and Conversion Theories." *Sociological Analysis* 50(1):1–22.

Kosmin, Barry, et al. 1991. *Highlights of the CJF National Jewish Population Survey* (a publication of the Council of Jewish Federations in association with the Mandell–Berman Institute–North American Jewish Data Bank). New York: The Council of Jewish Federations.

Lofland, John. 1977. "Becoming a World Saver Revisited." *American Behavioral Scientist* 20(6):805–818.

Lofland, John, and Rodney Stark. 1965. "Becoming a World Saver: A Theory of Conversion to Deviant Perspective." *American Sociological Review* 30:862–874.

Snow, D. A., and R. Machalek. 1984. "The Sociology of Conversion." *Annual Review of Sociology* 10:167–190.

3

From West Africa to Brooklyn: Yoruba Religion among African Americans

Mary Cuthrell Curry

Over the past three decades a quietly growing phenomenon has been part of the religious scene in the Western world. The Yoruba religion of Africa has become a part of communities and countries from which it was previously absent. This religion is intimately bound up with the cultural traditions of the people who practice it. They have taken it with them as they have migrated from Africa to Cuba to North and South America and, most recently, to Europe.

This chapter examines the reproduction and transformation of the Yoruba religion in the United States, using African American practitioners of this religion in Brooklyn, New York, as a case study. It is based on four years of field research, during which time I participated in religious activities and conducted intensive interviews with seven leaders and thirty members.

ORIGINS

The Yoruba religion (also known as the Religion or *Santeria*) is spreading rapidly in the United States as a result of Cuban immigration and efforts on the part of African Americans to import it. Structured as a mutual aid organization, it provides a support network to obtain jobs, places to live, and help in times of trouble. Its rituals offer intimate community to uprooted people who talk directly to the gods and who believe that the gods respond with advice about their problems.

The Yoruba religion's presence in the United States is the result of a two-stage process of migration: (1) the huge influx of Yoruba slaves to Cuba in the eighteenth and nineteenth centuries and (2) the emigration of Cuban refugees after the revolution of 1959.

Sections of Nigeria, Benin, Togo, and Ghana constitute the ancestral home of the Yoruba people. During the eighteenth and nineteenth centuries, a long civil war in this region resulted in the selling of war captives as slaves, who were taken to Brazil and Cuba. In order to preserve their religion within the Christian context of Cuba, the slaves transformed it to resemble local religious organizations. The Yoruba religion took the form of religious brotherhoods, or *cabildos*, and also acquired a new name—Santeria, from the word *santero*, which in Spain originally meant a carver of the images of saints. In this new social context santero came to mean "maker of saints" or a "creator of the path through which the deities could come to earth" and interact with human beings (James 1970). These African deities (called *Orisha*) were identified with Catholic saints, so that the practitioners of this pre-Christian religion could avoid persecution in a Catholic country.

During the nineteenth century the *Cabildos* became relatively independent from the Catholic parochial structure because there were too few priests to supervise them (Sandoval 1975, 1995). During the latter part of that century and the first part of the twentieth, the Cabildos were disbanded by law and went underground, practicing the religion in secret.

Prior to the 1960s, Cuban adherents to Santeria in the United States kept their religion secret. Initiations into the priesthood were done in Cuba. However, with the large influx of Cubans after the revolution, major rituals began to be conducted in the United States. At this same time, African Americans were beginning to seek new religions that would provide an identity outside the American mainstream definitions of Blackness. Many were attracted to the Yoruba religion because of its identification with West Africa.

The first African American Yoruba priest was Nana Oseijeman Adefunmi (born Walter Eugene King), who had been seeking an African religious expression for Black Americans. This search took him from Detroit, where he was born in 1928, to Cuba, where on August 28, 1959, he was initiated as a priest of Obatala (the most senior god in the Yoruba religion).

Adefunmi was not only the first African American priest initiated into the religion, but also the founder of the Yoruba Temple in Harlem. Many members of the African American community first became aware of the religion through participation in that temple. Because of their identification with Africa, African Americans dropped the name Santeria and called it the Yoruba religion. They also discontinued the identification of the Orisha with Catholic saints, which had been the major form of syncretism[1] in the Cuban version of the religion. They considered this syncretism of Yoruba and Catholicism to be no longer necessary, since the need for hiding the religion had disappeared with slavery. In addition, since most African American adherents to the Yoruba religion had been previously Protestant, Catholicism was not for them a mark of cultural identity, as it was for Cubans.

THE HOUSE OF OCHA

The Yoruba religion is organized into structures of ritual kinship called Houses. The word "House" describes a group of people, the relationship between them and lines of descent from the *Orisha* (deities of the Yoruba religion). A House of Ocha (a short form of the word Orisha) is called by the name of the priest who heads it, for example, Peter's House or Katherine's House. It is unclear when a new House can be said to exist. Some say after a priest has initiated three priests, while others maintain a new House exists when a priest has initiated eight godchildren.

Members of the House are considered to be the godchildren of the head of the House and godbrothers and godsisters to each other. Other terms modeled on kin relationships are also employed: grandparents in ocha, aunts and uncles in ocha, nieces and nephews in ocha, and so on. Of all these relationships, the most important is that between godparent and godchild. This is the central relationship of the social organization of Santeria (Gregory 1986:67). It implies the existence of links between parents and children, the living and their ancestors, and the Orisha and humanity as a whole.

Godparents and godchildren have complementary responsibilities. The godparent is responsible for the godchild's growth in the religion. She or he oversees all necessary divinations, sacrifices, and initiations for the godchild and has the duty to instruct the godchild in religious knowledge, ritual, and duties. Reciprocally, the godchild is expected to assist the godparent in rituals or do work in the godparent's home that is connected with religious activities.

There are two major hierarchies in the structure of the House: those initiated into the priesthood and those who have received the primary initiation of *ilekis*. Ilekis are bead necklaces strung according to the colors associated with each Orisha. For example, Shango's colors are red and white, and Oshun's are orange and amber. Ilekis are considered to extend the protection of the godparent's Orisha to the *alejo* (literally stranger-resident-in-the-House, that is, a person who has undergone the initiation of ilekis). Both the alejos and priests are ranked according to seniority, that is, in the order of initiation. In addition, all those who have been initiated into the priesthood outrank all those who have not.

The crucial stage of socialization into the Yoruba religion is initiation into the priesthood, which marks the final category of membership in a House. The initiate acquires an *Ojubona* (a secondary godparent). This person may or may not belong to the House of the godparent. The Ojubona assumes the responsibilities of the godparent if the godparent dies or is incapacitated. The role of Ojubona is a means of forming bonds within a House or between Houses. As time goes on, a priest may acquire godchildren and found a House of his or her own.

Very few practitioners of the religion have become priests, compared to the total membership. Peter's House, for example, which had over 300 members in 1976, had only sixteen initiations into the priesthood in the subsequent twenty years. During that same time period Katherine's House initiated eighteen priests. Among Peter's and Katherine's godchildren who are priests, only ten have initiated other priests. Some will undoubtedly initiate new priests in the future, which would make them godparents as well; however, others regard the role of godparent as burdensome and unrewarding.

Relationships between Houses can be formed in a number of ways. Subhouses of a line have built-in relationships. For examples, Houses whose heads are godsisters or godbrothers of each other will interact closely. Indeed, seen from the outside, they actually appear to constitute one House. Also, the godparents of a priest usually serve as secondary godparents for the first priest whom he or she initiates. Marriages between priests of different Houses provide yet another vehicle by which Houses generate relationships with each other.

Even though the Yoruba religion exists in Cuba, Brazil, Trinidad, and some parts of Haiti, all Houses in the United States have Cuban roots. This has occurred for two reasons, one historical and one structural. The historical reason is the exodus of priests from Cuba during the revolution. The structural reason is related to the way that the religion is organized in various countries. Outside of Cuba, the Yoruba religion is organized into temples that have hierarchies of priests with different functions. In order to transplant a temple, it is necessary to transplant the whole temple hierarchy. However, as the Cuban Yoruba religion is based in the home of one priest, to transplant the Cuban version of the religion requires fewer people.

If one were to trace each Yoruba line in the United States back far enough, one would eventually come to a small number of Houses in Cuba—possibly even one. However, many have not retained their Cuban roots. According to Gregory (1986) and Brandon (1983), some Houses of Ocha in New York City remain exclusively Cuban, while others are composed of entirely of Black Americans or Puerto Ricans. Still others are multiethnic. The diversity results because growth comes from the personal networks of priests. However, this diversity has also been a source of conflict among the different groups involved in the religion. For example, by all accounts (Cabrera 1970; Sandoval 1975, 1995; Murphy 1981; Brandon 1983), the number of Cubans involved in the religion in the United States is larger than in Cuba. For many of them, Santeria serves as a mark of Cuban social identity. This identity, however, is unlikely to appeal to all other ethnic and racial groups, especially since the Spanish language may be an obstacle for many African Americans. Also, because of the history of religious persecution in Cuba, Cuban Santeros tend to be secretive about their religious practices. This causes conflict with Black Americans, many of whom sought the religion for an enhanced sense of *African* identity and wish to proclaim it publicly.

> Black Americans further had to find ways to make Orisha worship relative to them in ways that were not real concerns for their Cuban elders. We were interested in the religion as an alternative to Western Christianity. Many of us had turned to Islam in this search—but others of us wanted something that was more specifically ancestral. And having found it we were not as inclined as had been the Cubans to hide our religion. (Weaver 1986:23)

Black Americans have known racial discrimination but not religious persecution. Moreover, Catholicism is more characteristic of Cuban ethnic identity. Not only are Black Americans not Catholic, but the very appearance of statues of saints (mostly white) is a negation of the meaning of the religion as fostering an African identity for them. Conversely, Cubans view the Black American desire to go back to the African Roots of the religion as a denial of the Cuban role in transmitting it. While some Cubans acknowledge the African origins of the Yoruba religion, others (while not denying it) downplay it considerably. I even heard one Cuban priest maintain that Spanish is a sacred language.

THE ROLE OF THE YORUBA PRIEST

The primary role of the Yoruba priest is to be a mediator between human beings and the divine. However, throughout the Americas, the priest is a counselor, physician,[2] psychologist, father/mother confessor, and advisor on practical problems, all rolled into one. Although the priest is the central figure in a hierarchical structure, she or he is also subject to democratic controls in a context with a familial ideology (Deren 1953:176). To navigate such a role successfully requires a degree of skill in social relationships not required of most people. Priests are judged by their character. If a priest is disagreeable or unknowledgeable or is judged to lack integrity, people no longer come to her or him. The priest retains the priesthood but is left alone.

There is no gender requirement for Orisha priesthood, although priests are more likely to be women than men. They may specialize in their functions. For example, some specialize in the performance of rituals. Others (specifically women) run the kitchen during the course of ceremonies. Some priests become scholars of the religious tradition by reading the books available to them. Some non-Cubans go as far as to learn Spanish in order to read the much greater volume of religious literature produced by Cuban authors. Some priests make the religion a very small part of their lives, while others have an emotional attachment to it and center their lives around it.

In the United States, the major function of the priest is to counsel people on all the problems in their lives. Many people first come to a priest when they have major problems that seem to defy solution. When someone presents a problem that is beyond the knowledge of a particular priest or when there is a need to perform an especially complex ceremony, the priest consults a ritual expert. Ritual experts function as consultants for a number of Houses. One of the primary ceremonies at which the presence of ritual experts is required is the initiation of a priest.

CONVERSION

Some people experience "intellectual conversion" (Lofland and Skonov 1983) before ever coming into contact with the religion. Intellectual conversion is a type of preconversion activity that occurs before social contact with the group concerned. The potential convert reads books, attends lectures, watches television shows, or engages in other forms of information gathering. With intellectual conversion we find minimal to nonexistent social pressure, varying temporal duration, and little psychological involvement. Belief exists prior to participation or even contact. Intellectual conversion is frequently the pattern followed by people who had Black Nationalist tendencies and sought the Yoruba religion as a means of developing a positive African identity.

However, the religion spreads in the Black community mainly through networks of friends and relatives. New members participate in the activities of a House for long periods of time without making a commitment. Little or no pressure is put on them to do so. This is what Lofland and Skonov (1983) call "experimental conversion." It takes place over long periods of time—months or even years. Some of the members of Peter's House have been involved as long as fifteen years, but report no obvious concerted pressure to make them become more involved.

The Yoruba religion does not actively seek converts. There are no missionary efforts at all. Currently most conversions occur through the personal networks of earlier converts. The members of Peter's House to whom I talked report that they first learned of Peter through a friend or relative. No one reports any pressure to become any more intensely involved or to obtain a higher stage of initiation. Indeed, some have reported that Peter has asked them not to refer any more people to him because of his workload as a priest and consequent inability to deal with more people.

Observation of the members of Peter's House reveals that there are four clusters of relatives; one consisting of a mother, her four children, and their spouses and children (totaling fourteen people); another of a group of three cousins, the spouse of one, and the children of another (totaling six people); a mother and her two children; and another group of two cousins. Additionally there are four groups of friends and a group who belonged to a cultural nationalist group before they joined Peter's House.

These people have been involved with the House for varying amounts of time. They are at different stages of initiation, but all have a great degree of intensity of involvement. Among those who are initiated into the priesthood, the length of involvement in the religion varied between two and fifteen years before their initiation.

In sum, the Yoruba Religion became established in the Black community in the 1960s (a period of intense turbulence and growing activism) through the search of some African Americans for a religious underpinning of their cultural identity. This search initially took the form of intellectual conversion. The quest for an acceptable Black identity by means of intellectual conversion still brings some converts to the religion today. However, many others are attracted through social networks or experimental conversion.

CONCLUSION

The Yoruba religion is one example of the transformation of a religious culture brought about by the migration of the practitioners of the religion from one society to another. Its organizational structure and certain aspects of its belief system were changed by the initial migration to Cuba. It is currently undergoing additional changes in the United States. At this point it is too early to tell what, if any, changes will occur in Europe, where the Yoruba religion has recently arrived. The social conditions of Cuban slavery and post-emancipation persecution produced a religious structure that proved the most transportable of all the Yoruba-derived religions in the Western Hemisphere. Social conditions in the African American community in the United States, especially in the urban North, provided an initial embrace of the religion as a survival of African heritage. However, this embrace produced (and is still producing) other changes, for example de-syncretization or the uncoupling of religious elements from the cultural tradition of Cuba, which had been characterized by, for example, the identification of the Yoruba gods with Catholic saints and the transformation of the term Santeria. It is likely that the Protestant culture encountered in the African American community in New York City greatly facilitated this desyncretization

The Yoruba religion is finding some acceptance in non-Cuban Latin communities and in white ethnic communities. However, the spread of the religion into these communities has not been widely studied. While the African American community emphasizes its African origins and Cubans emphasize its recent Cuban vintage, it can hardly be expected that other communities will find these issues equally compelling. What can be expected is that the spread of the Yoruba religion into other sectors of American society will produce new patterns of reproduction and transformation.

NOTES

1. Syncretism is the combining of different belief systems. In the Americas, many of the practitioners of African and Native American religions adopted certain characteristics of Roman Catholic belief—such as the veneration of saints—in order to avoid persecution.

2. In Haiti, Brazil, and Cuba one of the functions of a priest is that of herbalist. In the United States, this aspect of the priest's role has lost most of its prominence. Instead, if the diviner suspects medical problems, he or she advises the person to see a doctor.

REFERENCES

Brandon, George Edward. 1983. *The Dead Sell Memories: An Anthropological Study of Santeria in New York City*. Ph.D. dissertation, Rutgers University, the State University of New Jersey, New Brunswick, NJ.

Cabrera, Lydia. 1970. *Koeko Iyawo Aprende Novicia*. Miami: Ediciones Universal.

Deren, Maya. 1953. *Divine Horsemen: The Living Gods of Haiti*. London and New York: Thames and Hudson.

Gregory, Stephen. 1986. *Santeria in New York City: A Study In Cultural Resistance*. Ph.D. dissertation, New School for Social Research, New York, NY.

James, Edward. 1970. "Introduction." In *Shango de Ima: A Yoruba Mystery Play*, by Pepe Carril. English adaptation, with a preface by Susan Sherman and introduction by Jerome Rothenberg and Edward James. New York: Doubleday.

Lofland, John, and Norman Skonov. 1983. "Patterns of Conversion." In Eileen Barker (ed.), *Of Gods and Men: New Religious Movements in the West*. Macon, GA: Mercer University Press.

Murphy, Joseph M. 1981. *Ritual Systems in Cuban Santeria*. Ph.D. dissertation, Temple University, Philadelphia, PA.

———. 1994. *Working the Spirit: Ceremonies of the African Diaspora*. Boston: Beacon Press.

Sandoval, Mercedes Cros. 1975. *La Religion Afro-Cubana*. Madrid: Playor, S.A.

————. 1995. "Afro-Cuban Religion in Perspective." In Anthony M. Stevens-Arroyo and Andres I. Pérez y Mena (eds.), *Enigmatic Powers: Syncretism with African and Indigenous Peoples' Religions among Latinos*. New York: Bildner Center for Western Hemisphere Studies of the Graduate School and University Center of the City University of New York.

Weaver, Lloyd. 1986. "Notes on Òrìṣà Worship in an Urban Setting: The New York Example." Paper read at the Third International Conference on Òrìṣà Tradition, July 1–6, 1986, University of Ife Ile Ife, Nigeria.

4

Identity Reconstruction and Empowerment of South Asian Immigrant Women in Canada, Australia, and New Zealand

Helen Ralston

RELIGION, MIGRATION, AND IDENTITY RECONSTRUCTION IN EVERYDAY LIFE

Migration is an ongoing process that involves not only leaving a homeland and crossing territorial borders but also crossing social, psychic, and symbolic borders that define relations, membership, belonging, religious meaning systems, and worldviews of realities of everyday experience (Berger and Luckmann 1966; Berger 1967). It involves a sharp break in lived experience of cultural and religious identity, in group membership, and in a meaningful worldview in a birth country and reconstruction of a dynamic culture, identity, and worldview in a new settlement.

Culture, like identity, is not a static collection of customs, beliefs, and practices that women carry in their bodies or their baggage when they leave their homeland. On the contrary, culture and identity are continually being shaped and reconstructed subjectively and socially along many axes (such as race, gender, ethnicity, religion, and national origin) through relationships with other immigrants and with native-born residents of the settlement country. Race, ethnic, gender, class, and caste relations organize social life and imply, on one hand, a complexity of shared meanings and understandings in social relations in various spheres of a group's activities and, on the other hand, a recognition of boundaries and limitations in shared understandings and of differences in social relations (Barth 1969:15–16)—and, I would add, in relations of ruling—with other groups.

In this chapter I have drawn on Weber's (Gerth and Mills 1946:218) notion of religion as creating a "meaningful cosmos" out of a world that is "experienced as specifically senseless" and Berger's (1967:25) conception of religion as "the human enterprise by which a sacred cosmos is established." I have also adopted Dorothy Smith's insights about knowing society *from the standpoint of women* and making visible "relations in which each individual's everyday world is embedded"

(Smith 1987:185)—relations of power, oppression, and exploitation in the institutions organizing society, which she refers to as "relations of ruling" or the "ruling
apparatus" of society. In Smith's feminist sociological perspective, the concept
"lived experience" refers to practical activities of everyday life, things people do,
rather than to people's perceptions of and attitudes toward the situations in which
they find themselves.

I have explored practical religious activities—praying, meditating, chanting,
performing religious rituals and rites of passage, reading religious books, practicing
religious fasts and celebrating religious festivals, participating in religious
organizations, and visiting temples, mosques, gurdwaras, churches, and synagogues—in other words, what South Asian immigrant women do to reconstruct
their identity and to empower themselves in a new settlement.

SAMPLE SELECTION AND DATA COLLECTION

This chapter is based on studies that I conducted in four immigrant settlement
regions: Atlantic Canada (namely, the provinces of Nova Scotia, New Brunswick,
Prince Edward Island, and Newfoundland), Western Canada (the province of
British Columbia), Australia, and New Zealand. In each region, a case study
approach was used to collect data through in-depth interviews. Samples were
drawn from first-generation immigrant women aged fifteen years and over, in proportion to the respective Census distribution of women of South Asian origin in
each settlement region: 126 in Atlantic Canada, 100 in British Columbia, 50 in
Australia, and 10 in New Zealand. In all the studies, I and my research assistant,
Emily Burton, who conducted 45 interviews in Vancouver, attempted to adopt the
standpoint of the women, to see everyday life from their perspective, and to let their
stories be heard in their own voices.

PROFILES OF THE WOMEN WHO PARTICIPATED IN THE STUDIES

The women in all samples were of diverse national, linguistic, and religious
backgrounds. The term "*South* Asian" encompasses distinctly different categories
of people who trace their origin either directly to the Indian subcontinent (India,
Pakistan, Sri Lanka, Bangladesh) or else indirectly through their ancestors who
migrated to East Africa, the Caribbean, or Fiji. "South Asian" refers not so much
to personal qualities of individuals as to social characteristics that have been
constructed in historical and social relations in specific economic and political
contexts.

How South Asian immigrant women represent themselves varies in terms of
whom they are addressing. Few "South Asians" identify themselves as such. In my
studies, women frequently represented themselves in terms such as "Indo-
Canadian" or "Punjabi-Canadian." In everyday life, the term "immigrant woman"
refers not so much to *legal* status as to processes of identity construction that occur
through social relations. From the standpoint of dominant white citizens of the
settlement country, some women who are visibly and audibly different in char-

acteristics such as skin color, language or accent and in religious, dress, and food customs are identified as "immigrant women"—foreign, alien. By contrast, the term "immigrant woman" is seldom applied to white English-speaking Western women who enter Canada, Australia, or New Zealand from the United Kingdom, Ireland, Northern Europe, or the United States. From the standpoint of a South Asian immigrant woman, migration can mean an experience of "alienation"—a loss of identity consciousness and a meaningful worldview. To be identified by others as "alien" or "immigrant woman" is thus a social construction for some people who are actually *permanent residents and citizens* of a country.

Birth Country, Mother Tongue, and Religion

While the majority of women in the studies were born in India, there were fourteen different birth countries among the samples. Punjabi and Hindi were dominant mother tongues in all samples, but a diversity of eighteen Indian languages was represented, particularly in the Atlantic Canada and Australia samples. The women were affiliated with seven different religions, Hinduism and Sikhism being the most frequent, except in New Zealand, where Christianity dominated (see Table 4.1).

Table 4.1
Religious Affiliation of Samples of South Asian Women, from
Atlantic Canada, British Columbia, Australia, and New Zealand

Religious Affiliation	Atlantic Canada South Asian Women		British Columbia South Asian Women		Australia South Asian Women		New Zealand South Asian Women	
	Count	Percentage	Count	Percentage	Count	Percentage	Count	Percentage
Hinduism	69	54.77	40	40.00	14	28.00	3	30.00
Sikhism	17	13.49	40	40.00	9	18.00	1	10.00
Islam	17	13.49	9	9.00	11	22.00	1	10.00
Christianity	19	15.08	7	7.00	10	20.00	5	50.00
Zoroastrianism	3	2.38	3	3.00	—		—	
Judaism	1	0.79	—		—		—	
Buddhism	—		—		6	12.00	—	
None	—		1	1.00	—		—	
Total	126	100.00	100	100.00	50	100.00	10	100.00

Marital Status, Age, and Migration

Almost all of the women migrated as young married women in their child-bearing years, many as *social* and legal dependents of their husbands through an arranged marriage—or what some chose to call a "semi-arranged" marriage, where the daughter and male candidates were free to agree or disagree with a marriage proposed by parents.

IDENTITY RECONSTRUCTION AND EMPOWERMENT IN THE SETTLEMENT COUNTRY

Analytically, my intent is to provide an understanding of how the women recon-structed identity and a meaningful worldview and empowered themselves in the context of alienating and subordinating conditions of living.

Religious Activities in the Home

Although the immigrant women in all samples had unique stories to tell, 80 percent or more of them described religious activities, such as reading sacred books, worshiping at a household shrine, praying, meditating, lighting lamps, celebrating festivals, and listening to or singing Indian religious songs and chants as part of their everyday life. Two-thirds of Hindu women who engaged in religious activities at home did so on a regular basis. Images of favorite gods and goddesses (like the Great Mother God in the forms of Durga or Kali) and gurus (like the South India charismatic teacher Sai Baba) adorned shrines and living-room walls. In some instances, a guru from India taught children meditation and mantras in Sunday classes, which they then practiced at home with the mother. A British Columbia woman, who had migrated in 1960 at age twenty-two years, commented on her increased religious activity, "I worship more here. . . . In India in our home we had photos of gods and goddesses in a corner. I pray to the goddess Kali. Here I had my shrine after fifteen years. Slowly after that, [I worship more]. I find deep meaning now. I was young in India."

Some women observed customary religious fasts in deference to their husband. For example, an Atlantic Canada Hindu woman, who held a full-time senior posi-tion as an accountant and had resided in Canada for twenty-two years, reported, "I am a very religious person. I am a life member of the temple. . . . I worship every Monday. I still fast every Monday . . . a regular working day."

Religious gender roles in the family were sometimes changed; a Hindu mother performed a household *puja* (a ritual with lamps, songs, bells, and incense) that was normally the father's role in India. Canadian women who did not expect their children to practice religion as they did made comments like the following: "The children don't want to practice as Hindus." "My children are Canadian." "I don't expect the children to do those things but I want them to know their culture." Such comments reflected not only changed gender roles but also the importance of religion in identity reconstruction in a new settlement.

Nearly all Muslim women were religiously active at home. They varied in their performance of orthodox prayer rituals, some praying the customary five times a day, and others less frequently. A woman in Australia was interviewed during the Ramadan season of fast from sunrise to sunset. At sunset, the husband returned from work, the whole family prayed, and then the woman invited me to share their evening meal. Although the woman observed the religious custom of not attending mixed-sex English-language classes, her teen-age daughter told me that her mother did not expect her to wear the veil to school. "They are Australian," the woman said of her children. Thus, through selective religious activities, the woman reconstructed a *Muslim* Australian identity for herself and her children.

Among Sikh women, two-thirds engaged in religious activities, like reading the writings of founding gurus in the sacred Guru Granth Sahib or performing rituals at home, to teach their children as well as to affirm their own ethnoreligious identity. For example, an Australian woman described her early morning religious ritual, which followed customary purification by bathing:

I get up at six. . . . After a shower, then a few moments of prayer, I open the Guru Granth Sahib. My husband closes it after his shower and prayer. For us, [this prayer] gives continuity, from homeland to here. The children don't feel the same need. I could not pass the same values to the children. . . . I don't know why I didn't. It was my responsibility. Perhaps I didn't have time.

As with Hindus, for Sikhs, religious socialization of children is the woman's gender role. Women also performed rituals that were customarily the father's gender role in Punjab, India.

Among Christian women, almost all read the Bible (often in their mother tongue), prayed, and performed religious activities regularly in their homes. One Atlantic Canada Presbyterian woman, an immigrant from India who was educated in English-medium Christian schools, when asked about her initial settlement experience identified the customs and culture of Canada as fundamentally Christian and therefore familiar to her.

I didn't find anything a trouble, because, you know, the religion was there and the language. We were always brought up with the missionaries and white people— Americans and Canadians and English and Scottish people. So we were used to all their rules and regulations and eating habits, their religious practices and all those things, so we didn't find anything hard.

In her experience, the less "different" you were (in religion, culture, and language), the easier it was to settle in, to reconstitute your identity, and to interact with white Anglo-Canadians in everyday life.

A high percentage of women in all samples celebrated religious festivals in their household. However, Hindu, Sikh, and Muslim women worked hard at celebrating festivals in Canada or Australia that were part of everyday life in the homeland. Without a religious calendar and necessary ritual materials and symbols, they found it difficult to celebrate movable feasts. In addition, women lacked networks of kin and friends to help in preparation of meals, decorations, and festive activities. For example, an Atlantic Canada woman observed, "It's not fun to celebrate those festivals yourself. Celebration needs people. That's why all the time for Diwali I go to the temple. . . . You go there for a couple of hours, but in India Diwali is for weeks." A woman in British Columbia made a similar comment: "The spirit is different here. Diwali's a communal event in India. Here it's short and secluded. It's not a public holiday. Firecrackers are forbidden here."

Yet the women did what they could to teach their children and to share celebrations with neighbors of other cultures. Some Christian women noted that Christmas and Easter had been a *religious* festival in their homeland and had become a secular festival in the new settlement. When Christmas came, women of all religions would join in the secular celebrations as part of their new culture. Thus the women crossed borders and extended boundaries to redefine their identity and culture.

Religious Organization Activities

Where ethnic categories of people are residentially dispersed, ethnic reference groups can be constituted, maintained and activated by communication in what Etzioni (1959:258) has called "limited social situations" and in activities of core institutions, such as ethnoreligious and ethnocultural groups. Through communication, activities, and experienced differences in the "limited social situations" of such organizations, South Asian immigrants reconstructed personal and social identity consciousness and ethnoreligious worldviews. They reconstituted and reinforced ethnoreligious boundaries.

In all samples, a majority of women were affiliated with an ethnoreligious organization and attended services. The women described religious organizations, like temple, *gurdwara* (Sikh temple), mosque, and church, as key elements in transmission of cultural symbols, activities, and value-systems to the next generation. In fact, one might argue that such organizations are created precisely for the purpose of reaffirming and transmitting a shared meaning system and symbolic universe, a system of countervalues and standards of behavior that are "different" from those of the dominant culture of the settlement country. This objective is especially important in areas like premarital relations between boys and girls and in religiously prescribed dress codes, like Muslim girls wearing pants rather than shorts for athletic activities. Many women took children to temple, gurdwara, or mosque to communicate basic values through instruction in beliefs, rituals, and behavioral codes and to promote their children's social relations with families and youth of their own ethnoreligious identity, often with a view to marriage within the community. For example, a British Columbia woman who migrated in 1973, soon after her marriage, observed,

> I go to the temple so that my kids get some of their heritage. My son is involved and also works with a youth group. He's now very much Canadian. They need something [of their religious heritage] in their lives. They don't have to give up everything. A

melting pot is not a good thing. I'm a Canadian. I'm *Indo*-Canadian in eating, language, religion. I believe very strongly in multicultural Canada.

Many Hindu women visited temples. The absence or presence of regional and linguistic variations in temple rituals and style of worship was a key factor in determining participation in organized temple activities for their own identity reconstruction and for bringing up their children in the new settlement. An Atlantic Canada woman remarked,

> It would be very helpful if there were a temple where we could go every week like Christians do for Sunday service. If the children go once a week when they are young, . . . they can learn everything. That's a big misfortune that we don't have a common place where we can show them that it is our tradition. Even though I go to my basement to do my prayers, and my husband spends time too, the children think that it's a very unfamiliar thing. [But if] they see a lot of people of our community doing the same thing [at the temple], then they will have an emphasis on it. Otherwise if they think that it's very uncommon, they think it's not as important.

The possibility for specific regional and linguistic styles of worship depends largely upon having a sufficient number of Hindu families of that identity to support a subgroup. That situation is more likely to occur in large metropolitan centers like Vancouver or Toronto in Canada and Sydney and Melbourne in Australia. In smaller settlements of Atlantic Canada and in interior British Columbia, where there were few Hindu families, in the absence of a temple, they often met once a month in the house of one member or in a rented hall for special occasions. The religious worship was described as "a mixture in celebration" to accommodate the variety of members' identities. The gathering served to sacralize a generalized Hindu identity and to provide a context for social support. On the other hand, regional religious and cultural differences often came into play to create an experience of alienation. For example, Atlantic Canada women of South India origin described celebrations they attended as being North Indian, with *bhajans* [songs] and puja in Hindi, "We're lost . . . [it's] almost like another religion."

Where there is a high concentration of Sikh families—as in Vancouver, Canada; in Melbourne and Sydney, Australia; and in Auckland, New Zealand—there are several Sikh gurdwaras. All the Sikh women in British Columbia and Australia visited gurdwaras—for prayer, peace of mind, and celebration of the feasts of the ten gurus, but also for social events such as marriages, birthdays, anniversaries, and secular holidays. The only Sikh gurdwara in Atlantic Canada is located in metropolitan Halifax. All but two women in the Atlantic Canada sample visited the gurdwara. The women described it as a social gathering-place as much as a place of worship, where people shared in the *langa* (traditional meal) after the religious ceremony and met other Punjabi-speaking people and where they taught their children about religion and culture.

Two-thirds of the seventeen Atlantic Canada Muslim women regularly visited the mosque with husbands and children, whereas in South Asian countries it is customary for men only to pray at the mosque. Nine of the eleven Australia Muslim women visited one of several mosques for celebration of the feast of Id, but not for regular Friday prayers. In metropolitan St. John's, Newfoundland, Muslim women formed a chapter of the Canadian Council of Muslim Women, which met every two weeks for prayer, discussion of the Qu'ran, and general socializing. In Melbourne, Muslim women also met as a collective to talk of religion and social issues. In both Australia and Atlantic Canada, members of mosques and women's groups were of diverse ethnic and national origins and included native-born white Australians or Canadians, respectively. The mosque became the principal context for reconstruction of *religious* consciousness and identity. It seemed that Islamic religion, rather than national or regional origin, was the most salient marker of identity. Australian Buddhists, by contrast to Muslims, established temples for specific national groups—Sri Lankan, Thai, Vietnamese—where women participated in ceremonies.

In Atlantic Canada, Zoroastrian families were too few to support a temple. Halifax families gathered once or twice a month for religious and social celebrations. Children were taught religious beliefs, values, and practices and were formally inducted into the religion through the sacred thread ceremony. By contrast, in British Columbia, there were many Zoroastrians. Women visited a prayer hall regularly for religious, social, and children's instructional purposes and rented larger facilities for festivals. An Atlantic Canada woman described her religious gathering as "a small close community . . . our (extended) family." A British Columbia woman described such gatherings as "a comfort zone where religion, jokes, and food are shared." For women of both regions, the gathering was important for reconstructing ethnoreligious identity, for providing support net-works, for teaching children, and for redefining boundaries between themselves and other South Asian Canadians as well as native-born Canadians.

South Asian Christian women reconstructed their identity with the least discontinuity. They were affiliated with various denominations—Catholic, Angli-can, United (in Canada) or Uniting (in Australia), Pentecostal, United Baptist, or "born-again" Christians—whose organization, traditions, rituals, values, beliefs, and sentiments were most akin to those of their religion in the source country. In metropolitan Halifax, five Christian women belonged to the Allied Christian Association, an organization composed exclusively of Christians of Indian or Pakistani origin. For these women, a specific ethnoreligious organization was important in reconstructing their cultural identity.

In the majority of ethnoreligious organizations, patriarchal gender roles prevailed. However, several women made wry remarks, such as, "My husband is secretary; he used to be president. *I* do all the work." In general, men were in control and held the principal offices. For example, British Columbia gurdwaras were male dominated. The women avoided temple politics among male heads of families who sought control and management of the gurdwara activities and resources and sometimes aligned themselves with party politics in the Punjab, India. Women would attend only for social occasions and placed greater empha-sis on festival celebrations at home. In Vancouver, South Asian women's organizations used temple social gatherings, with the support of gender-conscious husbands, to present antisexist and antiracist skits and dramas that raised consciousness of wife abuse. Through these activities, women were empowered and whole families were educated to awareness that such abuses against women are reprehensible. By contrast, the Maritime Sikh Society in Halifax was exceptional. Atlantic Canada Sikh women performed rituals at the gurdwara. The society also elected an all-women executive, which was responsible for all temple-related activities—managing society money, recruiting Indian singers for celebrations, and organizing the langa after religious ceremonies.

In sum, besides being places for praying and offering an atmosphere of peace, ethnoreligious organizations provided a social context where people could meet and reconstitute consciousness of ethnicity, identity, language, tradition, beliefs, values, and shared meaning systems. They fostered the formation of a specific South Asian identity among children, as they grew up as citizens of the settlement country. They provided needed social, cultural, recreational, and spiritual services and integration within the settlement society, especially for newcomers. In some instances, they were a context for antiracist and antisexist resistance to alienation and discrimination. Women used ethnoreligious organizations to empower themselves, to negotiate and contest their subordinate position in social situations, and to promote change.

CONCLUSION

Through religious activities, women reconstructed a positive identity as *South Asian* Canadian or Australian or New Zealand women. Their "differences" established boundaries in identity separating them not only from other native-born and immigrant Canadian, Australian, or New Zealand women, respectively, but also from South Asian immigrants of specific regional, cultural, linguistic, and religious backgrounds.

The women's accounts suggested that for the overwhelming majority of them, religious activities in the household and in ethnoreligious organizations were an important factor in recreating a meaningful world, in reconstructing personal and social ethnoreligious identity, in empowering them, and in transmitting key elements of cultural identity to children in the alien context of the settlement country. In Hans Mol's (1976:1–15) terms, the women sacralized their ethnoreligious identity. They renewed and restored the "sacred canopy" (Berger 1967) that had been broken by the migration experience.

REFERENCES

Barth, Fredrik. 1969. *Ethnic Groups and Boundaries: The Social Organization of Culture Difference*. London: George Allen and Unwin.
Berger, Peter L. 1967. *The Sacred Canopy: Elements of a Sociological Theory of Religion*. Garden City, NY: Doubleday and Company.
Berger, Peter L., and Thomas Luckmann. 1966. *The Social Construction of Reality: A Treatise in the Sociology of Knowledge*. Garden City, NY: Doubleday and Company.

Etzioni, Amitai. 1959. "The Ghetto—A Re-evaluation." *Social Forces* 39:255–262.
Gerth, Hans H., and C. Wright Mills (eds.). 1946. *From Max Weber: Essays in Sociology.* New York: Oxford University Press.
Mol, Hans. 1976. *Identity and the Sacred: A Sketch for a New Social-Scientific Theory of Religion.* Oxford: Basil Blackwell.
Smith, Dorothy E. 1987. *The Everyday World as Problematic: A Feminist Sociology.* Toronto: University of Toronto Press.

5

Religious Views of Mainline Protestant Baby Boomers in the United States

Dean Hoge, Benton Johnson, and Donald A. Luidens

Since the early days of the United States, a few Protestant denominations have been central to American culture and American institutions. This group of denominations, called "mainline Protestants," consists of the Episcopalians, Lutherans, Presbyterians, Methodists, United Church of Christ, Christian Church (Disciples of Christ), American Baptists, and Reformed. Since the mid-1960's all of these denominations have experienced declines in numbers. The Episcopalians and the Presbyterians lost 30 percent of their members. Others lost 15 to 25 percent. The declines were steep in the 1970s and 1980s, less severe in the 1990s.

EXPLANATIONS FOR NUMERICAL DECLINE

Why did these declines occur? Sociologists have uncovered five facts key to an explanation. First, the high points of membership in most mainline denominations were between 1963 and 1967, but the rate of growth had actually begun to decrease in the early 1960s.

Second, researchers charting the membership trends saw that the curves were smooth, indicating that they were caused by underlying social factors rather than by specific changes in leadership or policy, which would produce abrupt breaks. This finding disproves a theory held by some analysts that denominational conflicts over social issues in the 1960s and early 1970s had caused membership losses.

Third, the denominations with the greatest decline since the 1960s were the ones with the highest levels of affluence and education.

Fourth, the cause of the decline was largely the reduced flow of young adults into church membership rather than any exodus of older members. This suggests that whatever was causing the decline was disproportionately touching young adults (Hoge and Roozen 1979:322–323).

Fifth, some historians argue that studies that start their analysis from the early 1960s are misleading. They point out that the 1950s were an unusual period of church growth and that decline in the 1960s and 1970s may show a return to normalcy. However, this pattern accounts for less than half of the decline in numbers.

RECENT RESEARCH EFFORTS

During the past three decades several studies have tried to assess mainline decline. Dean Kelley (1972, 1977) argued that strict churches grow while nonstrict churches decline and that mainline Protestantism has become less and less strict in recent decades, thus bringing its downturn. Other authors who have addressed the question of recent church trends are Coalter, Mulder, and Weeks (1996); Hadaway and Roozen (1993); and Roof (1993).

In the early 1990s we designed a study specifically to test theories of mainline decline by getting direct information from young adults (see Hoge, Johnson, and Luidens 1994). Since researchers have found that many Protestant youth drop out of church life when they are between sixteen and twenty-two years old and return later, we wanted to study a group old enough that many would have returned by the time we talked to them. So we chose persons thirty-three to forty-two years old at the time of interviewing. These persons were born between 1947 and 1956, the first ten years of the Baby Boom. Also, to simplify the task, we restricted the study to one mainline denomination, the Presbyterians. Since mainline denominations are similar theologically and culturally, we did not need to study a large number of them.

After evaluating research options we decided to do an alumni survey of confirmation classes. We approached twenty-three Presbyterian churches in five states in different parts of the United States, assured everyone of confidentiality, and asked if we could take random samples from their past confirmation lists. We knew that all the churches kept good records and that someone in each town could help us find where the confirmands are today.

THE SURVEY OF PRESBYTERIAN CONFIRMANDS

We worked in five different states and interviewed 500 confirmands by telephone. We discussed their religious histories, beliefs and doubts, evaluations of churches today, and central values in life. Then we talked with forty of the confirmands at greater length in person.

We found that these young Presbyterians were largely upper middle class, well educated, family oriented, and highly mobile. Sixty-three percent had earned a four-year college degree. Ten percent had never married, and another 24 percent had already been married and divorced. Sixty-two percent now belonged to a church, and 47 percent had attended at least twice a month in the past year. At least 75 percent had dropped out of church at one time, usually in their late teens or early twenties. Half of the dropouts (approximately 37 percent of the total sample) had returned to churchgoing, but only half of these had returned to Presbyterian churches.

In religious beliefs and practices it was a heterogeneous sample of people. We identified eight types, four of them "churched" and four "unchurched." Fifty-two percent were "churched," which was defined by two characteristics—they had to be members of some church when interviewed and to have attended worship services at least six times in the previous year. The other 48 percent, the "unchurched," did not meet one or both criteria.

The churched portion comprised four of the types: (1) people now active in Presbyterian churches (29 percent of the sample); (2) people now active in other mainline Protestant denominations (10 percent); (3) people who had moved to fundamentalist, conservative, or pentecostal churches (6 percent); and (4) people now active in any other denomination or group, such as Roman Catholics, Baptists, or Jehovah's Witnesses (7 percent). The unchurched formed four more types: (5) people who attended a church at least six times in the past year but are not members of any church (10 percent); (6) people who belonged to a church but had not attended six times in the past year (9 percent); (7) people who had neither attended nor become church members but still saw themselves as religious persons (21 percent); and (8) people who said that they no longer saw themselves as religious at all (8 percent).

In sum, the major loss in mainline membership was due to the many people who had stopped church involvement. Why did they stop? We asked them numerous questions about theological topics, such as their belief in the creeds, whether all religions have equal truth, and whether a person needs to go to church to be a good Christian. See Table 5.1, which gives the responses for the total sample and for the churched and unchurched categories.

The top section of the table shows that the majority hold a Christian worldview. They believe that Jesus Christ was God or the Son of God, and they believe that human beings should live in anticipation of life after death. Both churched and unchurched people have these views, and the unchurched people have not rejected Christian teachings. The middle of the table shows that the confirmands have mixed opinions about whether the only absolute truth for humankind is in Jesus. A majority do not believe that only followers of Jesus Christ can be saved. Roughly half believe that all the great religions of the world are somehow true.

The bottom section of the table tells us that these people are very individualistic in religious matters. The majority believe that an individual should arrive at his or her own religious beliefs independent of any churches or synagogues, and the vast majority believe that a person can be a good Christian without going to church.

In the entire table the differences between churched and unchurched persons are only moderately large. The unchurched have not rejected Christian teachings. Both the churched and the unchurched are generally Christian in their beliefs. At the same time many people—both inside and outside the churches—feel uncertainty about the special truth of Christianity, and most believe that individuals need to decide religious matters for themselves.

Table 5.1
Religious Attitudes of Presbyterian Confirmands (in percentages)

	Total Sample	Churched Persons	Unchurched Persons
Core Belief Statements			
What do you believe about Jesus Christ?			
He was God or the Son of God.	78	95	61
He was another religious leader like Mohammed or Buddha.	15	4	27
He never actually lived, or Don't know.	7	1	12
Human beings should live with the assumption that there is no life after death. Strongly or moderately agree.	10	6	15
Particularism and Relativism Statements			
The only absolute Truth for humankind is in Jesus Christ. Strongly or moderately agree.	60	81	38
Only followers of Jesus Christ and members of His church can be saved. Strongly or moderately agree.	29	45	12
All the different religions are equally good ways of helping a person find ultimate truth. Strongly or moderately agree.	55	47	65
All the great religions of the world are equally true and good. Strongly or moderately agree.	39	32	46
Individualism Statements			
An individual should arrive at his or her own religious beliefs independent of any churches or synagogues. Strongly or moderately agree.	63	50	77
Do you think a person can be a good Christian or Jew if he or she doesn't attend church or synagogue? Yes.	82	73	92

THREE QUESTIONS

We began this study of Presbyterian confirmands with three main questions. First, when these young adults select congregations for themselves after their teenage years, is there a general flow from mainline churches to conservative and fundamentalist churches? Many people were claiming that this was the case, since mainline churches have been declining and conservative churches have been growing. But we found that, of the total sample, only 6 percent had switched to fundamentalist, evangelical, or pentecostal churches. We also found that 48 percent were "unchurched." Put simply, the main flow of these confirmands outward from the Presbyterian denomination was into inactivity or no church commitment, not to conservative churches. This suggests that mainline Protestant churches cannot halt their decline by taking on more of the character of conservative churches.

A second question was whether these young adults were strong in the Christian faith, yet stopped churchgoing because of problems with the *institutionalized churches*. We found that this was true of *some* people who were disgusted with the churches because of their inadequate stands against racism or sexism or even for general reasons, such as boredom in Sunday worship. But not many. We found few objections to local congregations or pastors and almost no objections to denominational policies. In fact, we found very little knowledge of denominational affairs or interest in them. Therefore the problem of decline was not solely a rejection of institutional policies and leaders.

A third question was whether these people have strong faith in the truth of Christianity or whether a large number are relativists—believing that all religions have some truth and that Christianity is one option among many. It turned out that many are relativists, and this is crucial.

THE LAY LIBERAL

We uncovered a definite type of person among these confirmands whom we called the "lay liberal." Lay liberals are people with generally open-minded views about religion, social issues, and moral issues, but without the backing of an articulate theology. They have pieced together their beliefs for themselves. They are relativists regarding religion and do not believe that Christianity is truer than other religions. Some lay liberals said that Christianity is true "for them" or that it meets their needs, but they did not see this truth as universally valid. They said that religion is a good thing and that all religions have truth in one way or other. Lay liberals typically separate the doctrinal teachings of Christianity from its moral code. They strongly support responsible moral behavior and have a high regard for the teachings of Jesus.

We are not the only researchers to identify a large number of Christians who are unclear about doctrinal matters but dedicated to responsible moral living. Nancy Ammerman (1995) analyzed interviews with adult Protestants and Catholics and identified a category of persons she called "Golden Rule Christians." These persons are not very concerned with beliefs but are committed to living by the Golden Rule and making the world a better place. They define their religion by actions more than by creeds. Ammerman found that in mainline Protestant denominations approximately two-thirds of the members are Golden Rule Christians.

Lay liberals have some other clear characteristics. They are cautious about identifying the source of religious authority. What is a reliable authority for knowing ultimate truth? How can we be certain about life after death and about the way we should live? During the Reformation, the authority of the Roman Catholic Church and tradition was attacked and effectively supplanted by authority of Scripture. However, since then, higher criticism of the Bible and modern scientific inquiry have weakened Scripture's authority. If the church and the Bible are not reliable authorities, what can be the foundation of a person's faith? We found that lay liberals tend to respond to the problem of authority by relying on their own personal experience. This often leads to a sense of relativism, since one person's experience will be different from another person's, and there is no way to know what really is true.

Lay liberals are not interested in converting others to Protestantism. We asked everyone in the sample if the churches should send missionaries to foreign lands to convert people from other religions, and the lay liberals said *no*, since those foreigners have their own religion, which we need to respect. However, they were in favor of mission programs promoting *education* or *health*.

Lay liberals are very tolerant and open-minded regarding matters of belief and practice; this is one of their dominant characteristics. They tend toward inclusiveness rather than exclusiveness. They are reluctant to share their own faith with other people; they share the American assumption that faith is a private matter, to be discussed in public only if another person asks. They are good material for all kinds of leadership in a pluralistic society such as the United States today, since they are accepting of various religious views and ready to work with numerous groups.

Lay liberals believe in religious training for children. They want children to learn about the Bible and the Christian tradition, for the sake of exposure. They think children should choose their own religious commitments later; if the children then move away from Protestantism, that is all right, since it is *their* business.

Lay liberalism is a pragmatic response to the challenges of modern culture and pluralism. By personalizing Christianity and relativizing the truth, lay liberals do not challenge the veracity of other religious traditions. By downplaying specific Christian claims to authority, they can thrive in both Christian and religiously neutral settings (such as corporate business, government, international affairs, and science) today. Their position appears to be a solution to the problem of how to be a religious person in a pluralistic and secular world. Lay liberals tend to be more educated than average, which accounts partly for the concentration of them in mainline Protestantism. It also accounts for the greater membership losses in denominations having the most educated people.

How many lay liberals are there? We estimated that roughly half of our sample were lay liberals, which leads us to believe that maybe half of the membership of mainline Protestantism today is composed of lay liberals.

Where does lay liberalism come from? In our sample we found that it was a product of liberal education, cultural awareness, and international travel. Protestant young adults today have higher levels of education, cross-cultural awareness, and international experience than ever before in history. Mainline Protestants glory in that. For decades mainline Protestants have been urging open-mindedness and tolerance on their children. They push their children to get into the best colleges, usually secular colleges rather than religious ones, and pay thousands of dollars for them to travel to all parts of the world.

Religious boundaries are vanishing for young adults who grew up in Presbyterian churches. This means not just the boundaries between Christian denominations such as Presbyterians and Methodists or Presbyterians and Catholics, but also the boundaries between major religious families such as Christians, Jews, and Buddhists. What were once clear boundaries between truth and error are becoming less and less convincing to these young adults, and many of them are quite relativistic about religious claims and religious authority. As sociologist Peter Berger has argued, religious communities cannot maintain their power if they lack boundaries. They need what he calls "plausibility structures," which are communities of intense communication and interaction among members, having clear boundaries between insiders and outsiders (Berger 1967:45–51). If internal communications weaken and boundaries are routinely crossed, religious faith and identity weaken.

NEW ATTITUDES TOWARD CHURCHES

Their relativized and personalized experience of faith makes lay liberals selective consumers of churches. For the most part, they do not attend church out of obligation or family loyalty. They feel no guilt if they abandon churchgoing, and they feel little need to go for the sake of appearances or respectability. If they go to church, it is because they want a connection to God and to authentic people with life experiences similar to their own. They want a church home as a place to work out their faith, rather than one that provides all the answers.

The people in our sample told us about the main values of church involvement as they saw them. They described four values that, so to speak, churches had for sale. We called these values "the four commodities." Most important was religious education for children and programs to enhance family life. We asked the entire sample, "Would you want a child of yours to receive any religious instruction?" and 96 percent said yes. It was almost unanimous. Even the unchurched people usually said yes to this question. Most Americans see the church as a valuable resource for family life. The other three "commodities" were immersion in a community, support for personal needs, and inspirational experiences.

The young adults in our sample believe that churchgoing is not absolutely necessary for Christians. As Table 5.1 shows, 82 percent say that a person can be a good Christian or Jew without attending church or synagogue. (In a 1988 Gallup poll, 79 percent of all American young adults agreed with the statement.) The persons in our sample thought of churchgoing in consumer terms. That is, they hold that individuals should think of churches much as they think of retail stores. If the store has something valuable, buy it. If not, don't buy and don't go back. There is no obligation. Furthermore, these people feel little brand loyalty or, in religious terms, little denominational loyalty. In our sample Presbyterian identity was very weak. They didn't see what difference it made if they were Presbyterians, Methodists, or Lutherans. As several persons told us, one of the appeals of mainline churches is their relative openness to individualized interpretations of Christianity. They don't make dogmatic demands.

A consumer attitude toward churches does not produce the same level of commitment and loyalty as a traditional faith commitment. Church involvement by lay liberals was lower than by conservative or evangelical Christians. A congregation or denomination filled with lay liberals will have no trouble teaching open-mindedness and tolerance, but it will have difficulties over its identity. The questions "Who are we?" "How are we distinctive?" "Who are we not?" and "Are we different from open-minded humanists?" are not easily answered by lay liberal congregations.

IMPLICATIONS FOR MAINLINE PROTESTANT CHURCHES

Is religion on the decline in America? Or are only the mainline churches declining? Sociologists the world over have been arguing as to whether there is a long-term global trend toward secularization. The debate has raged for years. One distinction has proven to be necessary, that between religious *needs* and religious *institutional life*. The religious needs of human beings are not easy to identify and measure, but they are certainly strong and will continue to be. It is true that human experience has changed during the last century, but there is no evidence that basic religious needs have decreased.

Yet religious bodies do change. Denominations as we know them are only several hundred years old, and the fastest-growing denominations in America, such as the Mormons, Adventists, and Assemblies of God, are less than two hundred years old. Individual congregations change even more quickly. For sake of clarity we need to distinguish the histories of particular denominations and particular churches from underlying religious needs of humans. In market terms, the religious market is strong and eternal, but it changes in particulars—and the "firms" that service the market change as well.

This, we believe, is the most accurate view of the situation today. Religion is permanent, and trends toward secularization in one country or another or in one region or another are short term. Furthermore, they are self-limiting in that nonreligious societies tend to spawn new religious movements. Mainline denominations are experiencing declines in membership because of changes in young adults. These people feel less urgency for church involvement, and churches do not always relate to their most basic beliefs. Today many Protestant congregations are growing and many others are declining, but the overall picture is a gradual decline.

A related trend is a gradual detachment from denominational structures. Since the beginning of the 1990s, many mainline denominations have been unable to maintain their authority and their central programs. The members of the local churches are not sending money to denominational centers and to denominational programs the way they did two or three decades ago. Every national bureaucracy in mainline Protestantism has needed to downsize, and in some cases there have been drastic cuts of 20 to 40 percent. Local churches are making more decisions for themselves and relying less on denominational leadership. This is the beginning of a shift in power away from central denominations and toward local churches. The shift is also seen in the growing number of Protestant churches today that are nondenominational; they exist happily without any denominational connection, and some of them are thriving.

Why is this happening? One factor seems to be a skepticism about large national institutions of all kinds, a skepticism especially strong among young adults today. Social surveys prove that Americans have decreased their confidence in institutions since the 1950s—for example, in government, in big business, and in the mass media. Confidence in organized religion is down also (Niemi, Mueller, and Smith 1989; Morin and Balz 1996). Centralized institutions will need to adapt.

The most reasonable prediction is that denominations will survive, but in a restructured form. Future denominations will be less centralized, less expensive, and more in the form of networks than of bureaucratic pyramids. Congregations will increasingly work together in voluntary networks of churches and clergy. The future vitality of mainline Protestantism will depend more than ever on the creativity and persuasiveness of local congregations. It will depend on the ability of local churches to relate to the deepest feelings of the new generation.

REFERENCES

Ammerman, Nancy T. 1995. "Golden Rule Christianity: Lived Religion in the American Mainstream." Unpublished paper. Atlanta, GA: Candler School of Theology.
Berger, Peter L. 1967. *The Sacred Canopy*. New York: Doubleday.
Coalter, Milton J., John M. Mulder, and Louis B. Weeks. 1996. *Vital Signs: The Promise of Mainstream Protestantism*. Grand Rapids, MI: William Eerdmans.
Hadaway, C. Kirk. 1993. "Church Growth in North America: The Character of a Religious Marketplace." Chapter 17 in C. Kirk Hadaway and David A. Roozen (eds.), *Church and Denominational Growth*. Nashville, TN: Abingdon Press.
Hadaway, C. Kirk, and David A. Roozen (eds.). 1993. *Church and Denominational Growth*. Nashville, TN: Abingdon Press.
Hoge, Dean R., Benton Johnson, and Donald A. Luidens. 1994. *Vanishing Boundaries: The Religion of Mainline Protestant Baby Boomers*. Louisville, KY: Westminster/John Knox Press.
Hoge, Dean R., and David A. Roozen. 1979. "Some Sociological Conclusions about Church Trends." Chapter 14 in Dean R. Hoge and David A. Roozen (eds.), *Understanding Church Growth and Decline: 1950–1978*. New York: Pilgrim Press.
Kelley, Dean M. 1972. *Why Conservative Churches Are Growing*. San Francisco: Harper and Row.
———. 1977. *Why Conservative Churches Are Growing* (Updated Edition). New York: Harper and Row.
Morin, Richard, and Dan Balz. 1996. "Americans Losing Trust in Each Other and Institutions." *Washington Post*, January 28, pp. A1, A6, A7.

Niemi, Richard G., John Mueller, and Tom W. Smith. 1989. *Trends in Public Opinion*. Westport, CT: Greenwood Press.

Roof, Wade Clark. 1993. *A Generation of Seekers: The Spiritual Journeys of the Baby Boom Generation*. San Francisco, CA: Harper San Francisco.

6

Gender and Jewish Identity among Twenty-Somethings in the United States

Debra Renee Kaufman

Amazing grace, how sweet the sound
That saved a wretch like me.
I once was lost but now I'm found,
Was blind but now I see.

"When I hear 'Amazing Grace' I think *Shabbos* (the Jewish Sabbath)," a twenty-five-year-old male said to me as we sat around a table with nine of his other friends and ate communally from the spread before us in the small booth in the Ethiopian restaurant where we had agreed to meet. Just how complicated identity in a pluralistic society can be is evident in the ways that "Amazing Grace," redolent with meaning of a different time and place for one community, can invoke identity for members of another community.

In this group interview drawn from a snowball sample of fifty students from ten colleges along the eastern seacoast of the United States and from twenty personal interviews among Boston based residents between the ages of twenty and thirty, this young man was explaining in response to the question, "What things do you do in your life that make you feel Jewish?" that he spends almost every Friday night in the celebration of the Sabbath with his friends.

> We get together almost every Friday night, although we don't always go to *shule* [synagogue] and sometimes we don't even have Friday night dinner together or even light the candles or make the *kiddush* [prayer over wine] or *mozi* [prayer over the bread, challah], but we always folksing together. We bring our guitars and we sing. We sing Hebrew, Yiddish . . . songs from the sixties but we always, always end our evening by singing "Amazing Grace."

In this essay, I wish to contest the notion that there is a definable, easily recognized, monolithic and unambivalent complex set of emotions and attitudes and/or content that make up our identities. Erickson once referred to identity as "a term for something unfathomable as it is all pervasive" (cited in Meyers 1990:56). Like other theorists, I do not believe that identities derive from "natural" qualities or divisions. Instead, they are continually being produced, disseminated and struggled over (Connolly 1991:64). Although I am interested in the dynamic processes whereby the many components of identity are produced, in this brief chapter I shall not be able to pursue this continuous play among and between culture, history, and power, but rather shall confine myself to a more descriptive analysis of identity among young adults in the United States. Several important theoretical issues emerge from these findings. Identity requires difference, and it is contextual. As Connolly (1991:64) suggests, "Identity requires difference in order to be" and "it converts difference into otherness in order to secure its own self-certainty." Moreover, we learn our identities within certain moments of history and within certain parameters of class, race, gender, and ethnicity.

One finding that I shall reveal before I even present the data is that for both the male and the female young adults in this study, except for the three subjects who are strictly orthodox,[1] Jewish identity, in general, constitutes what has been called an ethnic solidarity based on stereotypical understandings of peoplehood and the peculiar characteristics of those people, rather than on a religious understanding of Judaism. Feingold (1991) calls this the possibility of being Jewish, but not Judaic. While the majority of identified American Jews may not be very well informed about the content of Judaic thought or theology or even the history of their people, they do seem to be involved, as my data show, in the political process of carrying on the culture in a "separatist, distinctive communal style" (Feingold 1991:72) or in the ways that mark them as different from others, even if that difference has to be continually created. Therefore, since those under study are predominately middle to upper middle class, ethnically similar, and of the same race, gender will be my focus. Gender, like identity, of course, is dependent on or constituted by the intersection of class, race, and ethnicity as well.

Hall (cited in Silberstein 1994:4) writes, "Identities are the names we give to different ways we are positioned by and position ourselves within the narratives of the past." One such narrative that has *not* been explored among this age group is the Holocaust. How do these young adults, for whom memory is fast becoming history, position themselves within this past event? In what ways does this narrative become, if at all, a part of their Jewish identities?

The question for me is, does the Holocaust provide themes and metaphors around which Jewish identity is constructed and positioned? Before the Holocaust, American Jewish identity, for most Jews, according to Meyers, was either a religiously based morality or a loose bond of ethnic solidarity. A rise in awareness of the Holocaust has produced in many individuals a much more "determined" Jewishness (1990:56). In fact, claims Meyers, the Holocaust is a major factor in sustaining Jewish identity since World War II. Seidler-Feller (1991) argues that in the absence of a positive motivation, the Holocaust becomes critical in sustaining Jewish identity. He reasons that the steady diet of Holocaust films, novels, memorials, and museums constitutes the set of institutional ways in which young adults of this generation create their identities. The focus then for most young people is on victimology, a political identity based on both perceived and real anti-Semitism and the historical reconstructions of being the victim.

Therefore, two issues are of particular concern to me: What part, if any, does the Holocaust play in the construction of Jewish identity; and are there gender differences in the ways in which Jewish identity is constructed for this population? For it is this generation of eighteen-to-thirty-year-olds who represent the future generation of Jews in the United States. Yet, despite the pivotal role it plays in understanding Jewish identity, this is a population for whom we have very little data. Several explanations may account for this neglect. For the most part, this generation is marrying later and bearing children later. In that Jewish identity has been measured, for the most part, through surveys aimed at those who are institutionally affiliated, we can see how a population that has yet to establish itself as members of the Jewish community might very well be overlooked. To date, our best measures of identity have come from activities identified through institutional participation (fundraising, synagogue attendance, Jewish Community Center activities). Since, typically, people of this age group live independently of their families of origin and are not yet involved in institutional Jewish life, we have seen very little in the literature reflecting their attitudes or opinions about Jewish identity.

Understanding Jewish identity is doubly confounded if it is measured through attitudinal surveys with only open-ended questions to touch upon the complexities of responses to such a manifold topic. Survey methods cannot plumb the depths of so pervasive a term as identity. To date, although several colleagues are concurrently engaged in qualitative research (Bethanie Horowitz, Arnold Eisen, and Steven Cohen), no in-depth interview studies have been published on Jewish identity among this age group. In this study, as in my book *Rachel's Daughters* (1991), I have engaged my sample in what I call "structured conversations," introducing a set of prepared questions that guide our recorded conversations.

THE STUDY

Just who are these young adults? They range from twenty to thirty years of age. The average age for the twenty personal interviews was twenty-six, for the group interviews twenty-one. They are in school, continuing with their education at the graduate or professional level, and/or currently employed. All have had some or are currently engaged in post-secondary education. Their estimated family-of-origin incomes range from $65,000 to $250,000 with almost all parents in professional and/or business careers. Those in the group interviews (fifty) came from all over the United States, heavily representing the Northeast, but also including Montana, Oregon, Texas, California, Illinois, Ohio, and Mississippi. Those in the individual interview sample were all from the Boston area, except for two (from New Jersey and California). Among the interviews there were eleven women and nine men. Among the group interviews there were thirty-seven men and thirty-three women.

Contrary to Seidler-Feller's (1991) and Meyer's expectations, the Holocaust, while present in the construction of Jewish identity in relation to their political identities, did not play as predominant a role in their overall Jewish identity. One thirty-year-old male puts it this way:

> I think there are a lot of people whose Jewish identities are very structured by memories of the Holocaust and the establishment of the State of Israel, and they are things I feel strongly about. Neither one is the primary event, however, that structures my Jewish life. . . . I really think . . . an emphasis on either of those two things really de-emphasizes the way in which one can, or sort of understand a Jewish experience that's in the present.

A twenty-eight-year-old female claims:

> Judaism is not just about the past . . . the Holocaust is a *big problem* [emphasis hers]. I mean, it's *crucial*, that we remember it. I've been to Poland, and I studied it, and read books, and it's awful. It's the worst thing to happen to the Jewish people, or any people, and we have to remember it, and read books, and tape testimonies from people and make movies, and have it immortalized, but what we *can't* do is become a cult of the Holocaust, where our sole identity is based upon guilt that we survived, or determination that it will never happen again, or just rooted in the tragedy. . . . Judaism is much more than that. . . . It has an affirmative message which predated the Holocaust, and which will go forward from that and that has to do with the land, and Jerusalem, and the food, and the music, and the culture, and the way you live your life.

A twenty-year-old male put it this way: "I don't like to think of it as something where the Jews have suffered through history and we have to protect it. . . . I don't deny it happened, that Jews have suffered a lot throughout the ages, but I don't think that's the reason that I choose to go on being Jewish. . . . I don't want to think of myself as a victim of history." A twenty-two-year-old female stated: "I think there are a lot of people who do things Jewishly not to give Hitler a posthumous victory. I don't do things for that reason. I like it, that's why I do it."

Although anti-Semitism is certainly a component, the strongest issues emerging in the construction of Jewish identity were not couched in terms of perceived or real anti-Semitism but rather the need to belong to a group one could call "your own." When asked what was specifically Jewish about that kind of group identi-fication, almost all believed that it had to do with belonging to a group of people who had a unique and long history and a distinctive culture. One twenty-six-year-old male put it this way: "I was born into this 5,000 year tradition, of which I am proud. . . . I feel an obligation to continue and perpetuate it." Another twenty-seven-year-old stated that the most comfortable part of being Jewish is that he identifies with "a community and a history and a tradition . . . notice I didn't bring up God. . . . Whether God exists, or doesn't . . . gave us the Torah or didn't, or brought us out of Egypt or didn't . . . it doesn't change our history or tradition, or all the great things about the Jewish people one way or another." "I don't buy into that 'we suffered, we suffered, we suffered, be Jewish' attitude," another twenty-six-year-old male claimed. "I'm just proud about where I come from and I want to continue that." A twenty-two-year-old female stated: "For me, Judaism, being Jewish, has always been kind of unusual, in that people say they are Irish Catholic, but you say you are just *Jewish* [emphasis hers]. It's like, it's your heritage *and* your religion. . . .When you're Jewish, it seems like everything is all rolled up into one. So it's a little bit different." A twenty-two-year-old male put it this way: "History and heritage; that's what defines me."

One theme that emerged from both males and females and across the age spectrum was the need to be a part of a community or a group with which you have something in common. Commonality came from difference, whether it was expressed as a unique sense of humor, a specific history, a way of looking at the world, a particular way of looking, or having a "typical Jewish mother." It was the distinctive parts of the community that these respondents felt they had in common with one another. Many spoke of humor as a part of that commonality, with Woody Allen as a trademark, while others mentioned a long line of comedians who had been part of both Hollywood and the New York Greenwich Village scene. The humor, many claimed, derived from being the other, from looking at the world from a unique perspective. Others spoke of the many Jews who made important contributions to the world, from Sigmund Freud to Albert Einstein to Isaac Stern.

Except for the very religious, the distinction Feingold (1991) makes between Jewish and Judaic held for this population, for few mentioned religion as key to their Jewish identity. Except for the very religious, few practiced daily Jewish rituals (praying three times a day for the men or keeping kosher, for instance). However, almost half kept the *Shabbat* (Sabbath) or at least honored that day by not working. Almost three quarters of the sample claimed that most of their friends were Jewish, yet only a minority of the subjects of the twenty personal interviews belonged to an organized Jewish group or, if they did, were nominal members of a group, occasionally participating in a synagogue service or attending a social function. Of those interviewed on college campuses, most belonged to or identified with the Hillel House, but this did not necessarily mean active membership. Yet, despite the infrequency of day-to-day activities, the majority saw themselves as Jews first and Americans second. Most lived in neighborhoods with many other Jews, maintained close ties with other Jewish friends and family, took Jewish studies courses when available or history courses covering, for instance, the Holocaust, and/or worked in professions where there were many other Jews. Most found that when they read the papers or listened to the news that stories about Jewish notables and, most particularly, about Israel caught their interest first. Many felt most comfortable among other Jews, even if the activities were not specifically Jewish in content. There were no notable gender differences.

Although most began by stating they did not lose family in the Holocaust or know anyone personally who did, many felt that anti-Semitism was still a real possibility and something about which Jews needed to be vigilant. The destruction of the Jewish people, not Judaism, was at issue. None used the word Judaism in this discussion or even referred to religion, but rather specifically referred to a people and a shared culture and past. Although the impetus for discussion of anti-

Semitism is the Holocaust and the insurance that it never happen again to Jews, the social justice engagement, when it occurs, is often on behalf of others who are experiencing forms of genocide or threatened genocide. For those expressing their politics in relationship to the Holocaust specifically (not, for instance, engaged in charity work because they are required as practicing Jews to do so), "never again" meant "never again to any people." This was seen most clearly for those involved in what was formerly Yugoslavia. Others felt that their work with Oxfam was another expression of their obligation never to see a population die out. For still others, it was human rights activities directed at South America, Africa, or Asia. The impetus for such involvement stemmed from their sense of duty as Jews and their own history as an oppressed people. Sixty percent of the sample spontaneously referred to the Holocaust during the conversations about identity. For most of the respondents, the Holocaust was seen as one of many moments in the history of anti-Semitism.

While the themes and issues raised did not seem to differentiate between men and women, upon repeated listening to the taped conversations, different foci emerged. For women, there was the sense that their identity was embedded in their everyday lives, both as women and as Jews. Men never referred to gender as an issue in their Jewish identities, although five did identify with the feminist movement and the concern about women in such a patriarchal structure as Judaism. A twenty-year-old female said, "I'm not a gung-ho feminist, but Jewish orthodoxy violates my female identity. I won't go to an orthodox service, but I do go to a traditional service where there is mixed seating. After all, I am at [woman's school] to enhance my identity as a woman."

There was no parallel among men for the following answer from a twenty-six-year-old female. In response to the question of why it is important, if at all, to call yourself a Jew, she answered, "It's extremely important. . . . In one way it's just so vital to who I am . . . it's how I identify myself. There's always the question, what are you first: "Are you a woman, are you a Jew, are you an American?" I think in different scenarios it changes. Another respondent recounted an incident in which she meant to answer by saying "I am a Jew" but said instead: "I'm Sara [fictitious name]." It was, she notes, "as if these things were identical." No male ever responded by saying, "I think of myself more as a male than a Jew," whereas a twenty-four-year-old female said, "I think of myself more as a woman. I pay more attention to women's issues than Jewish issues, 'cause I feel like . . . it has not affected me, my life, to date, being Jewish. Being a woman has."

One thirty-year-old spoke of her distress at being the only female in her Sunday school class and the fact that the congregation of which she was a part would not allow her to read from the Torah. It was not surprising that when asked about how larger changes in the society have affected her identity she responded by saying, "Well, . . . the whole women's movement. At some point, in the middle of junior high, it became extremely important to me, and that didn't fit with Judaism."

Another woman and the only one to mention bisexuality (although two men mentioned the importance of addressing gay and lesbian issues in Judaism, but not as personal statements) expanded on her experiences as a woman praying and singing out loud at the Western Wall and having ultra-Orthodox men throw chairs at her:

> I think there's something about being a woman and also being bisexual that are not dealt with. . . . That whole thing's being cast as a Jewish issue and as a religious issue, and as a . . . Orthodox issue. It's not. It's a feminist issue. It's a misogynist issue. It's an issue of control of women. It happens to be happening with a Jewish community and taking on the trappings of Jewish religious law. . . . But do I think that's authentically Judaism? No, I don't think that Judaism authentically prohibits women from singing . . . or from reading the Torah at the Wall. It's not my understanding of Judaism.

For men, there was a tendency to be more abstract in responses to the questions and in their conversations in general. For instance, when speaking about the relationship between their political and their Jewish identities, men more often spoke of the universal principles at stake, while women spoke specifically of the devastation to families and particularly to children. This was reiterated in the discussion of identity as well. Women talked of the day-to-day practical implications of the ways in which they did things as important to their Jewish identities, while men spoke of transcendence, of God, of theology, and of overarching principles and ethics of behavior, rarely grounding them in real-life examples.

But perhaps the most interesting differences came in the way in which women, compared to men, spoke about the consequences of difference, of separatism, and of a "distinctiveness" as Jews. Except for a few males who expressed concern about Israeli politics and the treatment of the Arabs by Israelis, only women seemed to connect their concerns about "others" with their own connectedness to the Jewish community. One twenty-two-year-old worried about not having non-Jewish friends. She said, "And I think that the healthy way of dealing, of being part of a minority group, is to have friends inside and outside the group. . . . I worry . . . that I'm not going to be able to maintain friendships with non-Jews." Another woman said, "Being involved with the Jewish community has made my social life much too homogeneous and that's something that I'm trying to do a little bit more outreach on and to try to cultivate some other relationships." Women were more likely to be concerned about the notion of a "chosen people" and its consequences for relationships. One twenty-four-year-old stated it this way:

> I think being Jewish makes me special because it makes me feel special. . . . I think my values are pretty good . . . but that doesn't make me a better person . . . this kind of differentness. . . . I think that it is a dilemma. I have had privileges that have allowed me to have amazing opportunities, but I'm not a better person. I'm not more deserving. . . . I haven't worked harder than the next person . . . it's tough. . . . I have a non-Jewish boyfriend and it's very tough to say . . . "you and I are equal and I respect your opinions as much as I respect mine, but I think mine are right." . . . Why do I want my kids to be raised Jewish? . . . Why is it so important to me?

SOME CONCLUSIONS

Both men and women see identity as couched in a need to be a part of a unique historical experience, a tie to a people and a past with a particular culture. Religion plays a lesser part in this understanding of Jewish identity than do culture and history. The Holocaust, while certainly a part of Jewish identity, is best seen as a part of political identities whereby social justice is directed toward others as much as other Jews, if not more so. Gender differences are clearest in the ways in which each sex narrates their understanding of identity and the consequences of "unique" and "different" and the way in which women deal with being female in a society that still maintains stereotypical views of them and in an ethnic religious community that is still prototypically male.

NOTE

1. The Orthodox comprise approximately 10 to 12 percent of the U.S. Jewish population.

REFERENCES

Connolly, William E. 1991. *Identity/Difference*. Ithaca, NY: Cornell University Press.
Feingold, Henry. 1991. "The American Component of American Jewish Identity." Pp. 69–81 in David M. Gordis and Yav Ben-Horin (eds.), *Jewish Identity in America*. Los Angeles: Susan and David Wilstein Institute of Jewish Policy Studies, University of Judaism.
Kaufman, Debra Renee. 1991. *Rachel's Daughters*. New Brunswick, NJ: Rutgers University Press.
Meyers, Michael. 1990. *Jewish Identity in the Modern World*. Seattle: University of Washington Press.
Seidler-Feller, Chaim. 1991. "Responses." Pp. 61–65 in David M. Gordis and Yav Ben-Horin (eds.), *Jewish Identity in America*. Los Angeles: Susan and David Wilstein Institute of Jewish Policy Studies, University of Judaism.
Silberstein, Laurence J. 1994. "Others Within and Others Without: Rethinking Jewish Identity and Culture." Pp. 1–34 in Laurence J. Silberstein and Robert L. Cohn (eds.), *The Other in Jewish Thought and History*. New York: New York University Press.

7

Canadian Evangelical Church Women and Responses to Family Violence

Nancy Nason-Clark

The Voices of Women Victims

But when I became a Christian, I was thankful to the Lord because I had a pastor who . . . knew what I'd been through, and he didn't judge me. And he was the type of pastor who was working with women who had been through . . . abusive marriages.

How can I go to my friends in the church when . . . I tell them I'm a Christian and admit that stuff like this is going on? . . . a lot of Christians have this ideal thing . . . what they're supposed to live like and what they're supposed to be like and what they're supposed to dress like . . . you know you're put into that cocoon.

The Voices of Women Helping Women Victims

I think that the best way . . . is to help her understand somehow that she doesn't have to be there. She doesn't have to stay. It takes a long time. . . . But if somehow, just love her enough, 'cause she's not getting any love. . . . And it's just to love her right out of that house . . . the bottom line is to get them out!

A girl that went to our church. We helped her to move . . . I got my daughter's boyfriend. . . . I got his army buddies to come up so that they could handle the [abusive] boyfriend if he came back while we helped her move everything out in a truck . . . this girl was only 100 pounds soaking wringing wet.

From the rugged shores of Newfoundland to the timbered coastline of British Columbia, groups of Canadian men and women meet together in some form of Christian worship that is evangelical in perspective. The worship style is often characterized by enthusiastic singing and traditional expository preaching in churches that demand a high level of commitment from their members. Closely associated with the emphasis on conversion and a personal relationship with God is their celebration of family life and family values.

Mothers are heralded as the emotional guardians of the home, though both men and women are supposed to nurture their children in both practical and spiritual ways. Passing on the story of evangelical faith and its associated lifestyle is considered central to the role of parenting. Believing that modern Canadian culture is rather hostile to their worldview, evangelical church families are urged to look out for one another and to stem the tide of secularism. But what happens when family life is marked by fear, tension, and violence rather than love and nurturance? In essence, where can and do these families turn when the reality of daily life does not match the Sunday rhetoric of marital harmony?

This chapter explores how women within the evangelical Christian tradition accommodate the reality of wife abuse within their notions about family living. With their explicit focus on family values, is this an environment willing and able to assist women who have suffered the pain and humiliation of violence? Or, do evangelicals simply sweep violence under the proverbial church carpet? When violence is disclosed, what advice is offered? Are women admonished to become better wives and in so doing to find favor with both God and their husbands? Or, are abused women empowered to gain control over their circumstances and thereby avert further violence?

Data for this chapter are drawn from an ongoing research program that involves several Christian denominations and the experiences of more than a thousand women abuse victims, pastors, lay members of congregations, and workers in the shelter movement.[1] Within this chapter, however, our focus is exclusively directed to those who are connected with the evangelical faith tradition.[2]

VIOLENCE AGAINST WOMEN: UNDERSTANDING THE PROBLEM

Conservative estimates suggest that one in every six women in the United States and Canada has experienced a violent episode at the hands of her marital partner within the last year (Straus et al. 1980; Statistics Canada 1993). This number increases to one in four for women who have at some point in their marital relationship been the victim of a violent outburst from their husband (Feld and Straus 1989). Typically family violence occurs "behind closed doors" in a carefully constructed context of shame and secrecy (Straus et al. 1980; *Fire in the Rose Project* 1994).

Pervasive societal notions about the sanctity and privacy of family life deter women from reporting the violence they experience and foster within them notions of guilt and embarrassment. While the roots of wife abuse can be traced to a belief in the subordination of women to male control (Dobash and Dobash 1979), contemporary roles, relationships, and institutions continue to make women dependent on men. The battery of women by their male partners is not linked directly to social class, ethnicity, or regional variables. Yet clearly some women are more vulnerable than others.

In 1993, Statistics Canada conducted a national survey among 12,300 women (aged eighteen years and older) concerning their personal experiences of physical and/or sexual violence. According to their reports, three in ten Canadian women have experienced at least one episode of victimization that was consistent with legal definitions of these offenses and thus against the law. In two out of five households, children witnessed the violence. Few women sought help from either the police (25%) or a social agency (24%). Most relied on friends (51%) or family (42%) for support. One in every five victimized women (22%) told no one about the abuse prior to its disclosure during the telephone interview.

Because wife abuse is not a direct result of specific religious, cultural, or background characteristics (Timmins 1995), all women are potential victims. Yet battered religious women have some unique problems and special needs that set them apart from other victims of abuse. As a result, religious victims of abuse tend to seek out help from their spiritual leaders when crisis occurs in the family relationships.

VIOLENCE AND RELIGION: CONTEXTUALIZING THE RELATIONSHIP

Religious communities teach and model values and practices that have spiritual as well as secular overtones. Considered in this way, churches and their leaders have the potential to alter or at least to challenge attitudes that reinforce violence in the family. Clergy have an important role in responding to the mental health needs of the North American public, for domestic violence has been regarded as one of the foremost pastoral mental health emergencies (Weaver 1993).

Abused religious women begin their search for help within their faith community (Horton and Williamson 1988), although they are often dissatisfied with the results (Wood and McHugh 1994). Secular counselors, on the other hand, seem to be particularly insensitive to the needs of religious victims, failing to challenge the erroneous religious ideation associated with their suffering (Whipple 1987). To put it simply, many abused religious women desire and need counsel and practical support from *both* their faith community and secular agencies.

CONDUCTING THE RESEARCH

The Religion and Violence Research Team, a multidisciplinary group of academic researchers and community partners at the University of New Brunswick, has conducted numerous projects with various faith traditions involving more than a thousand participants.[3] Using a variety of research methodologies—including mailed questionnaires, in-depth personal interviews, focus groups, telephone surveys, and community consultations—this program of research has sought to tell the story of what happens when an abused religious woman seeks help from her faith community.

In this chapter we discuss only data from Baptist and Wesleyan (or holiness) churches, their pastors, church women, and abuse victims. All ministers serving within these traditions in Atlantic Canada[4] were sent a mailed survey (70% responded; n = 343), a sample of 100 were interviewed at their churches, and thirty focus groups were conducted with church women (n = 247) around the region. Taken together, these studies allow us to see how evangelical churches respond to violence against women.

Producing a Safe Environment

I guess I'd see the church perhaps as a, a safe haven. A place where if they're at the end of their rope and have nowhere else to go, I would hope that the church would be one place . . . where they could be given some love and immediate attention.

It's not a safe place to come because once you get there . . . nobody knows what to do with you.

Church women were unanimous in the call for faith communities and their leaders to respond to abused women. Yet, they were aware of some of the limitations of clergy-only counsel and the problems associated with seeking help in a relatively closed community. As a result, church women felt that both clergy and lay people needed to become fully aware of the extent of male violence against women and to explore options that would enable more effective responses. They were neither complacent with the current level of support for victims nor disparaging of the help that was provided. In essence, they challenged themselves and their leaders to greater compassion and more "hands-on" practical support.

The Importance of Women-Only Networks

Women have a wonderful networking system that men just don't seem to share . . . we have the emotional reserves to be able to share.

One of the findings to emerge from our exploration of women's response to abuse was their level of sophistication in defining abuse and the variety of practical and emotional ways in which individually and collectively they had supported victims. In part, their knowledge of the prevalence and severity of abuse was rooted in their personal experience or that of their sisters, mothers, or friends. As a result, they showed high levels of compassion and little tendency to condemn those who found it difficult to escape an abusive environment. Church women were particularly aware of the advantages of women-only support to battered wives. In essence, the gender-segregated ministry profile of most evangelical churches actually produced a milieu that augmented women's opportunities to network with each other and to provide support to women victims. Though most of these women would be reluctant to label themselves feminist, they practiced a form of feminist empowerment in their support for the transition house movement and individual battered women.

DEFINING ABUSE

With physical abuse, 85 percent of the time, it's noticed. Somewhere along the line . . . somebody's going to see the results. And it isn't one bit worse than mental abuse . . . with mental abuse nobody is aware of anything.

In part because their knowledge of abuse was linked to the experience of victims they knew, evangelical women were rather inclusive in their definition of what constituted abuse. They realized that some scars were obvious and others were not. In fact, they discussed the long-term implications of violence and the low self-esteem of victims. They were aware of the challenges for both victim and caregiver on the road to healing and recovery. We found no evidence that church women as a group minimized the pain or the consequences of abuse. On the contrary, they were impatient with the slow (and often inadequate) response of their clerical leaders. And they were often disappointed with their own feeble attempts to bring support and empowerment to battered women in their congregation or community.

Encouraging Disclosures

I think just being more open about it . . . even from the pulpit talking about it. So if there are people that are in the congregation that are actually . . . suffering . . . they'll feel more comfortable to discuss it with someone.

Two in every three women in our study revealed that they had sought the advice of another woman in their own church for a family-type problem, and the majority had been involved in supporting at least one abused woman (Nason-Clark 1996). These data offer compelling evidence of an informal support network, where women seek to assist each other under the umbrella of their religious worldview. Rather than deny the existence of abuse within the household of faith, evangelical women made themselves available to each other and offered friendship and an environment where it was "safe" for a woman to disclose the pain she suffered at home. Despite their experience in this area, evangelical women were critical of themselves for missed opportunities to "hear the voices" of other victims. They lamented the fact that they seemed to have so little time to offer coffee or lunch in their home and through these signs of friendship to make themselves available to others.

THE RELIGIOUS SUPPORT NETWORK

Referrals

I had a neighbor . . . she was living in an abusive situation. So, I was put together with her through a . . . pastor friend. She just lived down the street from me, so [I] was basically just a listening ear.

Sometimes initial disclosures of abuse were made to the pastor rather than to a church woman herself. In these cases, evangelical women felt that clergy had a responsibility to ensure that the victim was put into contact with a woman-only support network. Such a network was believed to augment the counsel of the pastor and to offer enduring friendship and practical help over the long road to healing and recovery. Most women recognized that alone they were ill-equipped to provide *all* the care that an abused woman needed, and sometimes they felt rather overwhelmed by the responsibility. In such instances, they suggested that a woman seek help from a secular counselor, the transition house, or some other community agency. As a group, church women showed less reluctance than clergy to make secular referrals (Nason-Clark 1996). Moreover, they were much more sympathetic to the transition house movement than one might have anticipated (Beaman-Hall and Nason-Clark 1997a), though some were wary of the advice church women might receive in that context.

OFFERING PRACTICAL HELP

Taking children, being a listening ear, a grocery person, taxi driver. Just seeing a need and doing it before they have to ask, just to make their life easier.

The myriad of ways that evangelical women upheld abused women was impressive (Nason-Clark 1997); one in five who had offered support provided overnight accommodation, and more than 10 percent had given child care or financial help. Others provided transportation or furniture. But the most common response of evangelical women was their offer of a *listening ear*, a form of support that demanded neither that an abused woman cut all ties with her partner nor that she remain indefinitely in an environment where her physical and emotional health were put at risk. By their listening skills, evangelical women offered abused wives both safety and empowerment. They upheld their right to make choices, even if they did not always agree with the choices that were made. In fact, many evangelical women reported their personal disappointment when an abused woman would decide to return to an unchanged violent partner.

Reinforcing the Spiritual Journey

We need to be there for each other. . . . I think women's self-esteem is so low, especially in abusive situations. I mean, we need to let them know how much Christ loves them . . . and therefore as Christ's ambassadors, how much we love them. . . . Christ doesn't want them to put up with it.

Spiritual support involved traditional religious activities like prayer and Bible reading, but it also involved explicit counsel that God was on the side of the victim. Hearing condemnation of their husband's abuse in religious language proved to be very empowering for victims. It was a form of support that secular care providers were unable to offer. As religious women condemned the violence in explicitly spiritual terms, they reinforced the boundaries of their faith perspective, even as they provided spiritual healing for victimized women. We found little evidence that religious women offered one another "pat answers" or advice that would increase the risk of further violence.

GLOBAL ISSUES

Evangelical women in Canada have a long history of social action. Through practical care for others, they believe they enhance their credibility to share the gospel. Yet, they are tempered in their enthusiasm for the women's movement, in part because they believe that feminism is associated with selfishness, a "me first" attitude that brings it into direct conflict with the "others first" attitude espoused by evangelicals (Beaman-Hall and Nason-Clark 1997b). While there are ideological differences between transition house workers and church women, they are united in their condemnation of violence against women and desirous to make a positive impact upon the lives of abused women. Their differences notwithstanding, it is more accurate to portray church women and transition house workers as partners rather than protagonists (Beaman-Hall and Nason-Clark, 1997a). But, how can the barriers be addressed in ways that are sensitive both to the feminist roots of the shelter movement and to the pro-family endorsement of evangelical Christianity?

BREAKING DOWN BARRIERS BETWEEN THE SACRED AND THE SECULAR

> Secular organizations will tie the hands of the church and won't let them talk about . . . where their hope can come from . . . probably we can go so far together and then we have to separate.

There are five major obstacles to partnership between secular and sacred caregivers in the fight to eliminate family violence and to respond compassionately to the victims (Nason-Clark 1996:524–529). First, naming the problem is an obstacle. While feminists label wife abuse as male violence against women, clergy name it family violence, revealing their hesitation to lay responsibility for abuse solely in the hands of men. The second obstacle concerns the role of reconciliation. Since the concept of reconciliation is central to the gospel message, it is not surprising that conservative clergy are overly optimistic about the feasibility of reform in an abusive man's life and possible reconciliation with the wife he has abused. Third, clergy are reluctant to attribute wife abuse in Christian families to other than spiritual factors. If the origin of the problem is spiritual, then so too is its cure. Fourth, there is a low rate of referrals between secular and sacred caregivers. Both groups appear hesitant to offer women choices outside of the ideological frameworks in which they have been trained. And fifth, there is a great reluctance on the part of male ministers to condemn violence against women from the pulpit. The failure of clergy to condemn wife abuse clearly and unequivocally from the pulpit is often interpreted as indirect support for men's abusive actions (Brown and Bohn 1989).

Building Bridges between the Steeple and the Shelter

> There are some things [about abuse] that I don't think the church understands. . . . However, the secular organizations may not have the compassion that churches can show.

The potential of partnerships between secular and sacred caregivers in the fight to end violence cannot be overstated. Yet, there are some serious challenges ahead if cooperation between the transition house movement and churches is to be strengthened. These obstacles notwithstanding, many believe that the needs presented by abused women and their children outweigh professional loyalties and ideological positions. In an age of fiscal restraint and shrinking public budgets, it is in everyone's best interests to attempt to build bridges between groups committed to a common cause.

CONCLUDING COMMENTS

In this chapter we have considered ways in which conservative Protestants have accommodated the reality of wife abuse within their ideology of the family. Evangelical women respond to victims of battery by offering practical, emotional, and spiritual assistance. They support the transition house movement through tangible means that could be regarded as bridge building, attempting to narrow the chasm between religious caregivers and those employed by community agencies. The magnitude of the problem of wife abuse in Canada, as elsewhere, means that all institutions—religious and secular in nature—need to work together to respond to the needs of victims and to promote violence-free family relationships.

NOTES

I would like to acknowledge financial support from the following sources: the Louisville Institute for the Study of Protestantism and American Culture, the Social Sciences and Humanities Research Council, the Department of the Solicitor General, the Lawson Foundation, the Constant Jacquet Research Award of the Religious Research Association, the Department of the Secretary of State of the Government of Canada, the Muriel McQueen Fergusson Center for Family Violence Research, and the University of New Brunswick Research Fund.

1. The Religion and Violence Research Team is affiliated with the Muriel McQueen Fergusson Center for Family Violence Research at the University of New Brunswick. The research team, which is multidisciplinary, is coordinated by Nancy Nason-Clark; other members include Lori Beaman, Lois Mitchell, Sheila McCrea, Terry Atkinson, and Christy Hoyt, plus several graduate student assistants. Collaborative research projects are now underway with the United Baptist Convention of the Atlantic Provinces, the Atlantic District of the Wesleyan Church, the Maritime Conference of the United Church, the Maritime Division of the Salvation Army, and the Anglican Church (Province of New Brunswick). Analyses of some of the data reported in this chapter have previously appeared in Beaman-Hall and Nason-Clark 1997a and 1997b and in Nason-Clark 1995, 1996, and 1997.

2. Our discussion here is built upon data collected from United Baptist and Wesleyan (or holiness) churches.

3. Atlantic Canada includes the provinces of New Brunswick, Nova Scotia, Prince Edward Island, and Newfoundland.

REFERENCES

Beaman-Hall, Lori, and Nancy Nason-Clark. 1997a. "Partners or Protagonists? The Transition House Movement and Conservative Churches." *Affilia* 12(2):176–196.
———. 1997b. "Translating Spiritual Commitment Into Service: The Response of Evangelical Women to Wife Abuse." *Canadian Woman Studies* 17(1):58–61.
Brown, Joanne, and Carole Bohn (eds.). 1989. *Christianity, Patriarchy and Abuse: A Feminist Critique*. Cleveland: The Pilgrim Press.

Dobash, R. P., and R. E. Dobash. 1979. *Violence against Wives: A Case against the Patriarchy.* New York: Free Press.

Feld, S. L., and M. A. Straus. 1989. "Escalation and Desistance of Wife Assault in Marriage," *Criminology,* 27(1):141–161.

Fire in the Rose Project. 1994. Ottawa: Canadian Council on Justice and Corrections.

Horton, Anne, and Judith Williamson (eds.). 1988. Abuse and Religion: When Praying Isn't Enough. New York: D.C. Heath and Company.

Nason-Clark, Nancy. 1997. *The Battered Wife: How Christians Confront Family Violence.* Louisville, KY: Westminster/John Knox Press.

———. 1996. "Religion and Violence against Women: Exploring the Rhetoric and the Response of Evangelical Churches in Canada." *Social Compass* 43(4):515–536.

———. 1995. "Conservative Protestants and Violence against Women: Exploring the Rhetoric and the Response." Pp. 109–130 in Mary Jo Neitz and Marion Goldman (eds.), *Sex, Lies and Sanctity: Religion and Deviance in Modern America.* Greenwich, CT: JAI Press.

Statistics Canada. 1993. "The Violence against Women Survey," *The Daily,* November 18, 1993.

Straus, Murray A., Richard J. Gelles, and Suzanne K. Steinmetz. 1980. *Behind Closed Doors: Violence in the American Family.* New York: Doubleday/Anchor.

Timmins, Leslie (ed.). 1995. *Listening to the Thunder: Advocates Talk about the Battered Women's Movement.* Vancouver, B.C.: Women's Research Centre.

Weaver, Andrew. 1993. "Psychological Trauma: What Clergy Need to Know." *Pastoral Psychology* 41(6):385–408.

Whipple, Vicky. 1987. "Counseling Battered Women from Fundamentalist Churches." *Journal for Marital and Family Therapy* 13:251–258.

Wood, Alberta, and Maureen McHugh. 1994. "Woman Battering: The Response of the Clergy," *Pastoral Psychology* 42(3):185–196.

PART II

RELIGIOUS ORGANIZATION

In Part I we examined ways in which individuals relate to religion—their meaning systems, their identity, and their choices. Now we turn to the structure of religious bodies.

This may not be everyone's favorite view of the subject. We often hear people complain about "organized religion." And yet many people continue to attend churches and other places of worship. Perhaps what they are seeking is a sense of community, and not necessarily the imposition of structure. However, communities cannot exist solely on the basis of ideas and values. They must deal with practical considerations, such as where they will meet, how their buildings will be maintained, and who will be responsible for rituals and other group activities. When people are dealing with personal problems or seeking answers to religious questions, they may feel the need of someone to counsel them. When they become parents, they may look for someone to help teach their children about their faith.

Religions develop structures to accomplish all these tasks and others. On the local level the structure may be a congregation, that is, a group of people who gather regularly to worship together. They may choose clergy to carry out special religious functions, or the clergy may be selected by a centralized church administration. These are the usual patterns in Western societies of the religious division of labor—that is, the distinction between clergy, who are responsible for providing leadership and tending to the spiritual needs of the members, and the members themselves, or lay people. There are some exceptions, such those Quaker congregations that do not have full-time paid clergy but rather share the responsibility for pastoral care among the members, who are all regarded as ministers. In other parts of the world the patterns may be more complex, as in the case of Hinduism, in which religious functions are carried out by a large number of people with different roles.

The structures of religious bodies also differ according to whether they are closer to the model of a church or that of a sect. A church is a large organization that seeks to include everyone in its membership, including newborn babies. This is why churches in the Christian tradition baptize infants. Churches tend to have formal structures with highly centralized authority and complex theology. Historically churches have sought close alliances with political powers. The extreme example of a church would be a state religion.

A sect, on the other hand, is a body of people who generally prefer to be outsiders to the political system but special insiders within their congregations. Sects tend to avoid close alliances with governments, except to negotiate their right to exist free from persecution. Their congregations are usually small and close-knit and impose strict ethical standards on their members. Membership is exclusive. One must prove one's worthiness to become a member by the example of an ethical life. Some sects require the avoidance of alcohol, dancing, card playing, gambling, and other behaviors that violate the norms of the group. Children are not eligible for full membership, although a great deal of attention may be given to their religious education, to prepare them to become full members when they are older. Christian sects usually baptize people as adults or adolescents, not as infants.

For religions to carry out their mission, that is, to make their particular contribution to people's lives, they need to survive. The survival of large, established religions is taken for granted. It is in the smaller or newer religions that we see how the organizational issues are played out. The chapters in this section illustrate these issues by revealing various aspects of religious roles and structures. The first, by Dawid Venter, looks at Christian congregations in South Africa as they have attempted to deal with the larger social issue of racial segregation by integrating their own church communities. The next two chapters examine the religious division of labor in very different settings, through Bradley Hertel's description of the variety of Hindu priests and assistants in India and the analysis by Frank DeRego and James Davidson of role conflict and role ambiguity among Roman Catholic deacons in the United States. The role of clergy is also the subject of Edward Lehman's survey of members of Protestant congregations in three different countries who were asked about their views on the ordination of women. The other four chapters shift from the level of congregations to the broader one of denominations. Gilbert Cadena describes the experience of Spanish-speaking people in the Catholic Church in California. Ronald Lawson utilizes church-sect theory in examining the missionary work of Seventh-day Adventists in several parts of Africa. Jerry Pankhurst looks at the new free market of religions in post-Soviet Russia. The final chapter in this section, Susan Palmer's study of the Raelians, a French-speaking UFO religion in Quebec, shows what a religious organization needs to do in order to survive and grow.

These eight chapters illustrate the analysis of religion at the middle range of organizational structure. At this level, religion develops itself as a relatively autonomous unit of society. It is religion *as religion*, and not simply as one social force among many or as a meaningful set of values in the life of an individual. Without organizational structures there would be no such thing as religion to interact with the other social institutions or to serve people's individual spiritual needs.

8

The Inverted Norm: The Formation and Functioning of Racially Mixed Christian Congregations in South Africa

Dawid Venter

INTRODUCTION

Prior to the twentieth century, most Christian churches in South Africa expressed the ideal of racially mixed congregations. However, such congregations are rare today, as a result of the segregation enforced by the apartheid regime between 1948 and 1990. For instance, in a survey I conducted in 1997, church leaders could identify only 3.17 percent of congregations in the Church of the Province of South Africa (Anglican) as racially mixed.

When the white National Party assumed power in 1948, each South African was assigned to one of four racial categories: "whites," "coloreds," "Asians," and "blacks." Residential segregation was enforced and racial intermarriage forbidden. Although the English-speaking churches expressed opposition to this legislated discrimination, they generally showed pragmatic compliance. By 1964, Anglicans, Methodists, Catholics, and Presbyterians admitted that, with rare exceptions, "people of different races do not normally worship together in the same church" (Cawood 1964:52–61, 92). The initial ideal of mixed congregations was now inverted. However, some deliberately racially integrated congregations did emerge from the 1960s to the 1980s in defiance of the political system (Robertson 1994:2; Brain 1991:157).

In the post-apartheid era since 1990, racially mixed congregations have been multiplying faster than before. South Africa's present nonracial[1] ideology encourages cultural diversity across all sectors of society.

PURPOSE AND METHOD

My purposes in this chapter are to outline the social factors that contribute to the formation of racially mixed churches, using these to construct a threefold causal typology and to indicate how congregational structures are adapted to accommodate racial and cultural differences. My focus is on the three major English-speaking Christian denominations that claim never to have followed segregationist policies: Anglicans, Methodists,[2] and Roman Catholics. I collected the data that form the basis of this chapter over a period of five years, in the course of two major studies. The first was an in-depth case study of three Johannesburg congregations, conducted by means of surveys, interviews, and participant observation. The second is ongoing research on the total number of multiracial and multicultural congregations in the three denominations, using a postal survey and interviews.

I will now illustrate what mixed congregations look like through three mini-case studies. The reader should remember that congregational analysis only yields static impressions at a specific time.

THREE INTEGRATING CONGREGATIONS

Johweto Family Vineyard

This congregation was born out of a challenge in 1983 by Moekete Mpete, a young black man from Soweto, to Alexander Venter, a white pastor from Johannesburg, to experience life in Soweto.[3] "Johweto" embodies the vision of crossing racial and economic lines drawn by apartheid between the predominantly white city of *Joh*annesburg and the black township of So*weto*. The concept emerged in 1986 from an intense dialogue between Mpete's group and Venter's group. "Johweto" reflected the vision of the group "not to recognize two separate cities, separate churches, different worlds of experience, but to bridge the gap, make peace, seek justice, heal the broken, release the oppressed and [let] 'the two become one' in Christ" (Venter 1989b:1).

The political context was one of escalating state repression and counter-violence, with the government declaring a state of emergency in 1985. The issues discussed within the group related to apartheid, its effects, and solutions to these. White participants felt that they wanted to break racial barriers as an expression of solidarity with the black experience and as a form of repentance. Blacks wanted to have whites experience the conditions under which they lived. The first year was described as "very emotional, very confrontational." Soweto residents were not always happy about Johweto; a black church leader, well known in Soweto, was against the idea of a white-black church starting there. Some were angry with black Johwetans for mixing with whites.

Events in the wider society continued to affect Johwetans. For example, about 50 percent of black Johwetans were unemployed, prompting discussion on how to meet this and other needs through education and job creation (Venter 1989a:2). Johwetans also experienced psychological exhaustion from the intense interpersonal contact and physical and financial fatigue from traveling forty kilometers three times a week.

The congregation was very closely knit around the values of relationships, of being a family, of working among the poor, and of living in some form of community. By January 1993 half of Johweto's members were living communally, on two farms south of Johannesburg, a house in Soweto, and a house in Johannesburg. At its height Johweto comprised forty to fifty people, with a fifty-fifty black/white mix of six ethnic groupings. By 1995 Johweto had imploded because of internal friction between white members and the white pastor. Today it continues as a black congregation in Soweto.

Central Methodist Mission

The Central Methodist Church was founded in 1889 with a white congregation in the young mining town of Johannesburg. But when Reverend Peter Storey was appointed superintendent minister in 1976, he publicly declared that racial integration was his intention. This drew coloreds, Indians, and blacks to Central (Storey 1993:1). Storey followed up his declaration by appointing black staff members (*What a Family*, June 1980:1, May 1982:7; Storey 1992:4).

There was noticeable growth of black membership after the launching of an intentional three-step plan (Storey 1993:1–2): (1) a restaurant was established in Central's basement in 1978 to cater to all races (when this was still illegal under the Public Amenities Act), and white volunteers served black patrons; (2) a black/white contact program was introduced, called "My brother and me"; (3) Central's buildings were offered for anti-apartheid protest meetings.

In 1985 the church changed its name to Central Methodist Mission. This reflected a totally outward vision as part of a thirteen-point mission statement, the aims of which included becoming a racially inclusive community. By the mid-1980s, when blacks moved to the flatlands of inner Johannesburg in defiance of residential segregation, Central's black component had already surpassed 20 percent (Storey 1992:4, 1993:2). In response to this mix, some 200 white members left. In 1985 the first colored leader was appointed Society Steward (*Central Church News*, July 1985:3). By 1992 there were several racially mixed ministries, including evangelism, a preschool, and food and medical outreach to street people (Ching 1989:1; *What a Family*, November 1988:2; Storey 1992:5). Nevertheless, Central operated in a culturally assimilative mode. English language and culture dominated the services and hymns. The apparent desire among blacks to assimilate into a white English culture, along with a lack of guidelines for cross-cultural interaction, led to two problems at Central: (1) the black congregation preferred a more sedate Western worship style, despite various attempts to coax them into informal and spontaneous worship; (2) the black congregation was mostly uninvolved in the congregation's programs. This could have been based on the realization that, even had they adopted white Western values, their quality of life in the world outside the congregation would not change (see Mehan et al., 1994:97). They may also have been rejecting programs because of class differences between them and the leadership.

At the time of my research Central had a racially mixed leadership that looked after a congregation of about 350 people from ten language groups. Of these, English speakers formed just over one-third of Central's members, followed by Xhosa- (19%), Afrikaans- (10%) and Zulu-speakers (11%). Some 58 percent classified themselves as black, 22 percent as white, 16 percent as colored, and 4 percent as Asian. The congregation was becoming increasingly black because of white flight from the city (Storey 1993:2).

St. Francis Xavier Catholic Church

The third church is located in the west Johannesburg suburb of Martindale. At the time the church was built in 1929, Martindale was one of three freehold areas in Johannesburg where blacks could own land and live in a city otherwise reserved "for whites only."

St. Francis was a place of worship for different races from the start, because of the composition of the immediate neighborhoods. Most parishioners were black, with some coloreds and a small group of whites. Hymns were sung in Sotho and Zulu.

Black participation at St. Francis was effectively brought to an end on 10 February 1955 when, under the Group Areas Act of 1950, a police force of 2,000 began removing—at gunpoint—the first 110 black families to Soweto. By 1961 more than 80,000 blacks had been removed from Martindale and surrounding areas. During the 1960s St. Francis was more than half white, with some coloreds and Chinese. By 1982 about 80 percent of all parishioners were white.

Despite St. Francis's praiseworthy racially inclusive stance, cultural diversity had disappeared, partly because of the language preference of colored parishioners. In addition, a choir, which represented St. Francis's cultural mix by singing African-language hymns and using drums, ceased after conflict on a liturgical point, likely related to differences in cultural positions regarding official versus spontaneous forms of worship.

Group distinctions continued to play a role in the 1990s. Whites and coloreds usually sat separately from one another on Sundays. Coloreds and other ethnic groups were underrepresented in the various parish structures.[4] Of ten people at one meeting of the Pastoral Council, only one colored person was present. One colored person served on the liturgy committee, and one Indian in the Catholic charity organization, the St. Vincent de Paul Society. Small group meetings were rarely mixed, because they took place in previously segregated locations.

By 1993 St. Francis had a white priest and a colored and white congregation of 230 people, with a racial mix among the lay leaders. English speakers dominated numerically, with a smaller Afrikaans-speaking group, along with a sprinkling of other European languages. Parishioners included four Indian couples, some blacks, many coloreds (nearly 40%), and a majority of whites (nearly 60%).

St. Francis seemed to show a mixture of cultural indifference and assimilation, resulting in exclusionary practices. The underrepresentation of coloreds in leadership may also be interpreted as resistance from the dominated group to such practice.

This brings us to the discussion of what social factors contribute to the formation of racially integrating congregations.

EXTERNAL FACTORS CONTRIBUTING TO THE FORMATION
AND FUNCTIONING OF INTEGRATING CONGREGATIONS

At least five external factors contribute to the formation of racially mixed congregations in South Africa: (1) the presence of a political ideology or economic necessity in the wider society that drives toward interethnic cooperation; (2) proficiency in common languages and culture by at least one involved group, so that communication with the others can happen; (3) previous levels of Christianization, because among blacks in South Africa this process is always accompanied by a transmission of European culture; (4) urban location, as city residents are subjected to several assimilative forces that erode or alter their ethnocultural heritage; and (5) the predominance of white European cultures in society, as possession of white cultural forms is arguably seen as essential to obtaining a higher social status.

The dominant paradigm in the United States for describing the formation of mixed congregations is influx into a neighborhood by an ethnic group different from the dominant one.[5] Transitional congregations are caused by neighborhood change and tend to follow the following pattern: (a) ethnic demographic shifts occur in the neighborhood, eventually (b) affecting the composition of a congregation, and ultimately causing (c) a complete ethnic transition in both neighborhood and congregation. Demographic transition as a causal factor in some form or another remains a functional and accurate description for the genesis of many mixed congregations in South Africa. Congregations located in the center of Johannesburg experienced this in the 1980s, while congregations in Pretoria experienced demographic change in the 1990s.

Yet the South African examples show a range of causes of racially mixed congregations: (a) Inclusive congregations are formed almost as a side effect of a more diffuse inclusive focus, of which race is just one category. (b) Intentional congregations use race as a political-theological ideology to establish racial-ethnic unity, and racial issues are more explicitly worked through.

A TYPOLOGY OF INTERNAL FACTORS CONTRIBUTING TO
THE FUNCTIONING OF INTEGRATING CONGREGATIONS

Various internal options have evolved within racially mixed congregations. The structures that these congregations develop reflect their difficulty in trying to balance the need for functional unity with a felt obligation to maintain racial inclusiveness and cultural diversity. As will become clear, my typology represents a continuum with variations within and between two types—internally differentiated and internally integrated. Within these types, the congregations can be sorted into four major groups, which I call Class 1, Class 2, Class 3, and Class 4. I will describe each class in terms of examples that I came across in the course of my research.

Types with Internally Differentiated Structures

The Class 1 pattern (See Figure 8.1) is to develop a mixed congregation with integrated top structures, but which is segregated lower down. Sometimes there is a joint leadership, with two or more clergy from different ethnic-cultural backgrounds, and a joint lay leadership that is ethnically diverse. Separate structures are created to care for the different ethnic groups. These arrangements show that the congregation has some difficulty in bridging a perceived racial or cultural gap.

A Class 1 congregation is one in which there is a joint team of leaders but the services are segregated for some groups. There are at least two Class 1 types: (a) one with separate congregations, but with a joint leadership team (e.g., the Catholic parish of Kraaifontein, near Cape Town); (b) one with separate congregations that meet in the same building at different times, with joint leadership teams (e.g., the Anglican parish of Montclair near Durban).

Types with Internally Integrated Structures

These kinds of mixed congregation have integrated top structures, as well as joint structures of varying extent at lower levels in the same congregation. Varying degrees of cultural uniqueness are expressed in their program structures and services in a variety of ways. There are at least three classes of these congregations.

An example of Class 2 would be Central Methodist Mission in Johannesburg, which had black and white clergy as well as white, black, and colored lay leaders. Central's home groups were segregated, but the outreach programs were racially mixed. A second example is St. Francis Xavier Catholic Church, where a white priest oversaw coloreds and whites who met jointly for church services. Lay leadership and outreach was racially mixed, with some home groups segregated and others mixed. In both St. Francis and Central the services were in English with Western worship styles.

A Class 3 congregation would look like Johweto, which had a joint black/white leadership, with mostly racially integrated home meetings. Worship was conducted in most languages and styles of music of the cultural groups present, but English still dominated the services, discussions, and home groups. Outreach was by means of a culturally diverse ministry team. By 1995 sermons were either in English with translation into Sotho or the other way around. Outreach was by means of a culturally diverse ministry team, indicating that Johweto was becoming a Class 4 congregation (Venter 1994).

I have not yet come across a true Class 4 type in South Africa. The reason is that racially integrated churches tend to adopt two languages as a means of communication and at best use two styles of music in worship, namely Western and African. St. Joseph's Roman Catholic Church in Howick, KwaZulu-Natal comes closest to this type. St. Joseph's services include readings in English and Zulu, with a sermon delivered in English but translated into Zulu. Half of the eucharistic prayers are conducted in English, half in Zulu. The choir sings English and Zulu songs without accompaniment. Small faith groups are not integrated, but separated into language and neighborhood groups.

Table 8.1
Types of Mixed Congregations According to Internal Organization

	A. Internally differentiated structures	B. Internally integrated structures		
	Class 1: Montclair; Kraaifontein	Class 2: Central; Saint Francis Xavier	Class 3: Johweto	Class 4: St. Joseph (comes closest to this type)
Leaders	joint team	joint team or individual minister	joint team	joint team
Services	segregated services for some groups	joint Sunday services	joint Sunday services	joint Sunday services
Worship	one cultural style	one cultural style	two cultural styles	many cultural styles
Sermons	one language used	one language used	two languages, with translation	two languages, with translation
Programs	[inadequate information]	joint outreach, some segregated home groups	joint outreach, mostly joint home groups	joint outreach, segregated home churches
Pastoral care	by group—specific laity or clergy	by joint team or individuals	by joint team	[inadequate information]

CONCLUDING REMARKS

The evidence suggests that in South Africa dynamics in the larger society—such as political ideology, class convergence or divergence, assimilative forces, and a shared language—affect integration at the levels of the congregation and the neighborhood respectively. At the congregational level racially mixed congregations are formed through the intentional attempts of individuals to promote integration; while at the neighborhood level ethnic changes in the neighborhood around the congregation play a role, with people from other ethnic groups joining a previously white congregation.

Just how societal trends have influenced religion can be demonstrated by comparing how integrating congregations were formed before and after 1990. Historically the formation of racially mixed congregations can be described in terms of pre-apartheid, mid-apartheid, and post-apartheid periods. Congregations that emerged during the first and last periods deemphasize race, in contrast to those formed during the second period, which exhibit a more explicit focus on race as a basis for integration.

In the pre-apartheid era class distinctions resulted in ethnically segregated schools, churches, and eventually suburbs. A small number of congregations were integrated, such as St. Paul's Anglican Church in Rondebosch, but leadership was the exclusive preserve of white male landowners. Ironically, the master-servant relationship not only functioned to integrate these congregations but also resulted in segregated seating for different groups.

In the mid-apartheid period new integrating congregations emerged, mainly in the 1960s and the 1980s. During this period the state enforced geographic segregation. Congregants who joined racially mixed congregations were often bound together by a political ideology running counter to that of the apartheid regime. Certain integrated congregations provided a site for political meetings and so entered into a prolonged confrontation with government forces. Compared to the racial segregation prevalent in the wider society and in most churches, these congregations had a strong counterculture political identity and saw themselves as representative of what nonsegregated society should be.

In the post-apartheid era since 1990, integrating congregations have begun to emerge at a faster rate than in the previous two periods. Under the new regime previously homogeneous urban Christian congregations now have to manage an increasingly diverse racial, linguistic, and cultural membership. The year 1990 saw the release from prison of Nelson Mandela and the unbanning of the liberation movements, which gave concrete impetus to those aspects of apartheid legislation that had been repealed just prior to this date (for example, the removal of restrictions on geographic mobility). Most of the congregations that are now integrating are located in neighborhoods that became increasingly diverse.

More recently formed racially diverse congregations feed into and are supported by the dominant political ideology of nonracialism, as exemplified by Archbishop Desmond Tutu's espousal of the "rainbow-nation" slogan. Nonracialism pressures religious people to form or join integrating congregations and links up with historical attempts by church leaders to promote such expressions of pluralism. In addition many denominations have started exerting an increasing pressure on segregated congregations to integrate.

NOTES

1. Nonracialism, a term used in South Africa, is the belief that different racial groups should be integrated in the same institutions (rather than in separate ones), but that within such integrated institutions race should not play a role in people's relations with one another.

2. "Methodists" refers specifically to the Methodist Church of Southern Africa.

3. Information from this section comes from an interview with the Reverend Alexander Venter in Johannesburg on July 15, 1994.

4. At a report-back session of my research in 1993, some parishioners disagreed with my analysis, suggesting that it did not take into account the recent training of a large number of coloreds as catechists.

5. See Wilson and Davis (1966), DesPortes (1973), Davis and White (1980), Yon (1982), Leonard (1983), and Kwan (1990) for studies that illustrate this paradigm. For opposing views see Porter (1992) and Foster and Brelsford (1993).

REFERENCES

Brain, Joy B. 1991. *The Catholic Church in the Transvaal.* Johannesburg: Missionary Oblates of Mary Immaculate.

Cawood, Lesley 1964. *The Churches and Race Relations in South Africa.* Johannesburg: South African Institute of Race Relations.

Central Church News [Newsletter of the Central Methodist Church]. July 1985.

Ching, David A. 1989. Report on Evangelism Cluster for 1989. Unpublished report. Johannesburg: Central Methodist Mission archives.

Davis, James H., and Woodie W. White. 1980. *Racial Transition in the Church.* Nashville, TN: Abingdon Press.

DesPortes, Elisa L. 1973. *Congregations in Change: A Project Test Pattern Book in Parish Development.* New York: Seabury.

Foster, Charles R., and Brelsford, Theodore. 1993. *We Are the Church Together: Cultural Diversity in Congregational Life.* Unpublished report for the Consultation for Pastors in Culturally Diverse Congregations. Atlanta, GA: Emory University.

Kwan, Henry W. K. 1990. *An Alternative Model of Leadership Development in a Multi-Ethnic Church in New York City.* D.Min. project, Trinity Evangelical Divinity School, Deerfield, IL.

Leonard, Charles R. 1983. *A Study of Some Multi-Ethnic Congregations in Light of Church-Growth and the Homogeneous Unit Principle.* D.Min. dissertation, Eastern Baptist Theological Seminary, Wynnewood, PA.

Mehan, H., L. Hubbard, and I. Villanueva. 1994. "Forming Academic Identities: Accommodation Without Assimilation among Involuntary Minorities." *Anthropology and Education Quarterly* 25(2):91–117.

Porter, Mary E. 1992. "When the Stranger is Us: Identity and Vitality in the Racially Diverse Church." M.Div. research paper, Candler School of Theology, Atlanta, GA.

Robertson, R. J. D. 1994. "Engaging the Powers: Some Presbyterian Non-Violence." *Non-Violence News* First Quarter:1–10.

Storey, Peter S. 1992. "Thank You CMM, Thank You God." *What a Family*:4–6.

————. 1993. Personal correspondence with the author.
Venter, Alexander F. 1989a. Unpublished letter for benefit of Johweto's supporters locally and abroad.
————. 1989b. Johweto newsletter, January:1–2. Unpublished information document.
Venter, Dawid J. 1994. *The Formation and Functioning of Racially-Mixed Congregations.* Unpublished Ph.D. dissertation, University of Stellenbosch, South Africa.
————. 1995. "Mending the Multi-coloured Coat of a Rainbow Nation: Cultural Accommodation in Ethnically-mixed Urban Congregations." *Missionalia* 23(3):312–338.
What a Family [newsletter of Central Methodist Church]. June 1980, May 1982, November 1988.
Wilson, R. L., and Davis, J. H. 1966. *The Church in the Racially Changing Community.* Nashville, TN: Abingdon Press.
Zaaiman, Johann 1994. "Kerk en geloofsaffiliasie in Suid-Afrika" [Church and religious affiliation in South Africa]. *Nederduits Gereformeerde Teologiese Tydskrif* 35(4):565–574.
Yon, William A. 1982. *"To Build the City—Too Long a Dream": Studies of Urban Churches.* Washington, DC: Alban Institute.

9

The Variety of Hindu Priests and Assistants: A Brief Introduction

Bradley R. Hertel

People in Western societies commonly think of religious communities as made up of clergy and laity. The clergy are experts who oversee worship services, counsel those in need of guidance, and in other ways provide leadership. The laity are seen primarily as receivers of these services. However, the boundary between providers and receivers is likely to be blurred by the contributions to worship made by lay people. For example, in Christian circles worship is directly or indirectly facilitated by lay people serving as Sunday School teachers, lay readers, and choir directors, and in other ways.

The present study is of Hindu *functionaries*, that is, the priests who comprise the core of Hindu clergy, and many other supporting positions that facilitate religious practices. In Hindu society, there are many gods. They vary greatly in the range of needs they meet for their devotees and in the geographic areas where they are worshiped. Some are sought for a wide range of concerns; others meet only a few needs. The major gods are worshiped throughout the Hindu world. Many local spirits are worshiped by a tiny handful of devotees. Some gods are worshiped with animal sacrifice, others with only vegetarian food offerings. This wide range of gods requires numerous functionaries to help the laity fulfill their religious obligations.

To help make sense of the many kinds of Hindu functionaries, I have organized this chapter in terms of clusters or *complexes* of related positions. Some of the ties are among functionaries who provide similar services. For example, astrologers and palm readers both predict the future. Other complexes consist of functionaries who provide different but complementary services such as the Brahmin household priest and the low-caste funeral pyre tender, both of whom are essential for death rites.

There are complicating factors that make it difficult to construct a complete list of Hindu functionaries.[1] The breadth of duties associated with any given functionary title tends to be greater in villages. The variety of functionaries tends to be greater in towns and cities. Being born into a certain caste is essential for serving in some functionary positions and not so relevant for others. The positions and duties described below in nine complexes are illustrative but not necessarily comprehensive of the full range of Hindu functionaries.

FIELDWORK AND SETTING

This chapter is based on my observations and interviews in Bhojpur in northern India. The field work was done in various blocks of time between 1978 and 1992. Local Bhojpuri-speaking individuals assisted in interviewing hundreds of functionaries and lay persons varying widely in caste, sex, age, and education, and worship practices.

COMPLEXES OF HINDU FUNCTIONARIES

Individual Acting on His or Her Own Behalf

Hindus perform many devotional acts without intermediaries. These activities include the daily ritual bath, reading sacred literature, reciting prayers, fasting, and *puja* (worship) at a small worship site in the corner of a room in the home. Hindus also worship at minor temples and shrines without the presence of a temple priest. In some instances, these acts of worship are private, such as recitation of prayers and puja in the home. In other situations, worshipers perform unassisted devotional exercises in the midst of large gatherings, as in the daily ritual bath at a river or temple tank.

Family Member Serving Other Family Members

Hindus perform a wide variety of rituals that strengthen family bonds. Mothers, and sometimes fathers, take their children on weekly temple visits. Mothers play a large part in the planning and performance of rites of passage for their children, including the first haircut celebration for the happiness and long life of the child, most often held for five-year-olds. In conservative Bhojpur, the movement of women is restricted by their seclusion (*purdah*). Consequently, the groom's mother participates in prewedding rituals in her own village but does not attend the wedding, which for most castes is held at the bride's house.

Women perform devotional exercises to maintain and restore the health of family members, such as fasting for the well-being of family members and worshiping the goddess Shitala for protection of children from skin diseases. On Saturday mornings, women worship Sanni (Saturn) and pray for the long life, health, and happiness of their family members, especially husbands and sons. Young married women worship Santoshimata for assistance with conception. Mothers apply heavy mascara on their young children to make them less attractive and less likely to fall victim to the harmful covetous glance of a woman possessing evil eye.

Men serve as representatives of the family at weddings, death rites, and other large gatherings outside the home. Men and women are usually both involved in the worship of the *kul deota*, a god held as special by the members of a family. Men are far more involved than women in the worship of caste gods. Arranging the marriages of their adult children is a duty of utmost importance for fathers.

Sons are preferred for the role of *dahak* (chief mourner) to light the funeral pyre and for other death rites for fathers. Husbands are regarded as the ideal dahaks for wives. Siblings participate in annual celebrations in which they declare their loyalty and affection for their opposite-sex siblings and seek the gods' protection for them. There are numerous other ritual duties to refurbish bonds within the nuclear family, extended family, and clan.

Extrafamilial Household Priest

The *purohit*, or Brahmin household priest, is the archetypal Hindu priest, but by no means the only kind. The purohit visits the families he serves to perform monthly worship services in the home and oversees weddings, funerals, and other rites of passage. He draws up an astrological chart at the time of a birth; he or his successor later consults that chart to confirm that a prospective couple is well matched. He also helps the parents select an auspicious date for the wedding. The purohit provides amulets to protect clients from evil and prescribes atonement rituals when these are needed to restore balance in lives disrupted by sin.

Families of very low castes not served by Brahmins are served by priests from within their caste. These priests are general practitioners who perform rites of passage, especially weddings and funerals, and oversee any temple, shrine, or festival of that caste.

Individuals of many castes play roles in rites of passage and other household worship overseen by the purohit. The most important of these is the *Nai*, a barber-caste male who serves as the purohit's assistant. The Nai purchases the other items needed for a puja and arrives before the purohit to arrange these items at the puja site. He occasionally substitutes for the purohit to oversee weddings and death rites in low-caste families. The Nai cuts hair and fingernails for routine grooming and for ceremonial purposes. He shaves heads of young children at the first haircut rite of passage and the heads of male mourners over ten years of age. Since the diversity of his ritual activities and the range of castes he serves are broader than those of the purohit, the Nai is a leading figure for meeting the integrative function of religion in Hindu society.

The *Nain* (barber wife) oversees a number of rituals for women preceding weddings. She helps mothers organize the activities for children's first haircuts. The Nain also helps care for new mothers during the six or twelve days after delivery that they are considered polluted and live apart from other family members.

In Bhojpur, *Chamain* carries the dual meaning of "woman of the leather worker caste" and "midwife." Although most deliveries nowadays take place in hospitals and clinics, midwifery has not died out. Conception and birth are interpreted in both biological and spiritual terms. The arrival of a new baby represents the rebirth of a soul. The midwife leads the mother in prayers to the Goddess for safe delivery. She provides the Brahmin priest with the approximate time of birth so that he can draft an accurate astrological chart. Along with the barber wife, she cares for the mother and baby during the postpartum pollution period. Sometimes she serves as wet-nurse, making her all the more likely later to be called *Chachi* ("Auntie") by those she has delivered.

The *Dom* (funeral pyre tender) maintains the fires at cremation grounds. He hands a burning pole to the chief mourner and instructs him on where to light the body. Later the Dom tells the chief mourner when to strike the skull with a pole to free the soul for its onward journey. In Banaras, site of the most sacred cremation grounds in India, Doms' functionary duties are confined to overseeing cremations (Parry 1980). Elsewhere in Bhojpur, they blow a curly copper horn in wedding processions and major festivals. This role softens the denigration suffered by Doms through their close association with death.

A soul in transition is believed to have bodily needs but to be unable to meet those needs by itself. Throughout the mourning period, the dahak adds water to a clay pot hung from a tree at the outskirts of the village or town so that the newly deceased may drink. The *Mahabrahmin*, a very low-ranking Brahmin limited to certain death rites, removes the pot at the end of the mourning period. This task is considered dangerous because if done improperly, it might anger the unsettled soul.

There are many other contributors to the household rituals for which the purohit is chief overseer (Wiser 1958). The *Kumhar* (potter) makes disposable clay cups for guests at feasts and a clay elephant symbolizing long life and happiness that occupies a place of honor beside the bride and groom at their wedding. The *Lohar* (blacksmith) makes a large nail used in rituals to tether evil spirits to prevent them from disrupting important celebrations. These individuals are only illustrative of the many caste-related lesser functionaries who provide material goods and minor services for rites overseen by purohits.

Caste Priest

Many high and middle castes employ priests to maintain temples for gods associated with the origins or saints of those castes. To illustrate: Vishwakarma ("Builder of the Universe") is a god revered by members of castes whose traditional occupations are in the industrial arts: carpenter, blacksmith, potter, weaver, and the like. Men of these castes honor Vishwakarma at annual festivals. More devout men visit temples for their caste god throughout the year. Priests at caste temples may be Brahmins, holy men from the worshiping caste, or holy men from a third caste. Those low castes not served by Brahmin household priests have priests from their own castes for providing a simpler range of rituals and for overseeing annual festivals and temples or shrines for deities important to their castes.

Local Temple and Festival Priests

Many Hindu temples are for general gods that attract devotees of numerous castes. Most overseers of these temples are Brahmins whose occupational title is *pujari* ("temple priest"). The pujari opens his temple each day to allow worshipers access. He also looks after the god's needs by providing food and by closing the temple to give the god time to rest. If the temple is small and receives few visitors, he may also look after its physical upkeep. Temples with a daily stream of visitors have more than one pujari sharing responsibilities and income from devotees' donations. Some pujaris recite *katha* (stories glorifying god) on a day of the week associated with the primary god of the temple. At larger temples there is a temple association, a body of lay leaders who make decisions on priestly succession and who oversee the physical maintenance of the temple.

As a temple becomes more prominent, the range of services available to visitors increases. Many nonpriestly functionaries sell offerings for the gods: At first, flower and candy vendors appear only on the major day(s) of the week for that god. In time, an increase in number of visitors may lead to the daily presence of flower sellers and other vendors selling food, small toys, and souvenirs.

The *bhagat* is a low-caste priest whose authority rests on charisma and informal training from an experienced priest. Some bhagats are associated with temples for Kali or other deities, particularly those that are worshiped with animal sacrifice. Other bhagats lack temples, in which case they are inactive except during the annual festival for their particular deity.

The annual pujas overseen by bhagats are lively events that often attract large numbers of devotees from all castes. The bhagat and his closest disciples solicit donations of money and grain about a week before the puja to cover its costs. On the day before or morning of the puja, they clean the temple or sanctify a puja site in an open field. For the goddess Kali, there is a parade with musicians, devotees, and perhaps elephants and jeeps. The puja is centered around animal sacrifice and demonstrations by the bhagat that the honored god has heeded his call to attend the celebration. The bhagat confirms the god's presence by performing one or more extreme austerities without showing sign of pain or injury. Dipping hands in boiling milk, standing on sharp upturned swords, and fire walking are among the means by which bhagats show that they are blessed by the god or goddess. At the conclusion of the celebration, the bhagat or a close ally known as *mataha* may drink blood from the first of the sacrificed animals as a crucial step for utilizing the power of the god to cure the sick and/or to act as an oracle to make predictions concerning climate, crops, and the health of the villagers and their animals during the coming year. A low-caste "cutter" takes the life of the animals given to the god. Other assistants distribute the meat among the meat-eating celebrants who sponsored the puja. The *Chamar* (leather worker) plays a single-skinned drum at festivals for gods given animal sacrifice.

Priest at Pilgrimage Site

At pilgrimage centers the *pandas* (Brahmin pilgrimage center priests) associated with any one temple each have time slots throughout the week when they are entitled to serve. Some of the Brahmins associated with the most popular temples help visitors find accommodations and local transportation. Other Brahmins in pilgrimage centers sell "sacred threads" to be worn by high-caste men over the shoulder and chest to signify membership in one of the higher Hindu castes.[2]

Despite the high prestige of major temples in places of pilgrimage, pandas are commonly resented. A large flow of pilgrims may result in considerable income for them. Hindus take a dim view of high economic rewards for functionary duties. Stories abound of pandas encouraging pilgrims to pay for the right to take a side door into the temple to avoid standing in line. Such complaints reenforce the common image of pandas as greedy opportunists.

Experts in Predicting the Future

In India, astrology is considered a science deserving as much respect as astronomy or meteorology. Calendar makers are the most highly regarded astrologers and arguably the most influential of all Hindu functionaries. It is through their efforts that millions of Hindus schedule their celebrations throughout the year. As drafters and interpreters of life charts, purohits are the most numerous and visible Hindu astrologers. Far less common are skilled Brahmin specialists in astrology, found mostly in urban areas, whose predictions and advice are sought primarily by high-caste individuals. Non-Brahmin astrologers are sought for advice on career and other decisions but not for drafting life charts or advice on rites of passage.

Palm readers, like astrologers, are largely Brahmins viewed as having considerable potential for predicting the future. Many purohits use palmistry for a glimpse into the future, but not for drafting life charts or for decisions on mate selection. Most Hindus have more confidence in astrology because palm readings may be rendered inaccurate by changes in the lines of the hand due to aging and injury. However, others, reflecting the diversity of viewpoints central to Hinduism, claim that palmistry is more reliable, because astrologers often base their predictions on a life chart drawn up long ago by a third party who may have been misinformed about the time of birth. By contrast, the palm reader bases his predictions on evidence in his immediate presence.

At the bottom of the hierarchy of predictors are various non-Brahmins who may be subsumed under the term "lesser predictors." Some of these individuals are "little *ojhas*" (magicians, or shamans) who shake two small pieces of wood together in their hands and interpret the sound as having meaning for the client's future. Other lesser predictors use parakeets to select cards which are then interpreted, or a cow that walks in circles within a ring of men and boys until it stops in front of that individual predicted to marry soon, to go on a long trip, or to have some other major experience. Some bhagats become temporary oracles at the end of festivals. In a highly theatrical voice, signifying that he is no longer himself, the bhagat loudly announces his predictions for the coming year. Most of these predictions concern crops and health of humans and cattle, but he may also comment on other matters including local or national elections and even interna-tional relations.

Specialists in Healing and Protection

In Bhojpur, physical and mental illness are interpreted as having one of three general sources: (a) accidents and natural causes, (b) sin, and (c) unsettled spirits of the dead and practitioners of black magic. Brahmins are the main providers of relief from the first two sources. Brahmins dominate in various schools of medicine, including the ancient Ayurvedic herbal medicine, modern Western allopathic medicine, and homeopathy and naturopathy. If one's household priest proves unable to prescribe atonement rituals adequate for removing the ill effects of sin, the sinner, one or two male family members, and their purohit may travel to a *dharma gurudeo* ("religious judge"), a rare Brahmin specialist able to advise on the steps to be taken to offset the suffering from serious sins (Hertel and Singh 1985).

Purohits are active in a variety of protective rituals known as *baandana*. Some of these rituals serve collective needs, for example, the tethering of spirits before major rites of passage and festivals. Other forms of baandana are for the protection of individuals. One's Brahmin household priest provides amulets and other charms for this purpose. Non-Brahmins including vendors outside of temples and ojhas also provide amulets to prevent misfortune.

Non-Brahmin specialists are the chief providers of relief from suffering attributed to unsettled spirits. The bhagat and mataha at the annual Kali puja perform faith healing and exorcism but they are ordinarily available only on that one day of the year. "Great ojhas" (magicians who are viewed as having considerable power) are available throughout the year to perform rituals to assist women to conceive. Some magicians specialize in exorcism, or *bhut utaarna* ("spirit removal"). The most respected and feared exorcists are believed able to perform *bhut lorna* ("spirit placement"), black magic in which an unsettled spirit is imposed on an unsuspecting victim. Whereas ojhas and other exorcists are usually male, the *daiyn* is a childless woman whose covetous, uncontrollable "evil eye" cast on young children can cause them harm. Most women believed to have this power are viewed as pathetic rather than willfully malicious. Occasionally, a daiyn is seen as intentionally harmful, in which case villagers rally behind a great ojha for protection.

Idealized Role Models

Hindus hold a large variety of individuals in very high esteem. Revered elderly family members, favorite school teachers, the family's household priest, an accomplished artist or athlete, or a widely respected political leader can symbolize spiritual excellence. Two broad categories of idealized role models deserve special attention. *Sadhus*, or holy men, represent the ideal of a nonmaterialistic simple life close to the gods and nature. They serve to remind others that it is possible to live a highly spiritual life without social and material comforts.

A wide range of spirits of the dead also reenforce ideals for humans to follow. Belief in spirits supports belief in reincarnation and in the doctrine of karma. One example will help to show the part played by spirits in shaping the behavior of the living. Brahmins who die prematurely either by murder or accident become spirits known as *brahms*. As spirits, they cannot be seen, but they remain active in society. If their death came by murder, they might seek revenge against the murderer or his family. Fearing reprisal, those individuals are likely to propitiate the victim at a small shrine built by his family to honor him. In time, stories may be told of cures and other benefits that came to people who showed their respects at that site. As his reputation grows even larger, a minor spirit earlier feared and propitiated by only a few people can become a regional godling revered and worshiped by many thousands of devotees. Belief in the power of murder victims to take revenge helps protect Brahmins—and to a lesser extent, members of other castes—from violence. Belief in brahms serves to reenforce the high rank of Brahmins and helps to show that in the Hindu worldview there is no clear line between this world and the next.

CONCLUDING COMMENTS

Hindu functionaries vary immensely in kind and in the breadth of their duties, in the extent to which their services are available through other providers, in the geographic scope of their reputation and following, and in the timing according to which their services are sought. Male Brahmins are key providers especially for rites of passage and worship at temples for major deities. Women are important in rituals for the well-being of family members and for rituals involving children. Low-caste functionaries are the primary providers of rituals pertaining to the dangerous transitions of birth and death; they also are the leading functionaries associated with exorcism and worship of those gods requiring animal sacrifice. In the end, the extraordinary array of Hindu functionaries reflects not only the complexities of Hindu social structure but the tremendous diversity in the powers of the gods they serve.

NOTES

I wish to thank Rana P. B. Singh, Lalta Prasad, and Vinita Sharma for their indispensable help with the field work for this study. I wish also to thank Meeta Mehrotra for translating many of the taped interviews and for her comments on earlier drafts of this chapter.

1. Hinduism is a culture or set of regional and linguistic subcultures that permeates the lives of its adherents. The boundaries between religious and secular activities and roles are much less clear than in Western society. For overviews of Hinduism as culture, see Babb (1975), Chaudhuri (1979), Hertel and Mehrotra (1996), and Milner (1994).

2. See Vidyarthi (1978) and Vidyarthi, Saraswati, and Jha (1979) for descriptions of pandas and other functionaries at Hindu pilgrimage centers.

REFERENCES

Babb, Lawrence A. 1975. *The Divine Hierarchy: Popular Hinduism in Central India*. New York: Columbia University Press.
Chaudhuri, Nirad C. 1979. *Hinduism: A Religion to Live By*. New Delhi: B. I. Publications.

Hertel, Bradley R., and Meeta Mehrotra. 1996. "Authenticity in Hinduism—Who, What, How?" Pp. 229–250 in Lewis F. Carter (ed.), *The Issue of Authenticity in the Study of Religions*, Vol. 6 of Religion and the Social Order. Greenwich, CT: JAI Press.

Hertel, Bradley R., and Rana P. B. Singh. 1985. "Brahmin Judges in Traditional Hindu Society." *Deviant Behavior* 6:363–381.

Milner, Murray, Jr. 1994. *Status and Sacredness: A General Theory of Status Relations and an Analysis of Indian Culture*. New York: Oxford University Press.

Parry, Jonathan P. 1980. "Ghosts, Greed, and Sin: The Occupational Identity of the Banares Funeral Priests." *Man* 15:88–111.

Vidyarthi, L. P. 1978. *The Sacred Complex in Hindu Gaya* (Second Edition). Delhi: Concept Publishing Company.

Vidyarthi, L. P., B. N. Saraswati, and Makhan Jha. 1979. *The Sacred Complex of Kashi: A Microcosm of Indian Civilization*. Delhi: Concept Publishing Company.

Wiser, William H. 1958. *The Hindu Jajmani System: A Socio-Economic System Interrelating Members of a Hindu Village Community in Services*. (First published in 1936). Lucknow: Lucknow Publishing House.

10

Catholic Deacons: A Lesson in Role Conflict and Ambiguity

Frank R. DeRego, Jr., and James D. Davidson

Churches, like most other organizations, place people in various positions, or statuses, such as priest or minister, choir director, or parish council member. Each status is related to a role, or a set of expected behaviors related to one's position. Sometimes these roles are clear and consistent, in which case people have relatively little difficulty carrying out their responsibilities. At other times, roles are unclear or involve lots of conflicting expectations. Role conflict and ambiguity make it difficult, if not impossible, for people to perform effectively.

The Roman Catholic Church recently created a social position that is fraught with role conflict and ambiguity. That position is known as the "permanent diaconate."[1] People who occupy this position are called "deacons." While deacons derive considerable personal satisfaction from their work with the church, they also report a number of problems that can be traced to conflicts and ambiguities inherent in the diaconate.

In this chapter, we show that the main reason the diaconate is so fraught with conflict and ambiguity is that it was a compromise solution to the problem of the worldwide priest shortage. We also show that in the United States, where the diaconate has spread most rapidly, deacons experience frustrations and identity problems that are rooted in the conflicts and ambiguities inherent in their role.

A BRIEF HISTORY OF THE DIACONATE

The order of deacons thrived in the first three centuries of the church (Olson, 1992: 28). Closely aligned to the office of bishop, deacons were entrusted with the administration of temporal affairs such as the vital work of charity, as well as spiritual matters such as teaching and liturgical functions (Cunningham 1987:268–269). As monasteries developed into communities of men dedicated to prayer and service, the deacon's role in social welfare diminished. However, deacons' responsibilities in areas such as teaching prospective converts and performing sacraments such as baptism and Eucharist grew to the point that the Council of Nicea (325 C.E.) limited the power of deacons as a way of protecting the jurisdiction of presbyters (i.e., priests) (Cunningham 1987:269). As a whole range of lay ministries were conflated into the ministry of the priest, the authority of priestly ministry increased. Sacramental ministries in relation to baptism and the Eucharist also were conflated into the role of priests, furthering diminishing the importance of the diaconate. By the twelfth century, the office of deacon lacked any of the independent significance it had held in the first four centuries of the church (Olson 1992:62). It became little more than a transitional step to the priesthood.

The diaconate remained a transitional step toward priesthood until Vatican II, a worldwide council of Catholic bishops held in Rome between 1962 and 1965. In a document entitled "Dogmatic Constitution on the Church," the Vatican Council restored the diaconate as a "proper and permanent rank of the hierarchy" (Abbott 1966).

According to council documents, deacons are ordained clergymen "dedicated to the People of God . . . in the service of the liturgy, of the Gospel and of works of charity" (Flannery 1992:387). They are called "to administer Baptism solemnly, to be custodian and distributor of the Eucharist, in the name of the Church, to assist at and to bless marriages, to bring Communion to the dying, to read the sacred Scripture to the faithful, to instruct and exhort the people, to preside over the worship and the prayer of the faithful, to administer sacramentals, and to officiate at funeral and burial services" (Flannery 1992:387). In other words, they can perform all the duties of priests except for the sacrament of reconciliation, the anointing of the sick, and the consecration of the Eucharist.

What precipitated the restoration of the permanent diaconate? While other considerations were probably involved (Hoge 1987), the main one was the bishops' concern about the growing shortage of priests, especially in Third World countries (Olson 1992:363). One of the key factors often linked to this shortage is the church's requirement that priests be celibate males—a requirement that excludes women and married men from the priesthood. The bishops' concern over the priest shortage and the related matter of priestly celibacy is evident in council documents citing the fact that "laws and customs of the Latin Church in many areas render it difficult to fulfill [sacramental] functions, which are extremely necessary for the life of the Church" (Flannery 1992:387).

The bishops were sharply divided over the restoration of the permanent diaconate. The principal bone of contention was the idea of allowing married men to become deacons. On this issue, there were two distinct schools of thought. One group of bishops correctly observed that the change would overturn more than a millennium of tradition establishing the connection between celibacy and ordained ministry. Such a change, they argued, would lead the church down a dangerous slippery slope. If the church allowed married men to become deacons, was a married priesthood far behind? This group of bishops viewed married life as incompatible with the sacramental and pastoral duties of an ordained minister.

A larger group of bishops saw the permanent diaconate as a "leaven in the loaf." Because the permanent deacon lived in the workaday world and, it was assumed, would be married, his ministry would directly relate to the lives of the people he served. Unlike the priest, whose lifestyle of celibacy was seen as distant from the laity, the permanent deacon would be an example to the community of faith-filled loving service (Winninger 1993).

In the end, a majority of bishops were favorably disposed to the restoration of a permanent diaconate that included married men, but they insisted that "the law of celibacy must remain in force" for the priesthood (Flannery 1992: 387). Thus, whether they realized it or not, the bishops' vision of a permanent diaconate included role conflict and ambiguity. Deacons would be ordained, but they also could be married (although widowed deacons could not remarry); they would share married life with other lay people, but they also would be considered clergy.

Table 10.1
Global Distribution of Deacons

	N	%
North America	12,287	56.2
United States	11,175	51.1
Canada	760	3.5
Mexico	352	1.6
Europe	6,425	29.4
Germany	1,940	8.9
Italy	1,539	7.0
France	1,018	4.6
All others	1,928	8.9
Central/South America and the Caribbean	2,579	11.8
Brazil	760	3.5
Puerto Rico	358	1.6
Argentina	328	1.5
All others	1,141	5.2
Africa	327	1.5
Asia	132	0.6
Australia and Oceania	123	0.6

Source: Pistone (1997)

At the time we are writing, there are approximately 21,900 deacons in 121 countries. Most deacons, 68 percent (N = 14,866), are in North and South America; 29 percent (N = 6,425) are in Europe. The other 3 percent are located in Africa

(N = 327), Asia (N = 132), and Australia and Oceania (N = 123). Although bishops expected the diaconate to expand most rapidly in relatively poor countries where the priest shortage is most acute, these nations account for only 19 percent of all deacons (see Table 10.1 on page 91). Eighty-one percent of all deacons are in affluent countries, where the priest shortage is less severe.

Fifty-one percent of all deacons are in the United States. Figure 10.1 shows that there has been a steady growth in the number of American deacons since 1977 (*Official Catholic Directory*, 1977, 1982, 1987, 1992, 1997). The number of American deacons has steadily increased, from only 1,900 in 1977 to 11,788 in 1997. During the same period the total number of American priests has declined from

Figure 10.1
Priests and Deacons in the United States, 1977–1997

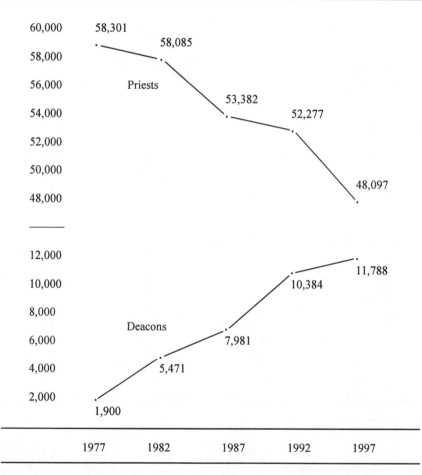

Source: Official Catholic Directory

58,301 to 48,097. Thus, compared to 20 years earlier, there were approximately 10,000 fewer priests but almost 10,000 more deacons in 1997.

ROLE CONFLICT AND ROLE AMBIGUITY

There have been three studies of the diaconate in the United States. The first (hereafter called the 1981 study) was done by the American Bishops' Committee on the Permanent Diaconate (Hemrick and Shields 1981). It collected data from deacons, deacons' wives, priests who serve as deacons' supervisors, and bishops. In the mid-1980s, Dean Hoge conducted separate surveys of priests, lay adults, and college students. All three surveys included a few questions about the diaconate. These results were reported in Hoge's (1987) book *The Future of Catholic Leadership*, which we call the 1987 study. The Bishops' Committee on the Permanent Diaconate recently sponsored a third study, which we call the 1996 study (see NCCB 1996). Like the bishops' earlier study, this one included data from deacons, their wives, and their supervisors. It also included data from lay members of parish councils. Thus, we now have the benefit of data collected at three points in time over a fifteen-year period. All three studies indicate some satisfaction with the diaconate but also point to frustrations that are rooted in role conflict and ambiguity.

The 1981 study indicated high levels of satisfaction with the diaconate. Hemrick and Shields (1981:13–25) found that 88 percent of deacons "would seek ordination if they had to do it over again"; 64 percent said they "have the authority to carry out the responsibilities assigned to them"; 78 percent felt "sufficiently qualified for their ministry"; and the vast majority were optimistic about the growth of the diaconate in the United States. Data from deacons' wives, supervisors, and bishops also indicated overall satisfaction with the diaconate program. Satisfaction was highest among wives, supervisors, and bishops who had the most direct involvement in deacons' ministries.

Hoge (1987:184–192) found that more than 80 percent of college student leaders, about two-thirds of adult lay people, and half of priests feel that the increasing number of deacons helps the church. He concluded that all groups "support increases in deacons and lay ministers" (Hoge 1987:198).

The bishops' 1996 study concluded that the diaconate has been "hugely successful" and that there is "widespread and enthusiastic acceptance of the ministries performed by deacons" among lay leaders in the church. Deacons themselves are very satisfied with their roles, and their "wives describe themselves as supportive of their husbands' ministry and their family as greatly enriched by his ordination" (NCCB 1996:1).

Role Conflict

Nevertheless, the permanent diaconate also has its problems. Some of these are rooted in role conflict (Kahn et al. 1964), which deacons experience when they face incompatible demands from bishops, priests, and lay people. The 1981 report showed that this conflict was related to several factors: The priests with whom deacons worked most closely had far more theological training than deacons; celibate priests and married deacons had different lifestyles; some priests saw deacons as intruding upon the priestly role; priests expected deacons to invest more time in their ministries, while deacons (who worked at their ministries an average of 13.7 hours a week) also had commitments to their families and full-time jobs; and most deacons received no salary or compensation from the church for such activities as continuing education and annual retreats, a situation that was likely to "place unfair economic burdens on the deacon or his family" (Hemrick and Shields 1981: 51). Deacons volunteered comments on other areas of role conflict. Seventy-one percent of those offering comments "said they would like [church law] changed to allow them to administer [the Sacrament of the Sick]"; 58 percent "asked that the law concerning blessing be changed"; and 45 percent "said the law should be changed to allow widowed deacons to remarry."

Data from deacons' wives, supervisors, and bishops corroborated deacons' concerns with role conflict. Though generally supportive of their husbands, some deacons' wives offered comments pointing to role conflict. Two-thirds of the wives volunteering their own observations said that "their husband's ministerial work takes time away from the family, and 21.4 [percent] say they feel their husband has been taken advantage of by their parishes." Supervisors reported that "the majority of conflicts which deacons experience can be traced to their relationships with pastors or other priests" (Hemrick and Shields 1981:38). Only 53 percent of supervisors believed that priests "desire and support the permanent diaconate" (Hemrick and Shields 1981:37). Supervisors said that deacons' least satisfying experiences involve "aspects of the ministry of the Word such as preaching, public speaking, and teachings"—situations in which the often-conflicting expectations of priests and lay people are most salient and most stressful (Hemrick and Shields 1981:38). Sixty-nine percent of bishops said they know about "conflict between deacons and priests"; 32 percent knew of "conflict between deacons and the laity" (Hemrick and Shields 1981:41).

Hoge's study of deacons showed that only 3 percent of all deacons worked full time for dioceses or parishes (Hoge 1987:193). Serving essentially as volunteers and working so few hours a week, permanent deacons did not provide the full-time professional presence desired by priests. Some Catholic lay people also argued that the restoration of the permanent diaconate increased the clericalization of the church and detracted from lay roles and responsibility (Hoge 1987:195). Catholic feminists, for example, contended the restriction of the diaconate to married men perpetuates male domination in the church. They are keenly aware that there were deaconesses in the early church (Olson 1992; D'Antonio et al. 1996:111–112), a situation that many would like to restore. In addition, religious sisters and lay women who serve as administrators of parishes that do not have priests are aware that ordination gives deacons a status higher than theirs (Wallace 1992:126).

The latest study shows that role conflict continues to center on differing expectations between clergy and laity over the permanent diaconate's place in the organizational structure of the church. Priests, who sometimes have difficulty sharing authority with deacons (Hoge 1987:196), are not convinced that the diaconate has helped the church. Deacons and their supervisors are concerned that deacons' limited service in traditional functions and the perception that permanent deacons are simply "priest adjuncts" distorts the meaning of the permanent deacon's role in the church (NCCB 1996:14). Lay people are mainly concerned with the availability and quality of religious services in the parish. Insofar as deacons provide needed religious services, they are accepted. But if anyone, ordained or not, could provide the same service, the laity would be equally satisfied.

Role Ambiguity

In addition to role conflict is the problem of role ambiguity. People experience this ambiguity when they lack "adequate role-relevant information, as when information is restricted or when role expectations are not clearly defined" (Rogers and Molnar 1976:599). Role ambiguity is related to the predictability of responses to one's behavior and the clarity of behavioral requirements or expectations (Rizzo, House, and Lirtzman 1970). In the deacon's role, ambiguity is a result of placing the deacon in both the secular and the ecclesiastical worlds.

Role ambiguity was very evident in the 1981 study. Deacons had uneven access to information because of wide differences in their training, as 44 percent had mostly academic training, 27 percent mostly pastoral training, and 20 percent mostly spiritual training. Thirty-five percent felt a need for more pastoral/field training, 20 percent wanted more training in dogmatic and moral theology, and 16 percent wanted more ascetic theology and prayer.

More than half of deacons had no job descriptions or formal work agreements with parishes. Almost one-third said they were not sure how their supervisors felt about the diaconate. The supervisors themselves reported that their own roles in relation to the deacons were ambiguous. While some met frequently with deacons, others met only occasionally. Only 40 percent of supervisors said that lay people understand the diaconate and its role in the church. Summarizing supervisors' responses, Hemrick and Shields (1981:38) concluded that "they report role ambiguity as the major source of frustration, whether it concerns the deacon 'vis-a-vis' other clergy or the deacon 'vis-a-vis' the laity."

Ambiguity was also evident in bishops' responses. One quarter of bishops were very involved in work with deacons, half were only somewhat involved, and another quarter were not very involved. Almost half of bishops questioned the adequacy of deacon-formation programs, and only one-third viewed their deacons as very effective ministers. When asked to identify major problems with the diaconate programs in their dioceses, bishops pointed to poor screening/lack of guidelines for choosing candidates, nonacceptance by priests, inadequate formation, role confusion as to what a deacon is expected to be and do, nonacceptance by the laity, and excessive clericalism/prima donnas (Hemrick and Shields 1981:43).

Hoge also pointed to the lack of role relevant information, arguing that the permanent diaconate is a status without an adequate job description. "The role of the deacon is inadequately defined. The problem is traceable to the definition of the office of deacon, which is stated in terms of a status, not in terms of a job to be done. It is a theologically defined status without any training for a specific job" (Hoge 1987:195).

Despite the fact that priests and laity alike downplay the clerical status of the deacons (Fichter 1992), the "leaven in the loaf" has taken on a decidedly clerical look, with deacons performing many highly visible roles that historically have been the province of priests alone (Rice 1997). Thus, the 1996 study shows that lay leaders are inclined to see deacons as "making up for the priest shortage" (NCCB 1996: 6). The report concludes, "Except for the theologically sophisticated, it seems entirely natural that laity would views their deacons as either underqualified priests or overqualified laity" (NCCB 1996:8).

Fewer than one-third of parish council members say they have a "very good" understanding of the diaconate; even fewer are convinced that lay people really understand the role of deacons (NCCB 1996:35–36). By and large, lay leaders have little or no input into the job descriptions or mission statements of deacons and seldom, if ever, meet with deacons to discuss their ministries (NCCB 1996:38–40). When asked about the future of the diaconate in their parishes, 41 percent of parish council leaders expected it to grow, but 59 percent disagreed or were not sure what the future would bring (NCCB 1996:37).

These ambiguities are expressed in deacons' continued concern with identity (NCCB 1996:7–8,14). Data from the 1996 study show that permanent deacons "thought a large majority of parishioners, priests, and lay staff with whom they worked did not adequately understand the identity of the deacon" (NCCB 1996:7). Forty-one percent of deacons' supervisors agreed with this observation. The majority of lay leaders surveyed narrowly identified deacons with parish-based sacramental activities (NCCB 1996:13) and viewed ordination as unnecessary for the duties deacons perform (NCCB 1996:13).

CONCLUSION

In their effort to preserve the priesthood for celibate males, while responding to the growing shortage of priests, Catholic bishops at Vatican II created a new position called the permanent diaconate. They did not appreciate the conflicts and ambiguities inherent in their vision of that position (Gaine 1991; Rice 1997).

Role conflict and ambiguity are not merely conceptual problems. They adversely affect the actual relationships among deacons, priests, and lay people. Priests are frustrated that deacons, who tend to work limited hours and cannot perform certain sacramental functions, do not provide the relief that the priests are looking for. Lay people tend to view deacons as "underqualified priests or overqualified laity" (NCCB 1996:8). No wonder deacons report identity problems.

It also is no wonder that the diaconate, as Hoge (1987) has pointed out, remains "under heavy fire in the United States." Some bishops have stopped ordaining permanent deacons (Gaine 1991:252).[2] Other church leaders have called for changes, including a review of the sacrament of orders (ordination), clarification of priests' and deacons' roles in liturgy, more focus on diocesan ministry, and more stringent qualifications for preaching (Rice 1997). However, changes of this sort are not likely to be made until church leaders and lay people reach some level of mutual accommodation regarding a position that was born in controversy and is inherently fraught with role conflict and ambiguity.

NOTES

1. There is an important difference between the "permanent diaconate" we examine in this chapter and the "transitional diaconate," which is a short-term status through which seminarians pass on the road to ordination as priests (Cunningham 1987; Olson 1992).

2. Hoge (1987:194) reports that 144 of 185 dioceses had diaconate programs in the mid-1980s. In its 1996 study, the NCCB got responses from 127 dioceses. More recent evidence from CARA indicates that only 127 dioceses have active diaconate formation programs. Only 104 of them "submitted reports of students enrolled during 1996–97, thirteen others are between training cycles or reorganizing and therefore have no students presently enrolled, and fourteen did not submit information for analysis" (CARA 1977:7).

REFERENCES

Abbott, William M. 1966. *The Documents of Vatican II*. New York: Corpus Books.

CARA. 1997. "More Than 2,100 Prepare for Permanent Diaconate." *The CARA Report*. Spring: 7.

Cunningham, Agnes. 1987. "Deacon." Pp. 268–270 in Joseph Komonchack, Mary Collins, and Dermot Lane (eds.), *The New Dictionary of Theology*. Wilmington, DE: Michael Glazier.

D'Antonio, William V., James D. Davidson, Dean R. Hoge, and Ruth A. Wallace. 1996. *Laity: American and Catholic*. Kansas City, MO: Sheed and Ward.

Fichter, Joseph. 1992. *Wives of Catholic Clergy*. Kansas City, MO: Sheed and Ward.

Flannery, Austin. 1992. *Vatican Council II: The Conciliar and Post Conciliar Documents*, Collegeville, MN: The Liturgical Press.

Gaine, Michael. 1991. "The State of the Priesthood." Pp. 246–255 in Adrian Hastings (ed.), *Modern Catholicism: Vatican II and After*. New York: Oxford University Press.

Hemrick, Eugene, and Joseph Shields. 1981. *A National Study of the Permanent Diaconate in the United States*. Washington, DC: United States Catholic Conference.

Hoge, Dean R. 1987. *The Future of Catholic Leadership: Responses to the Priest Shortage*. Kansas City, MO: Sheed and Ward.

Kahn, Robert L., Donald M. Wolfe, Robert P. Quinn, J. Diedrick Snoek and Robert A. Rosenthal. 1964. *Organizational Stress: Studies in Role Conflict and Ambiguity*. New York: John Wiley and Sons.

National Conference of Catholic Bishops (NCCB). 1996. *A National Study on the Permanent Diaconate of the Catholic Church in the United States, 1994–1995*. Washington, DC: United States Catholic Conference.

Official Catholic Directory, 1977, 1982, 1987, 1992, 1997. New Providence, NJ: P. J. Kenedy.

Olson, Jeannine E. 1992. *One Ministry, Many Roles: Deacons and Deaconesses through the Centuries*. St. Louis: Concordia.

Pistone, John. 1997. "Among Brothers." *Deacon Digest*, March/April:7–8.

Rice, Nick. 1997. "Will the Diaconate Become Parochialized?" *Origins* 26 (May 8):746–749.

Rizzo, John J., Robert J. House, and Sidney I. Lirtzman. 1970. "Role Conflict and Ambiguity in Complex Organizations." *Administrative Science Quarterly* 15 (June):150–163

Rogers, David L., and Joseph Molnar. 1976. "Organizational Antecedents of Role Conflict and Ambiguity in Top-Level Administrators." *Administrative Science Quarterly* 21:509–610.

Wallace, Ruth A. 1992. *They Call Her Pastor: A New Role for Catholic Women.* Albany, NY: State University of New York Press.

Winninger, Paul. 1993. "The Deacon and the Lay Person." In National Conference of Catholic Bishops, Committee on the Permanent Diaconate, *Foundations for the Renewal of the Diaconate.* Washington, DC: United States Catholic Conference.

11

Attitudes to Women's Ordination in Protestant Congregations in the United States, Britain, and Australia

Edward C. Lehman, Jr.

One of the most important recent developments in Western religious organizations is the women-in-ministry movement. During recent decades, increasing numbers of women have entered theological seminaries and rabbinical schools aspiring to become ordained priests, ministers, and rabbis. Hundreds of those women have been placed as ordained religious leaders of congregations. Some observers expect these changes in the sex composition of the pastoral ministry to modify the future image and practice of ministry (e.g., Weidman 1985; Nason-Clark 1987).

Given its potential impact on the church, the movement has also been highly controversial. The issues have been debated regularly in official denominational meetings. In those discussions the proponents of women in ministry typically promise that women's unique ministry style will help solve some of the church's problems (e.g., Ice 1987), while the women's detractors predict that the change bodes only catastrophe for the community of faith. Where denominations decided to ordain women, their supporters rejoiced, but some others who opposed the decision changed their denominational loyalties by switching to more misogynistic groups.

THE RESEARCH QUESTION

What do ordinary church members think about these issues? That is what we ask here. In most media coverage of discussions of the women-in-ministry movement, the focus has been on what church officials say about it. Missing has been any consideration of what ordinary people in the pews have to say. This is a significant omission, because those lay members constitute the fragile organizational and financial base on which church leaders sit. Without lay participation all grand denominational structures and programs would wither and fade from the scene. The ultimate fate of clergywomen will be determined not in the denominational offices but in the pews. Thus it is important to know what lay church members think about women in ministry.

This chapter reports the results of surveys of lay church members undertaken in three societies—the United States, the United Kingdom, and Australia. Each study was undertaken by the author expressly to determine the attitudes lay members held toward women in ministry. In the United States, the studies involved two denominations that had already officially endorsed women's ordination, the American Baptist Churches and the United Presbyterian Church, USA. Both of these bodies are representative of "mainline" Protestantism in America and the kinds of attitudes one might find there (Lehman 1979, 1985).

In the United Kingdom, four denominations were involved—the Anglican Church, the Baptist Union, the Methodist Church, and the United Reformed Church. The United Reformed Church came into existence through an organic merger of the former Congregational and Presbyterian churches. The Anglican Church, of course, represents the semiofficial religious body of British society, dating back to King Henry VIII. The Baptists, Methodists, and United Reformed represent groups that were formerly "dissenters" from the state church, and they portray "free church" tradition. Those four organizations comprise most of "Protestantism" in England (Lehman 1987).

There were two denominations involved in the Australian work, the Anglican Church of Australia and the Uniting Church. The Anglican Church of Australia enjoys the longest tradition there, but it doesn't have the extensive ties to official Australian society that Anglicans enjoy in England. The Uniting Church came into being a few decades ago through a merger of former Methodists, Congregational-ists, and Presbyterians. These two bodies represent "mainstream" Protestantism in Australia (Lehman 1994).

Each survey of members in all three countries involved a national sample of about 400 lay persons in each denomination. The sampling was done with the cooperation of the leadership in each body, which was very important in obtaining the members' cooperation. As the response rates to these surveys ranged between 85 and 93 percent, it is unlikely that nonresponse bias is a problem in the data. All of the research was done by the author with no denominational interference.

In each country, the sample was stratified by sex in order to obtain roughly equal proportions of men and women. The procedure was successful, in that the samples contained about 50/50 women and men. However, the differences between men and women in their receptivity to women in ministry were usually so small as to be statistically nonsignificant. Where sex differences did emerge from the analysis, (1) they were very slight, and (2) the women tended to be more receptive than the men.

ATTITUDES TOWARD WOMEN IN MINISTRY

Social-psychologically, attitudes toward women in ministry involve characteris-tics endemic to attitudes toward anything. They involve perceptions, feelings, and predispositions to act toward the attitude object—what people *think* about it, how they *feel* about it, and how they are *motivated to act* toward it. This constellation of responses we call "attitudes," and they are present whether the attitude object is another person, a group, an event, or even an abstract idea. These three aspects of attitudes are referred to as their "dimensions." There is (1) a "cognitive" dimension—what people *think* about the object, (2) an "affective" dimension—how they *feel* about it, and (3) a "behavioral" dimension—how people are prepared to *act* toward the object.

The studies of attitudes toward women clergy incorporated those distinctions—(1) what church members think clergywomen are like, (2) how they feel about clergywomen (liking or disliking), and (3) how they are prepared to act toward clergywomen.

What Church Members Think

Recently, whenever women have sought entry into occupations typically dominated by men, they have usually confronted stereotypes that paint females in a bad light. This pattern has been observed in many fields, such as law, medicine, corporate management, and higher education (Epstein 1988). People with negative attitudes tend to accept the stereotypes as true, while those who have positive attitudes more typically reject them. We incorporated several of those stereotypes in the church member surveys. We report on three of them here.

Women as Excessively Emotional. One stereotype of clergywomen holds that they are too emotional to be able to handle religious leadership effectively. As the image goes, their temperament is simply not suited for ministerial work. Women are not sufficiently rational, systematically organized, calculating, and assertive to do what the job demands. In the end, therefore, they will fail. A masculine temperament is what is required to run a church.

To measure differences in church members' tendency to hold this stereotype, we asked them whether they agreed with the following statement: "A woman's temperament is just as suited for the pastoral ministry as a man's." Disagreement with the statement indicates acceptance of the stereotype.

Women as Weak Leaders. Another stereotype women face in seeking entry into male-dominated occupations is that they are weak leaders. It portrays women as likely to crumble under the pressures of organizational realities. Accordingly, women will not be able to represent the organization to its publics forcefully enough to insure that the objectives of the organization will be reached. They will not be able to suppress or otherwise direct the internal conflicts endemic to work organizations including religious congregations.

The survey contained the following item to measure the extent to which church members hold that stereotype: "Congregations requiring strong leadership are more likely to get it from a man than a woman." Agreement with the statement indicates endorsement of the stereotype.

Women as Unable to Handle Role Conflict. The third stereotype involves role conflict, the cross-pressures that derive from the demands of two or more roles when those expectations are mutually exclusive. This image of clergywomen typically focuses on the conflicting requirements of home and work. Even when holding down a full-time job, women (more than men) are usually expected to be good parents and homemakers, and the stereotype asserts that they cannot do both tasks well. As women confront those dilemmas and find them impossible to handle, the stereotype asserts that they are likely to suffer emotional problems such as excessive guilt feelings, frustration, mood swings, and somatic symptoms.

To measure differences in viewing female clergy in this way, the survey asked the lay members whether they agreed or disagreed with the following statement: "Women who try to be both full-time ministers and wives and mothers are likely to have emotional problems due to all the demands placed on them." Agreement with the assertion indicates acceptance of the stereotype.

How Church Members Feel

Our feelings about other people at times are different from our ideas about them. Some white people, for example, may not accept the stereotype that portrays nonwhites as undesirable neighbors, but their concern about property values in their neighborhood may lead them to have negative feelings about nonwhite families buying homes around them. If they accept the stereotype, of course, they will readily resent desegregation of housing in their community.

Similarly, what people *think* female clergy are like is not always consistent with how they *feel* about having women as their religious leader. If lay members believe the stereotype of clergywomen as weak leaders, they will not *want* a woman in that position. However, they may hold perfectly nonstereotypical images of female clergy, but they may not want a woman for other reasons—such as the fear that introducing female leadership in their church will result in other members leaving the congregation. Feelings and ideas do not always match.

Accordingly, we incorporated the affective dimension of attitudes in the research by asking about the lay members' *preferences* for men or women performing various clergy roles for their congregation. The survey instrument contained the following item: "Listed below are several church positions and activities typically associated with the pastoral ministry (or, 'the priesthood'). Please indicate whether—given the choice—you would PREFER to have a man or a woman in the position or if you really have no preference." The choices given were: prefer a man, no preference, and prefer a woman. The roles listed included the following four items: parish priest (or pastor), serving Holy Communion, preaching a sermon, and personal counseling.

How Church Members Are Prepared to Act

People's overt actions do not always match their ideas and feelings. Some freely act out their thoughts and feelings, while others do not. For example, some restaurant owners who view members of minority groups in their community in terms of negative stereotypes do not want to serve them as customers. However, in view of civil rights legislation, they will typically serve minorities who enter their place of business for fear of legal action if they do not. Conversely, some employers will discriminate against minority job applicants even though they themselves are not prejudiced against them, if they perceive that local norms call for them to exclude minority-group members in their work force. Prejudice and discrimination—feelings and actions—do not always go hand-in-hand.

Similarly, lay persons will act either to accept or to reject clergywomen, and those actions may or may not be consistent with what they think and feel about them. A person may hold no prejudices about clergywomen, but because others in the congregation who are prejudiced against female clergy threaten to disrupt the congregation through schism or withholding financial contributions if a woman is installed, they will try to exclude the woman candidate in the name of congregational solidarity (see Lehman 1985). They themselves are not prejudiced, but they will discriminate in such circumstances. We wanted to know how lay church members are prepared to act toward women in ministry.

At the time each survey was conducted in England and Australia, the Anglican Church there had not yet officially endorsed the policy of ordaining women to the priesthood. To measure their tendencies to act toward women in ministry one way or the other—to accept or to discriminate—we asked the following question: "If you were asked to vote on the issue of ordaining women as Anglican priests today, how would you vote?"

The situation was different in the free churches in England, Australia, and the United States. There, as the acceptance of women as ordained ministers and pastors was already a matter of denominational policy at the time of the research, the question asked of the Anglicans would not make sense. Instead, we asked lay persons in the free churches the following item:

> If a search committee in your church recommended a woman as minister, and if tensions arose in the congregation because of that recommendation, which of the following actions do you think the search committee should take?
>
> a. stick with their recommendation and try to convince the church to call the woman,
> b. withdraw the woman's name and recommend a man,
> c. do nothing, but let the majority of the church decide what to do.

Church members indicating that the committee should stick to their guns (option "a") are showing no readiness to discriminate against women candidates. Those who chose either of the other answers were indicating a willingness to discriminate against a woman, at least in the name of majority rule.

Each survey included these questions along with items to gather other information. In a few instances the exact wording of the questions was varied slightly to accommodate uniquenesses of expression found in a particular society or denomination.

RESULTS

What did we find? How do lay church members in these societies respond to the women-in-ministry movement? As shown in Table 11.1, the picture is both complex and fairly consistent across societies. The data indicate wide divergences in church members' reactions to clergywomen. Some members are receptive to the idea of female church leadership—usually a majority of the members. Others are more inclined to reject the idea. Those patterns tend to be fairly constant across societies.

Table 11.1
Responses of Lay Members Indicating Acceptance of Ordained Clergywomen in the United States, United Kingdom, and Australia (in percentages)

Indicators	United States	United Kingdom	Australia
Stereotyping:			
Women who try to be both full-time ministers and wives and mothers are likely to have emotional problems due to all the demands placed on them.	45	30	47
Congregations requiring strong leadership are more likely to get it from a man than a woman.	57	54	63
A woman's temperament is just as suited for the pastoral ministry as a man's.	77	83	79
Role Preferences:			
pastor/priest	47	51	61
serve Holy Communion	73*	68	77
preach a sermon	63	78	82
personal counseling	71*	61	67
Support with Actions:			
what committee should do (free churches)	32	35	56
how vote (Anglicans only)	—	61	70

*Data from the Presbyterian Church only.

Tendencies to Stereotype

Between about one-third and one-half of the lay members reject the idea that women priests and pastors will experience emotional problems due to role conflicts between work and home. Thus between one-half and two-thirds of them believe this stereotype is accurate. Slightly fewer members rejected the stereotype in England than in the United States and Australia. In discussing this issue, we also learned that many of those who thought such problems would be prevalent believed that at root the problem was with the *husbands*, not the working wives, because men typically refuse to assume a proper share of household responsibilities when their wife is employed full time. In that situation, the pressures would be hard for most women to handle, they thought.

Slightly more than one-half of the lay members said they thought a woman was just as likely to give churches strong leadership as a man. Again the proportion reporting that opinion is slightly lower in England than in the other two societies, but the differences between societies in this case are statistically nonsignificant.

The vast majority of church members believe that women are just as temperamentally suited for the pastoral ministry as men. On average only about 20 percent of church members believe that men's temperament is more suited for ministry than women's. Once again, the proportions differ very little from one society to the next.

Overall, then, the general tendency is for most lay church members to reject stereotypical images of clergywomen and to view women in ministry in relatively open terms (except in the case of role conflict between work and home). A similar pattern was observed concerning other stereotypes, in that most members rejected them (Lehman 1979, 1985, 1994).

Role Preferences

What did the church members say they *want* regarding whether their religious leader is male or female? The answer depends on which role one is considering.

As concerns preferences for the incumbent of the position itself—the parish priest or pastor—about one-half of the lay members said they really had no preference for a male or a female. That means, of course, that about one-half did have preferences, and it tended to be for a *man*. (Only 2 percent or less stated that they preferred a female.) The proportion of members in Australia indicating no preference is slightly higher than that found in the other two places. That pattern is explainable by the fact that the Uniting Church in Australia at its founding established the acceptance of women's ordination as a criterion of membership in the denomination. That organizational norm would account for the higher figure in Australia. There was little difference between the United States and the United Kingdom concerning this role preference.

The pattern is a bit different concerning some of the things priests and pastors do, that is, preach sermons, conduct Holy Communion, and offer pastoral counseling. Between about two-thirds and three-fourths of the lay members said that it makes no difference to them whether the person performing those roles is a man or a woman. Overall, the differences among the three societies are not great.

Those patterns also indicate some inconsistency between gender preferences concerning the position of priest/pastor itself and the things the incumbent does. While half of the members prefer a male cleric, only about half of those having that preference also want a man to perform any of the three clerical functions. A significant number of people are saying, "I don't care who performs ministerial functions, but I want a man as my priest/pastor." This pattern obviously raises the question of why they prefer a male minister but don't care who does specific forms of ministering. The answer probably is that there is something more sacred about the position itself—THE PRIEST, THE PASTOR—than about the functions the incumbent performs—preaching, offering sacraments, and giving advice. The position itself is elevated higher than its functions.

Predispositions to Act

What overt actions can we expect from lay church members concerning the issues of ordination and placement of women as priests and ministers? The answer depends on the particular question that was asked about the matter. Among the free churches, between one-third and one-half of the members stated that the case for appointing a woman as ordained pastor should be pressed even in the face of serious congregational conflict. There was virtually no difference in the proportion of members taking that position in the United States and England—about a third. Slightly more than one-half of the members of the Uniting Church preferred that stance, which is greater than in the other two countries. As noted before, this difference is likely to be an artifact of that denomination's specification that acceptance of women in ministry is a test of fellowship.

The proportions of lay Anglicans in England and Australia who stated that they would vote in favor of ordaining women as priests are about the same—about two-thirds. This proportion of Anglicans saying that they would not discriminate against female candidates is higher than the figures observed in the free churches. This difference is most likely a direct result of the difference between the indicators used for the two types of church. The item used with the free churches posited a situation of congregational conflict—a threatening situation for most lay church members. The item used for the Anglicans did not. Finally the higher proportion of Anglicans unwilling to discriminate against women in Australia most likely is an artifact of timing. At the time of data collection in Australia, the Anglican Church in England had just recently voted to ordain women. This fact was widely discussed in Australia, and it probably elevated the number of people saying that they too would vote to ordain women.

CONCLUSIONS

What does the analysis tell us? Several generalizations derive from the patterns observed in Table 11.1.

Most church members tend to reject stereotypes of female clergy. About one-half of the members said they thought women could handle the potential role conflicts between work and family. Two-thirds to three-fourths of the members stated that women's temperament was just as suited for the pastoral ministry as a man's and that women are just as likely to be strong leaders as men. The prevailing images tend to be positive.

A majority of lay church members also said that it made no difference to them whether a man or a woman performed ministerial functions of preaching, counseling, and observing Holy Communion. But about one-half of the members stated a preference for a man in the position of priest/pastor, suggesting that the position is somehow viewed as more sacred than the functions.

Most of the Anglicans in England and Australia indicated that they would vote for women's ordination, prior to their denomination's officially taking that position. But in the face of congregational conflict and potential schism over the issue in the free churches, only about 30 to 50 percent of members said they would press the issue of accepting a woman as pastor.

The differences in receptivity to women in ministry between the three societies is negligible. Whether the church members in one society appear more or less receptive to clergywomen depends on which facet of receptivity one is considering, and typically the differences are not great.

Finally, it would be a mistake to overgeneralize about what "the lay church member" thinks about the ordination and placement of women as clergy. There is simply too much diversity in church members' statements to pretend that church members' attitudes are monolithic. What we can say, however, is that more church members appear to accept women in ministry than resist them.

Even though a majority of lay church members indicate endorsement of the women-in-ministry movement, the minority of members who are opposed have the potential of carrying more influence on congregational decisions than their numbers would suggest. As shown in the relative hesitancy to support clergywomen in the face of congregational conflict over the issue, the opponents of women's ordination and placement have a powerful social tool to use in pressing their point, i.e. the threat of congregational schism and decline in financial resources. The tendency frequently observed for the minority to press their case vociferously often makes the liberal majority misread the facts of the situation and allow the minority to block women's appointments. It is unfortunate that they usually do not also know that the threats of congregational decline rarely materialize (See Royle 1984). With clergywomen at the helm, most congregations continue to meet the religious needs of their members. The church continues to be the church.

REFERENCES

Epstein, Cynthia Fuchs. 1988. *Deceptive Distinctions: Sex, Gender, and the Social Order.* New York: Russell Sage Foundation.

Ice, Martha Long. 1987. *Clergywomen and Their World Views: Calling for a New Age.* New York: Praeger Publishers.

Lehman, Edward C., Jr. 1979. *Project SWIM: A Study of Women in Ministry.* Valley Forge, PA: American Baptist Churches.

———. 1985. *Women Clergy: Breaking through Gender Barriers.* New Brunswick, NJ: Transaction Books.

———. 1987. *Women Clergy in England: Sexism, Modern Consciousness, and Church Viability.* Lewiston, NY: Edward Mellen Press.

———. 1994. *Women in Ministry: Receptivity and Resistance.* Melbourne, Australia: The Joint Board for Christian Education.

Nason-Clark, Nancy. 1987. "Are Women Changing the Image of Ministry? A Comparison of British and American Societies." *Review of Religious Research* 28(4):331–340.
Royle, Marjorie H. 1984. "Women Pastors: What Happens after Placement?" *Review of Religious Research* 24(2):116–126.
Weidman, Judith L. 1985. *Women Ministers: How Women Are Redefining Traditional Roles* (Revised Edition). New York: Harper and Row.

12

Latinos and Latinas in the Catholic Church: Cohesion and Conflict

Gilbert R. Cadena

The United States of America is itself a new model of a multiethnic country, and the state of California is the prototype of a new country.
—Cardinal Peter Shirayanagi of Tokyo, Japan[1]

Latino Catholic religiosity in the United States reflects the changing dynamics of a multicultural nation. Euro-American Catholicism is being radically transformed from the bottom up as Latinos are changing the face of the church and challenging their historical relationship with it. This is happening in relation to an ethnic group that is growing quickly because of immigration and a high birthrate, within a larger societal context characterized by economic changes and ethnic conflicts. Southern California provides a clear case of this situation, showing social cohesion and social conflict both within the church and in the larger society. The Los Angeles metropolitan area, with its recent population changes and its tremendous diversity, may be seen as a microcosm of the United States of the future. This chapter will examine tensions between Latinos and the Catholic Church, drawing on McGuire's (1997) analysis of religion as a source of both cohesion and conflict. Before discussing the religious situation, however, let us look at some recent social and economic changes that have occurred in the Los Angeles area.

THE SOCIAL AND ECONOMIC CONTEXT OF LOS ANGELES

There is no longer an ethnic majority in Southern California. The 1990s represents a shift from the "traditional" race relations model of a Euro-American majority and an African American minority to a new model of multiethnic diversity. Today, in Los Angeles County, Latinos are the largest ethnic group (44 percent), surpassing Euro-Americans (35 percent). Asian Americans (11 percent) now outnumber African Americans (10 percent).[2] Between 1970 and 1990 Latinos increased by 236 percent and Asian Americans increased by 451 percent (Cheng and Yang 1996). It is projected that by the year 2040 Latinos will constitute 69 percent of the Los Angeles population, Euro-Americans 14 percent, Asian Americans 11 percent, and African Americans 6 percent. Thus, in terms of demographic shifts, both Euro-Americans and African Americans are losing their traditional social location, as Latino political strength and Asian American economic power increase. Furthermore, the Los Angeles region has the largest immigrant population of any city in the United States, with one-third of its residents born outside this country (Waldinger and Bozorgmehr 1996). Of the 3,351,000 Latinos in Los Angeles County, three-quarters are of Mexican descent and about 20 percent are Central Americans. Slightly less than one-half are immigrants. Los Angeles is now the second largest metropolitan area in the United States. It is projected that by the year 2020 Los Angeles will surpass New York as the largest metropolitan area.

The demographic changes in Los Angeles have been accompanied by economic disruptions. The 1980s and 1990s were characterized by changes that were linked to developments in the global economy. Los Angeles, like many major cities, experienced deindustrialization. There was an increase in layoffs as a result of corporate downsizing, the relocation of factories to countries with cheaper labor, and decreases in defense-related industry.

A recent study comparing income distribution from 1959 to 1989 shows that the income gap in Southern California is widening between Euro-Americans and people of color (Allen and Turner 1997). For example, in 1959 Chicanos[3] were paid about 81 percent of the median income of Euro-American men. By 1989 Chicano income dropped to 61 percent. For Mexican immigrants, income decreased from 66 percent in 1959 to 39 percent in 1989.

Latinos had the highest labor force participation in the region with 80 percent, compared to 74 percent of Euro-Americans and 64 percent of African Americans. However, in 1990, of those living in poverty, 57 percent were Latinos, compared to 16 percent of African Americans, 17 percent of Euro-Americans, and 10 percent of Asian Americans.

These demographic and economic changes have contributed to ethnic tensions in the region, resulting in a political mobilization against immigrants and people of color. The recession of the early 1990s encouraged the blaming of immigrants and people of color for the effects of decisions by government and big business. The year of 1994 saw the passing of Proposition 187, the "Save Our State" initiative, which attempted to exclude undocumented immigrants from public social services, health care, and public education.[4] A year later Proposition 209, the antiaffirmative action initiative, also passed, restricting the use of ethnicity, race, and gender as criteria for selection in jobs, government contracts, and post-secondary school enrollment.

Border hysteria fueled by both Republican and Democratic politicians and public officials contributed to the scapegoating of immigrants for California's economic problems, and a punitive welfare reform of 1996 targeted both undocumented and legal immigrants. Another initiative scheduled for 1998 will attempt to dismantle twenty years of bilingual education, imposing an English immersion standard for all students. These political issues have been reflected in divisions within the Catholic Church.

THE LOS ANGELES ARCHDIOCESE

The Archdiocese of Los Angeles is the largest in the United States with about 3,673,000 Catholics (*Official Catholic Directory* 1997). Latinos comprise about 70 percent of this number, or 2,571,000, making the Latino population of this one archdiocese larger than the total population of any other diocese in the country, including New York and Chicago (Foy and Avato 1997). Euro-Americans comprise about 19 percent of the archdiocese, Asian Americans 8 percent, and African Americans 3 percent.[5] In the parish churches 102 ethnic groups worship, with weekly masses celebrated in fifty-five languages (Wirpsa 1997). Of the 285 parishes in the archdiocese, fifty are predominately Latino, ten Latino/Asian American, nine Latino/African American, two African American, and two Asian American (*Official Catholic Directory* 1997).

Latino ministry in Los Angeles, as in most dioceses across the country, is focused on immigrant ministry. The archdiocese incorporates aspects of Latino culture in weekly services, such as Spanish masses, music, and Latino popular devotions. Evangelization classes are offered in Spanish and with attempts to help immigrants adjust and integrate to U.S. society. A Spanish-speaking newspaper, *La Vida*, is published weekly. The Office for Hispanic Ministry works with five pastoral coordinators representing each of the regions in the archdiocese. All the auxiliary bishops know some Spanish, and all new priests ordained in the archdiocese must know a second language.

The archdiocese has six colleges, fifty-one high schools, and 229 elementary schools (Foy and Avato 1997).[6] Latinos outnumber all other ethnic groups in enrollment in the elementary schools (46 percent) and in the high schools (39 percent). However, at the college level, Latino enrollment is less than 20 percent.

Inequality between Latinos and Euro-Americans is also reflected in the parishes. Many churches are characterized by social class inequality and are located in racially and ethnically segregated neighborhoods. The political controversies over recent legislative initiatives have been carried into the church, with lay people of different class and ethnic backgrounds taking opposing positions on immigration, affirmative action, and bilingual education.

RELIGION AND SOCIAL COHESION

If religion is a system of shared meanings that unifies people and links them to a common history, then religion contributes to the social cohesion of society and of groups within it (Durkheim 1965). This cohesion is achieved through collective identity, shared meanings, and nationalism (McGuire 1997).

Religion provides collective identity as it strengthens its members in their common goals. Latino Catholic identification has remained fairly consistent over the generations. In the California Identity Project, the majority of Latinos identified as Catholic, with the first generation showing the highest rates (79 percent) and the second and third generations showing only slightly lower rates (74 percent and 77 percent respectively) (Hurtado et al. 1992).

Shared meanings are greatly enhanced by symbols, which may foster group unity, especially when they are integrated with rituals. Participation in rituals links the individual to the larger society and provides the members of a religion with a sense of boundaries. Rituals enhance a group's consciousness and strengthen the individual's commitment to the group's expectations and goals. Churches encourage individuals to seek the good of the group rather than their own interests. Commitment and consensus are expected within religious groups, and churches use negative sanctions for noncooperative members (for example, excommunication and the denial of access to sacraments). Religious rites renew these representations by rekindling the group's consciousness of its unity. In addition, they strengthen the individual's commitment to the group's expectations and goals.

Popular religion is an example of Latino religiosity as it is maintained and transformed from generation to generation. As Diaz-Stevens has noted, popular religiosity "possesses a certain core cohesion which gives it its essence and gives evidence of particular characteristics," but "it is also always expanding, contracting, adding on and subtracting. Common examples are devotions to patron saints of a particular parish or specific region in Latin America" (Diaz-Stevens 1994:21).

An example specific to Los Angeles is the devotion to the eighteen-inch high image of Our Lady of Zapopopan, the Patroness of Jalisco, Mexico. For the past eight years this statue has been making an annual journey of 2,000 miles to visit churches in Los Angeles. Also known as *La Generala* ("The General"), this image of Mary is said to have played a role in preventing a bloodbath during the Mexican war of independence against Spain. Mozingo and McDonnell give an account of the devotions accompanying this journey of the statue: "Wherever she goes, celebrations of the Mass and rhythmic recitations of the rosary accompany her, along with the occasional shouts of 'Viva la generala!'. . . Supplicants show respect by approaching on their knees. Many light candles and provide donations. Others leave *milagros*, tiny metal talismans traditionally linked to miracles" (Mozingo and McDonnell 1997:6).

Devotion to Our Lady of Guadalupe is the most visible and persistent symbol of Mexican and Mexican American identity (Elizondo 1994:122). This particular image of the Mother of God represents "acceptance, dignity, love and protection" at the individual level. Politically, her image has been in the forefront of Mexican and Chicano social movements, from Mexican Independence in the 1820s to the United Farmworkers movement today.

In Los Angeles, Our Lady of Guadalupe is also part of popular art, from murals and posters to T-shirts and tattoos. Small shrines in places of business, calendars from bakeries, and medals in jewelry shops reflect her image throughout the city. An exhibit dedicated to Guadalupe art has been displayed at the Self-Help Graphics Gallery for the past several years during the months of December and January. For Chicanos and Chicanas, Guadalupe provides a historical memory linking the indigenous people of Mexico to the Christian conversion of the Americas and the contemporary reality of the United States. In other words, it is a symbolic representation of three distinct historical and religious epochs. In the Los Angeles archdiocese, there are nine churches named in honor of Our Lady of Guadalupe.

Religious identity also contributes to sentiments of nationalism by enhancing the sense of solidarity as a people. It brings people together in a central, unifying cultural experience. Within the United States Catholic Church, assimilation into Euro-American culture has been the primary pastoral policy aimed at immigrants and people of color. As a reaction, some Latinos are attempting to link their Catholic heritage to their indigenous or pre-Christian roots. Among second- and third-generation Chicanos, a number of popular religious practices have emerged.

Celebrations such as the *Dia de los Muertos* ("Day of the Dead"), celebrated each year on November 2, provide a way for individuals and families to commemorate ancestors and deceased family members, friends, and heroes. This celebration brings people together as they build altars, participate in processions to cemeteries, share meals, and listen to music and poetry. *Dia de los Muertos* was first celebrated with indigenous ceremonies more a thousand years ago. Today Chicanos continue to celebrate it every year at churches, parks, art galleries, cemeteries, and college campuses. At California State Polytechnic University, Pomona, for example, the annual ceremony includes a procession through the campus, a community altar, speakers, poetry, music, *folklorico*, and sharing of bread. Participants are invited to bring photos and offerings of food to the altar. Stories and testimonies commemorate individuals who have recently died. Theologian Virgilio Elizondo writes of *Dia de los Muertos*:

> We celebrate together that death does not have the final word over life and that life ultimately triumphs over death. Our family and our *pueblo* is so strong and enduring that not even death can break it apart. . . . Society might take our lands away, marginate us and even kill us, but it cannot destroy us. For we live on in the generations to come and in them the previous generations continue to be alive. (Elizondo 1994:129)

RELIGION AND SOCIAL CONFLICT

As religion contributes to self-identity and group identity, boundaries between members and nonmembers can also intensify and contribute to conflict. Religion contributes to social conflict on at least three levels: conflict within a religious group, conflict among religious groups, and conflict between religious groups and the larger society (McGuire 1997).

Conflict within a Religious Group

Within religious groups, conflict between members and leaders arises when power is concentrated among a small number of individuals. Religious hierarchies reflect unequal roles of power and authority. This conflict is exacerbated if the inequality is related to ethnicity.

In the Los Angeles archdiocese, ethnic stratification exists at most levels. Euro-Americans control most leadership positions, financial resources, media, priesthood, and the Chancery. Cardinal Roger Mahony leads the archdiocese along with six auxiliary bishops. Of these auxiliaries, only one is Latino. Of the six secretariats in the Chancery, only one is headed by a Latino. Similarly, only one person on the twenty-member editorial board of the archdiocesan newspaper is Latino.

Of the 440 active diocesan priests, about 18 percent are Latino. Latinas account for about 30 percent of 2,000 religious sisters. Without sufficient leadership reflective of their cultural heritage, many Latino Catholics choose either to participate in family religious traditions or to leave the church. Among women, Latinas are not part of the official leadership structure of the archdiocese, although many are involved in unpaid activities in parishes.

While Euro-Americans are in the minority among students at parochial schools, they comprise the majority of teachers and principals. As the statewide debate over bilingual education in public schools intensifies, the church has remained relatively silent when it comes to assessing its own limited bilingual programs. It has generally maintained an English-only policy.

Latinos at Loyola Marymont University in Los Angeles account for about 17 percent of the student body. Among the more than 250 faculty members, there are six Latino tenured or tenure-track faculty. There are no Latinos at the upper levels of administration. The only Latino department head is the chair of the three-person Chicano Studies Department.

Ethnic conflict is also manifested in political issues. The votes on the propositions against immigrants and affirmative action were split along ethnic lines. The majority of Euro-American Catholics supported the measures, while the majority of Latinos voted against them. Cardinal Mahony and the auxiliary bishops condemned the two propositions. This led to conflict with Euro-American lay people who disagreed with them.

Conflict between Religious Groups

As religious boundaries are defined, they can contribute to conflict with outsiders and other groups. Since the 1970s, the monopoly of Catholicism among Latinos has been challenged. Storefront evangelical and pentecostal churches are growing in most Mexican/Chicano neighborhoods, as are Latino subgroups within larger churches. There are more than a thousand Latino Protestant congregations. Many have organized efforts to bring in new members that target recent immigrants, families, youth, gang members, and neighborhoods. Recruitment methods include public street witnessing, daily radio and television programming, concerts, staged productions, rallies, and picnics.

Latino Protestant pastors far outnumber Latino Catholic priests. Many of the pastors are immigrants themselves, and they speak the language of the people. Charismatic leaders, independent of hierarchical control, emphasize the primary use of the Bible and individual conversion. Congregations are small and able to address people's immediate needs.

Evangelicals and pentecostals appear to have an affinity to poorer, less educated people, in contrast to Catholicism, which generally has more of a focus on middle-class sectors. Some may be drawn to Protestantism because of personal difficulties resulting from conflicts and dislocations in the larger society or because of discontent with the Catholic Church. In some cases, conversion is a reaction to Catholic authoritarianism, mega-parishes, Euro-American clerical and congregational discrimination, insensitivity to Latino cultural practices, and a lack of Spanish masses in some churches. Converts are looking for deeper spiritual experience with committed members. Conversion to smaller Protestant churches provides an alternative source of sacred meaning, community, and answers to religious questions.

Latino conversions to evangelical and pentecostal religions have created tensions between Catholic and Protestant churches and at times between individual family members. As more Latinos convert to Protestantism, a struggle over the definition of Latino culture and identity plays out in the community. Many evangelicals and pentecostals criticize Catholic devotions to saints and to Our Lady of Guadalupe, as well as cultural processions, the sacraments, religious icons, and other Catholic traditions. To some Catholics, Protestantism is an attack on Latino cultural identity.

Conflicts within families can occur when conversion is seen as the adopting of the Euro-American ethos and culture. Intense religious commitments pull the individual away from family activities. The strict dress codes and restrictions on makeup, dancing, and drinking characteristic of some Protestant churches may produce tensions, particularly during family celebrations.

Conflict between Religious Groups and the Larger Society

Religious conflict is also an expression of fundamental economic relationships. The dominant class attempts to impose its ideology and power on subordinate classes. As a reaction, groups may use religious ideas and organizations to legitimate their interests.

In 1985, 400 women known as the Mothers of East Los Angeles (MELA) organized to stop a proposed $100 million state prison scheduled to be built in their predominantly Latino neighborhood. East Los Angeles had become a dumping ground for prisons, freeways, and landfills. With five prisons already in the Eastside, more than 14,000 inmates were housed within two miles of thirty-four schools (Sahagun 1992). The proposed new prison would have added 1,450 more inmates. MELA worked with 47 civic organizations, called the Coalition against the Prison in East LA, including two church-related community organizations, the United Neighborhoods Organization (UNO) and the East Valleys Organization (EVO). A priest, Father John Moretta, and two Catholic parishes became deeply involved in this effort. They organized rallies, marches, candlelight vigils, letter-writing campaigns, news conferences, and trips to Sacramento, the state capital. After successfully stopping the prison, MELA continues to organize around community issues. For example, it blocked proposals to build a hazardous-waste incinerator and an above-ground pipeline to carry oil from Santa Barbara to Long Beach through East Los Angeles.

CONCLUSION

The Catholic Church of the twenty-first century will reflect the changing multiethnic and multilingual makeup of its membership and civil society. The 500-year influence of Catholicism will continue to provide cohesion for many Latinos, although the resistance of the Catholic leadership to change and the challenge of Protestant congregations will undermine Latino loyalty to the church. Throughout their history, Catholic Latinos have persevered with deep religious commitment, despite continual ethnic conflict within Catholicism. This commitment and this conflict, existing simultaneously, provide some insights into the tensions Latinos experience within the Catholic Church.

This situation raises numerous questions. Will the church wait until changes in civil society force it to respond to Latinos, or will it take the initiative to contribute to a new model of inclusion? Will the church develop ways to share power with Latinos, women, and lay people in general, or will the shrinking hierarchy attempt to centralize its power even more? Will Latinos position themselves at all levels of the church's infrastructure, or will they leave the church? How will the church respond to the increasing impoverishment of Chicano working-class and immigrant labor in contrast to the economic mobility of the Euro-American professional/ managerial class? As the multiethnic and immigrant backlash increases, will church leaders and laity defend multiethnic society or will they passively allow the attacks to continue? Will the church be strong enough to defend the newer immigrants as it did those from Europe at the turn of the century?

In many ways, the Catholic Church is one generation ahead of civil society in relation to the Latino resurgence. The church is attempting to make some small changes of inclusion, but will it make the more sweeping changes of power-sharing needed to make Latinos truly part of the church? The archdiocese views Latino ministry as a minority ministry, just like Asian American and African American ministry. Rather than accepting Latino ministry as the normative ministry, with Euro-American ministry as a minority in the archdiocese, it continues to marginal-ize the largest group in the area. Individual Latinos may serve in leadership positions, but as a critical mass, Latinos do not have any significant power.

The conflict Latinos experience both internally and externally to the church may further distance them from Catholicism if church leaders are not supportive of Latino concerns and Latinos are not empowered to become part of the religious decision-making process. Since Latinos include both immigrants and those born in the United States, the church must develop a pastoral plan to work with both of these sectors. As Latinos become the majority population in the Catholic Church and in Southern California, the church must not ignore the second, third, and subsequent generations who may not fit within either an immigrant or a Euro-American model of ministry.

NOTES

1. Quoted in "Cardinal Sees New Energy in California Melting Pot." *National Catholic Reporter*, October 1, 1996:5.
2. The data are reported in relation to Los Angeles (LA) County, LA city, LA region, and the LA Archdiocese, depending on the source.
3. The term "Chicano," or for women "Chicana," refers to people of Mexican ancestry born in the United States, as distinct from recent immigrants from Mexico. "Latino" and "Latina" refer to all people with Spanish surnames, born in the United States, in Mexico, or in other parts of Latin America.
4. Most sections of the bill were struck down by the courts.
5. These figures are close approximations.
6. All numbers are rounded to the nearest 1,000.

REFERENCES

Allen, James P., and Eugene Turner. 1997. *The Ethnic Quilt: Population Diversity in Southern California*. Northridge, CA: The Center for Geographical Studies, California State University.

Cheng, Lucie, and Philip Yang. 1996. "Asians: The 'Model Minority' Deconstructed." Pp. 305–344 in Roger Waldinger and Mehdi Bozorgmehr (eds.), *Ethnic Los Angeles*. New York: Russell Sage Foundation.

Diaz-Stevens, Ana Maria. 1994. "Analyzing Popular Religiosity for Socioreligious Meaning." Pp.17–36 in Anthony Stevens-Arroyo and Ana Maria Diaz-Stevens (eds.), *An Enduring Flame: Studies on Latino Popular Religiosity*. New York: Bildner Center for Western Hemisphere Studies.

Durkheim, Emile. 1965. *The Division of Labor in Society*. New York: Free Press.

Elizondo, Virgilio. 1994. "Popular Religion as the Core of Cultural Identity in the Mexican-American Experience." Pp. 113–132 in Anthony Stevens-Arroyo and Ana Maria Diaz-Stevens (eds.), *An Enduring Flame: Studies on Latino Popular Religiosity*. New York: Bildner Center for Western Hemisphere Studies.

Foy, Felician A., and Rose M. Avato (eds.). 1997. *Catholic Almanac*. Huntington, IN: Our Sunday Visitor.

Hurtado, Aida, David Hayes-Bautista, R. Burciaga Valdez, and Anthony Hernandez (eds.). 1992. *Redefining California: Latino Social Engagement in a Multicultural Society*. Los Angeles: Chicano Studies Research Center, University of California at Los Angeles.

McGuire, Meredith B. 1997. *Religion: The Social Context* (Fourth Edition). Belmont, CA: Wadsworth.

Mozingo, Joe, and Patrick McDonnell. 1997. "Sacred Sojourn." *Los Angeles Times* (May 15): B1,6.

Official Catholic Directory. 1997. New York: P. J. Kenedy and Sons.

Sahagun, Louis. 1992. "Mothers of Conviction." *Los Angeles Times* (September 16):B1,4.

Stevens-Arroyo, Anthony, and Ana Maria Diaz-Stevens (eds.). 1994. *An Enduring Flame: Studies on Latino Popular Religiosity*. New York: Bildner Center for Western Hemisphere Studies.

Waldinger, Roger, and Mehdi Bozorgmehr (eds.). 1996. *Ethnic Los Angeles.* New York: Russell Sage Foundation.
Wirpsa, Leslie. 1997. "Heading West for Good Liturgy." *National Catholic Reporter* (October 2):4–5.

13

Mission Churches and Church-Sect Theory: Seventh-day Adventists in Africa

Ronald Lawson

INTRODUCTION

Seventh-day Adventism was born in the United States. It emerged from the Millerite movement, whose leader, William Miller, had gathered a considerable following as a result of his preaching throughout New England and upstate New York that Christ would return on October 22, 1844. Although Miller had stated that it was not his intention to found a new religion, his followers were typically expelled from their churches. After the bitter disappointment and humiliation of the failed prediction, which silenced Miller himself, some of his followers continued to cling together, convinced that truth underlay his prophecy. While they awaited the end of the world as they knew it, they studied the Bible intensely and gradually arrived at a set of beliefs and norms that separated them from mainstream society.

Their urgent apocalyptic belief meant that they rejected the American Dream, for they believed that the nations were about to be destroyed with the return of Christ. Their insistence on observing Saturday as their Sabbath when a six-day work week was almost universal closed most avenues to employment. Their norms included vegetarianism, a refusal to take up arms, and prohibitions against coffee, tea, alcohol, smoking, dancing, theater, gambling, card playing, fiction reading, jewelry, and makeup. Moreover, Adventism's view of itself as God's Remnant people, the one true church and chosen vehicle of God's final message to the world in the last days, its declarations that other religious groups were "apostate," its brazen challenges in its evangelistic meetings to clergy of other denominations, and its expectation of persecution from the American state all tended to create bitter antagonisms.

These boundaries were strengthened by the close ties among Adventists, whose lives usually centered around their church. They attended church-run schools, often worked for the institutions developed by the church—hospitals, schools, health-food factories, and publishing houses—and were frequently drawn by educational opportunities and economic and social ties to live in what became known as "Adventist ghettos." Their social norms made it difficult for them to associate with others, caused employment problems, and sometimes had legal repercussions.

Early Adventism thus closely fits the definition of a "sect," which has been described by Stark and Bainbridge as a religious group in a high "state of tension" with "its surrounding sociocultural environment" (1985:23). This tension has three elements: difference, separation, and antagonism (1985:49–50).

However, church-sect theory predicts that if a sect grows, it is likely to lower its tension with society and thus move from sect toward "denomination." This has been true of American Adventism, whose level of tension with society has fallen sharply in recent decades. The growth and accreditation of Adventist educational and medical institutions has required participation in society and provided members with opportunities for upward mobility. Adventist hospitals have become increasingly orthodox, the five-day work week has removed many of the problems with Sabbath observance, and Adventist dietary and smoking prohibitions have won credibility as a result of medical research. At the same time, Adventism has pursued good relations with governments, switched its stance on military service, and sought better relations with other churches. Adventists have in effect postponed the apocalypse, working hard to maintain the separation of church and state in the United States, and thus to avoid the fulfillment of their prophecy that the "final events" will include persecution at the hands of the federal government (Lawson 1995:337–338, 1996).

Meanwhile, Adventism has spread around the world and is now active in 207 countries. Most of its recent growth has been concentrated in the developing world (see Table 13.1). Consequently, the proportion of its membership located in the United States has declined steeply: only 9 percent of the 8.8 million members lived there at the end of 1995.

Table 13.1
Seventh-day Adventist Membership
Developed versus Developing Worlds: 1960 and 1995

	1960	%	1995	%	Increase (%)
Developed World[a]	553,592	44.5	1,234,037	14.0	122.9
Developing World[b]	691,533	55.5	7,578,518	86.0	995.9
World Totals	1,245,125		8,812,555		607.8

[a]North America, Europe, Australia, New Zealand
[b]The rest of the world

Sources: General Conference 1961, 1996

What are the dynamics of these mission churches? Are their trajectories similar to that followed by the mother church in the United States? Is church-sect theory applicable to groups imported into other societies? This examination of Adventism focuses on Africa. After exploring the relevance of church-sect theory to international Seventh-day Adventism, I will broaden the analysis by testing it against the experience of Jehovah's Witnesses and Pentecostals.

The research reported here is part of a larger study of Adventism, which includes more than 3,000 in-depth interviews in fifty-five countries, thirteen of which are in sub-Saharan Africa. These interview data were supplemented by secondary sources. The data concerning Jehovah's Witnesses and Pentecostals were drawn entirely from secondary sources.

THE DATA

Adventists planted foreign missions on all continents during the last quarter of the nineteenth century. While their growth in what is now known as the developed world has remained relatively slow, so that the majority of members there today were born into Adventist families, the situation in much of the developing world is strikingly different. Because evangelistic strategies have been increasingly successful there in recent decades (see Table 13.2), Adventists there continue to be predominantly first-generation converts. Researchers have found that such a membership is likely to be highly committed and sectarian (Niebuhr 1929). We would therefore expect Adventism in these developing countries to show higher tension with society than in the developed world.

Table 13.2
Seventh-day Adventist Membership by Continent: 1960 and 1995

Continent	1960	%	1995	%	Increase (%)
Africa	241,575	19.4	2,902,171	32.9	1101.4
South America	140,717	11.3	1,610,668	18.3	1044.6
Asia	171,712	13.8	1,497,676	17.0	772.2
Inter-America[a]	111,861	9.0	1,331,835	15.1	1090.6
North America[b]	332,400	26.7	838,898	9.5	152.4
Europe	190,800	15.3	336,269	3.8	76.2
Oceania[c]	56,060	4.5	286,199	3.2	410.5
World Totals[d]	1,245,125		8,812,555		607.8

[a]Mexico, Central America, Caribbean
[b]United States, Canada, Bermuda
[c]Includes Australia and New Zealand, slow growth areas, as well as many Pacific Island groups with rapid growth
[d]Includes 8,839 members in the Middle East not listed above in 1995

Sources: General Conference 1961, 1996

However, the data suggest that Adventism there is much less sectarian than expected. It is increasingly following a direction similar to that taken in the United States. Several factors have contributed to this situation:

Adventists were initially much less separated in the developing world because of the manner in which they were received. In the United States, for example, Adventists were stigmatized by the dominant Christian churches and denominations as heretical and sectarian because they were small and different. In Africa, however, the local people did not distinguish among the missions, seeing them all "as part of the process of western cultural importations, rather than as special brands of them" (Assimeng 1986:53). Adventism found this pluralistic religious context, where it was not forced to compete with a dominant group, advantageous. Its missionaries, unlike Adventists in the United States, frequently joined ecumenical bodies, partly because these negotiated issues with colonial authorities (Assimeng 1986:222–225). Consequently, tensions between Adventism and these environments were lower; it was less sectarian. Moreover, because Adventism shaped its proselytizing strategies around educational and medical institutions, these activities helped it to build a positive reputation and to involve itself more deeply in these societies.

New members are attracted to Adventism because it is seen as offering opportunities for upward mobility. This is so in spite of the fact that missionaries are usually conservative members who emphasize that the world will soon end. Adventism has attracted converts because its schools offer members avenues for advancement. Adventist missionaries saw education as the keystone to evangelization: Elementary literacy became a prerequisite for baptism, for it was essential if the people were to read the Bible and study Adventist doctrine; schools were also the means of preparing workers for the church. However, when they realized that education was a key means of upward mobility in rapidly changing societies, graduates began taking lucrative secular jobs rather than filling church positions. A missionary in East Africa complained that the Adventist schools there were "largely a waste of training effort and money. . . . [It is not our purpose to train teachers] to provide the government and other agencies with educated help" (Flaiz 1950:30).

This trend continued as Adventism added the higher layers to its educational system, and administrators now lament that most students enroll in programs where there are few opportunities for church employment, ignoring the needs of the rapidly expanding church. A striking confirmation of this pattern occurred at the Adventist University of Eastern Africa, in Kenya, in the early 1980s. Protesting that having the church's name on their degrees would limit their employment opportunities, students staged demonstrations and strikes and eventually forced the University Council to change the institution's name to the "University of Eastern Africa."[1]

However, in recent years Adventist schools have become less important as a means of upward mobility for members in Africa, because Adventism is growing so rapidly there that it is impossible for the church to keep up with the demand for educational institutions. In Kenya, for example, where mission schools supported by government "grants-in-aid" were once the only source of education, most Adventists are now educated in government schools, and those attending the remaining church schools receive an inferior education (Nyaundi 1993:241–242). This situation is repeated in many parts of Africa. Since Adventism's reputation as a vehicle for upward mobility has been so important in attracting converts, it seems likely that the tarnishing of this image will eventually impact Adventist growth rates. Nevertheless, the vast concern for, and experience of, upward mobility among Adventist members in Africa has left them with an experience that is closer to that of American Adventists than the predominance of converts and the emphasis on sectarian teachings among the missionaries would have led us to expect.

Adventists have become politically prominent in some countries. The rapid growth of Adventism and the upward mobility among its members have transformed Adventists into a political presence in parts of the developing world. In Uganda, for example, the vice president (who was formerly the prime minister) is an active Adventist. A similar process has occurred at a more local level in other countries where the Adventist presence is more geographically concentrated, as in the provinces around Lake Victoria in Kenya. These developments took church leaders in the United States by surprise, for Adventists have rarely walked the corridors of political power in this country.[2]

Such political participation indicates that Adventists have become heavily involved in their societies and are not the objects of widespread antagonism. That is, it indicates that they have moved a considerable distance from sectarianism.

Adventists have established close relations with governments. Adventists have actively sought to reduce political tensions with governments and have been especially successful in establishing relationships with authoritarian regimes. These have often involved "exchange relationships," where Adventists have gained religious liberties and favors in return for helping to legitimate the regimes.

In Kenya, for example, Adventists fostered a close relationship with the regime of President Daniel Arap Moi, who in return arranged to provide them with land and a charter for their University of East Africa. In 1988, when the General Conference staged its Annual Council in Nairobi, the speech of the then Adventist world president, Neil Wilson, was reported in the press under the headline, "SDA head lauds Kenya for upholding freedom" (Nyaundi 1993:209). This public support was offered to Moi at a time when he was under attack from the National Council of Churches of Kenya for brutalizing opposition leaders and attempting to make constitutional changes designed to help him retain power in spite of his growing unpopularity.[3]

Adventists have thus frequently demonstrated a wish to be involved rather than separate. In courting good relations with governments, they have set out to prove that they are cooperative, not antagonistic, and to assuage any hostility or suspicion toward them.

Socialization of new members has sharply diminished. Beginning in the early 1980s, Adventist leaders placed increased emphasis on growth, promoting evangelism as a major proselytizing strategy in the developing world and pressuring evangelists and pastors with high goals for new converts. As a result, the growth rate for the world membership increased sharply, from 69.6 percent during the decade 1970–1980 to 92.4 percent during 1982–1992 (derived from General Conference 1993) (See Table 13.3). The bulk of this increase occurred in developing countries. The most dramatic change in procedures as a result of the adoption of this new policy occurred in Africa, where would-be converts had previously been required to be members of a baptismal class for two years before being admitted,[4] but are now typically baptized at the end of a three-week evangelistic campaign. Moreover, post-baptismal nurture largely disappeared, as pastors were forced to turn their attention to attracting the next wave of prospective recruits.[5]

Table 13.3
Adventist Growth: The Time Taken to Add Each Million Members, 1848–1996

Size	Time Taken	Dates
1 million	107.1 years	1848–1955
2 million	14.7 years	1955–1970
3 million	7.9 years	1970–1978
4 million	5.1 years	1978–1983
5 million	3.3 years	1983–1986
6 million	2.7 years	1986–1989
7 million	2.3 years	1989–1991
8 million	2.4 years	1991–1994
9 million	2.3 years	1994–1996

Source: Yost 1995:28, updated

A factor isolated by Wilson is significant here. He found that those sects that he defines as Revolutionist, or urgently apocalyptic, tend to move much more slowly from sect toward denomination than those he defines as Conversionist. This is because the former demand that converts have considerable knowledge before they are admitted, while the latter add new members rapidly without a great deal of prior training and socialization (Wilson [1959] 1967). In terms of this analysis, Adventism in Africa has shifted sharply towards becoming a Conversionist sect over the past decade or so: The grounding of converts in the sectarian teachings and separating lifestyle of Adventism is now often much weaker than in earlier decades. According to Wilson, such a change is likely to reduce sectarianism and foster denomination-like characteristics.

Member commitment has weakened significantly. Given the pressure for rapid growth and the consequent pattern of reduced socialization of converts, it is not surprising that the apostasy rate is high. The official statistics show an apostasy rate that was equal to 26.7 percent of conversions in the developing world during 1995. However, interview data suggest that this is a serious undercount. The system of record-keeping, which was designed in the United States, often proves too complex for those who must report from churches where the standard of education is lower, especially when pastors can be rewarded for rapid growth rates or penalized for slow growth. Consequently, the one datum these churches can be relied on to report accurately is the number of baptisms. Deaths and apostasies are likely to be ignored, while transfers often result in people being counted as members by two or more congregations. There is no doubt that the apostasy rate is a serious problem. For example, during the three years before my visit to Kinshasa, capital of the Congo, two evangelistic campaigns had resulted in 1,500 baptisms. However, at that point only 50 of these members, a mere 3.3 percent, were still attending church.[6] The data suggest that this kind of situation is common.

A cultural factor in Africa amplifies, and helps explain, the seriousness of the "apostasy problem" there. Africans do not share the Western understanding that commitment to one faith precludes adherence to others: "In Africa, it is very rarely the case that a person is exclusively a member of only one religious movement at any particular time, and very few movements succeeded in imposing the exclusivity principle" (Assimeng 1986:16). Indeed, many Africans see advantages in identifying with several religious groups, for this in effect gives them multiple insurance policies, or access to different kinds of magic that will be effective in varying circumstances. Consequently, some persons who respond to the call of an Adventist evangelist to be baptized and who thereby become members of the Adventist Church may respond similarly some months later to an invitation from a Pentecostal preacher.

During the early years of their missions in Africa, Adventists insisted that converts and those preparing for baptism withdraw from their villages and form a new Adventist village that was built around the church and church school (Nyaundi 1993:93–94,108–117). This had the effect of strengthening ties to the church. However, that practice was later abandoned. The long period of training in baptismal classes was also designed to cement commitment; however, as noted earlier, this practice has also been discarded.

Given the evidence of limited commitment among Adventist members—with poor socialization, focus on opportunities for career advancement, multiple memberships, and high apostasy rates—it is not surprising that many members have proved willing to compromise the standards of their faith in the face of difficulties. The major test for Adventists has usually been observance of their Sabbath on Saturday. American Adventists fired for refusing to work when scheduled on that day have fought the issue all the way to the Supreme Court (Lawson 1997). However, African students reported that when they were faced with the problem of classes and exams being scheduled on Saturday—which is a regular occurrence at all educational levels in the former French and Belgian colonies and is increasingly an issue in several former English colonies—most of them participated rather than risk educational penalties.[7] The weakening of commitment among Adventists reduces tensions with society, since this renders them more ready to compromise and therefore less different—and thus less sectarian.

To summarize: Adventism is growing so rapidly in much of Africa that it is still largely a first-generation religion there. However, contrary to what this fact might lead us to expect, it is not stridently sectarian in tone. Indeed, to invoke Stark and Bainbridge's three markers of tension between a sect and its sociocultural environment, it is far less different, antagonistic, or separated from society than when its American forebears had a similar proportion of first-generation converts.

TWO CONTRASTING EXAMPLES

I am not arguing, however, that this trajectory is typical of all imported religious groups in Africa. Assimeng's study of Jehovah's Witnesses, for example, finds that they were, and are, the most apocalyptic of all the imported Christian groups; they have remained much more separate from other religious groups and from government; and, since they refused to build and operate schools, they have not provided their followers with a means for upward mobility (1986:53–113). In some countries in particular, such as Zambia and Malawi, their "relationship with political authorities . . . has been characterized by acute strain" (1970:112). Here, then, is a group that Wilson would classify, like early Adventism, as a Revolutionist sect; however, the Jehovah's Witnesses have remained highly sectarian and have therefore followed a totally different path from Adventism.

Yet another extraordinarily different path has been followed by Pentecostals. Wilson classified them, in First World countries, as a Conversionist sect ([1963] 1969:365); however, when imported to Africa and Latin America they mutated to Thaumaturgical (magical). Assimeng found that "Their concern with salvation and the advent tends, in day-to-day practice, often to be eclipsed by their distinctive teachings of Holy Ghost power, spirit blessings and physical manifestations—particularly glossolalia. These charismata—and especially the 'gift' of divine healing—have been popularly embraced in Africa where traditional religion was itself strongly thaumaturgical, instrumental and expressive" (1986:xiii). In Nigeria, where the impact of Pentecostalism has been greatest, it took on a number of indigenous characteristics: for example, it seemed to confirm from Scripture the traditional witchcraft theories of disease (Assimeng 1986:150).

INTERPRETATION

What is the explanation of these differing patterns? The connections between imported religious groups and their sponsoring global organizations can play a key role in shaping the directions taken. When the structure of a global church and its relationship with its national branches are centralized and hierarchical, as with Adventists and Witnesses, its influence can be compelling. In this case, the central organization is likely to export the patterns of the relationships between the religious group and its surrounding environment that developed in the group's home base.

Adventism has considerably reduced tension between itself and American society over time: Adventists there have become comfortable, patriotic Americans. Meanwhile, the patterns that created these changes were transferred to Adventists abroad. International Adventism was soon typified by the centrality of its institutions, as these were promoted as the chief means of Adventism's evangelistic outreach. However, these institutions soon performed the additional functions that they served in the United States, such as providing opportunities for the upward mobility of members—and thus of helping to reduce tension between Adventism and the societies where it was located.

The relationship of Jehovah's Witnesses in the developing world to their central organization, the Watch Tower Society (WTS), which is also located in the United States, was also crucial. But in this case the outcome was the reverse to that with Adventists: The patterns that had prevented the tension between American Witnesses and their surrounding society from abating to any discernible degree were exported throughout the international organization. For example, it was the WTS that decided that Witnesses should "eschew all association and co-operation with other missionary bodies" to build schools, and should not recognize secular authority, which greatly heightened tensions between Witnesses and newly independent African countries (Assimeng 1986:53,218; 1970:100). Such decisions had the effect of keeping Witnesses separate and bolstering antagonisms against them, thus maintaining their sectarianism.

Pentecostals contrast strongly with these examples. They exhibit much greater variety because the absence of a single centralized umbrella group has allowed the local churches to blend much more closely with the environments in which they have found themselves.

This chapter, which began with the assumption that church-sect theory has proven useful in understanding and predicting the evolution of schismatic religious groups such as Adventism in the United States, has shown that the theory is also relevant to the evolution of religious groups introduced through missionary endeavor. Furthermore, it has proven useful in accounting for the different profiles developed by global church organizations in those cases—Adventists and Witnesses—where their umbrella organizations are structurally centralized and hierarchical.

NOTES

1. Information from interviews.
2. Information from interviews. There are currently three Adventist members of Congress, which is the highest such number to date.
3. Several similar examples are cited in Lawson (1996).
4. They had often also been exposed to Adventism during several years in church-run schools.
5. Interviews.
6. Interviews.
7. Interviews.

REFERENCES

Assimeng, Max. 1970. "Sectarian Allegiance and Political Authority: The Watch Tower Society in Zambia, 1907–1935." *Journal of Modern African Studies* 8(1):97–112.

———. 1986. *Saints and Social Structures*. Legon, Ghana: Ghana Publishing Corporation.

Flaiz, T. R. 1950. "Medical Missionary Objectives." *Ministry* 23:5.

General Conference of Seventh-day Adventists. 1961. *98th Annual Statistical Report—1960*. Takoma Park, MD: Office of Archives and Statistics.

———. 1993. *130th Annual Statistical Report—1992*. Silver Spring, MD: Office of Archives and Statistics.

———. 1996. *133rd Annual Statistical Report—1995*. Silver Spring, MD: Office of Archives and Statistics.

Lawson, Ronald. 1995. "Seventh-day Adventist Responses to Branch Davidian Notoriety: Patterns of Diversity within a Sect Reducing Tension with Society." *Journal for the Scientific Study of Religion* 34(3):323–341.

———. 1996. "Church and State at Home and Abroad: The Evolution of Seventh-day Adventist Relations with Governments." *Journal of the American Academy of Religion* 64(2):279–311.

———. 1997. "Seventh-day Adventists and the U.S. Courts: Road Signs along the Route of a Denominationalizing Sect." Paper presented at the Annual Meeting of the Association for the Sociology of Religion, Toronto, Canada (to be published in the *Journal of Church and State*, forthcoming 1999).

Niebuhr, H. Richard. [1929] 1957. *The Social Sources of Denominationalism*. Cleveland: Meridian.

Nyaundi, Nehemiah M. 1993. *Religion and Social Change: A Sociological Study of Seventh-day Adventism in Kenya*. Lund, Sweden: University of Lund Press.

Stark, Rodney, and William Sims Bainbridge. 1985. *The Future of Religion*. Berkeley: University of California Press.

Wilson, Bryan R. [1959] 1967. "An Analysis of Sect Development." Pp. 22–45 in Bryan R. Wilson, *Patterns of Sectarianism*. London: Heinemann.

———. [1963] 1969. "A Typology of Sects." Pp. 361–383 in Roland Robertson (ed.), *Sociology of Religion*. Baltimore: Penguin.

Yost, F. Donald. 1995. "Changes Ahead? The Numbers Say 'Yes!'" *Dialogue* 7(2):28–29.

14

Russia's Religious Market: Struggling with the Heritage of Russian Orthodox Monopoly

Jerry G. Pankhurst

The radical transformation of the Soviet Union under the leadership of Mikhail Gorbachev in the 1980s and its breakup into fifteen separate states in 1991 opened the way for one of the most extraordinary periods of societal change that any nation has experienced short of war. While Gorbachev's policy of *perestroika* (reconstruction) was motivated largely by the desire to improve the economic performance of the Soviet Union, all institutions were deeply affected by the loss of authority of the Communist regime and the widespread social disorganization that such sweeping changes entailed. Religion, coming out of the shadows of Communist atheist control, was no exception.

Many observers have thought that the disruptive societal change itself was cause for the Russian and other peoples of the former Soviet Union to turn to religion to find moral anchorage and national identity. Times of rapid social change entail major sociocultural dislocation, which in turn calls forth cultural patterns of renewal and reintegration that often take religious form. It would seem natural that the people would feel a great loss with the discreditation of the central ideology of Marxism, and they might be expected to seek out a different value system to embrace.

It turns out that, with widespread disillusionment with Soviet Communism, the end of the 1980s was a good time to present religion to the people of Russia as an alternative moral system and a focus for national identity. The process of filling the ideological vacuum, however, was and is not as simple as the replacement of one set of beliefs by another. Just as the overall reform policy of perestroika was stimulated in important ways by global forces in the economic and political spheres, forces of global interrelations and of a new free market in religion added complex factors to the process. These factors have led to cultural change that is taking Russia more and more away from its ancient religious heritage.

This chapter provides an overview of the development of an open market for religion in Russia, the largest of the fifteen new states that were created out of the former Soviet Union (FSU). It uses a model of religious economy that has proven to be extremely useful in understanding the American religious scene and the circumstances in some Western European countries.[1] Under the Soviets the Russian Orthodox Church held a virtual monopoly in the religious sphere. Although this monopoly did not apply to Jews nor to traditionally Islamic or Buddhist populations, for the historically Christian majority the only real religious option was Orthodoxy.[2] In the post-Soviet period, that monopoly is being challenged by a whole spectrum of faiths. These include, most notably, evangelical and pentecostal Protestants, a reestablished Roman Catholic Church, and a series of indigenous sects—growing out of the Orthodox tradition—and cults, which represent new religious phenomena for Russia (cf. Hadden and Pankhurst 1993). The ultimate consequences of this new and vibrant diversity cannot yet be foretold for certain, but there seems no question but that it will have a profound effect on the future of Russian society.

RELIGION'S PLACE IN RUSSIAN SOCIETY

According to the historical record, the society called *Rus*, the ancient precursor to Russia, adopted Christianity in about 988, when Grand Prince Vladimir converted to the Byzantine faith. The thousandth anniversary of that momentous cultural change was celebrated in 1988, and the Gorbachev government took the opportunity to establish a new relationship with the Russian Orthodox Church as part of its general reform processes (cf. Pankhurst 1996). In the political struggles that marked the final period of the Soviet Union, it was difficult to provide a focus for Soviet national identity that was similar to the old Soviet ideology. However, Boris Yeltsin and other change-oriented leaders stressed national autonomy for the many "republics" of the Soviet Union, with full expression of their cultural heritages as a means to establish the national identities of the fifteen states-to-be (Laba 1996). For Russia, the ancient Russian Orthodox Church was a natural vehicle for this identity formation and moral development. By the beginning of the 1990s, public opinion polling found that the church was already the most trusted social institution, surpassing the government and comparable only to the military in this measure of prestige. Given these dynamics, it is not surprising that some significant portion of the ardor for religion in Russia today takes the form of very patriotic, nationalistic appeals (Dunlop 1996).

The growth of the Russian Orthodox Church during the years since 1988 has been impressive. Davis's (1995) data shows a 90 percent increase in the number of parishes between 1988 and 1994, when the number had grown to 12,800. The yearly rate of increase has been slowing since 1991, but it appears that growth in number of parishes continues through the present.

However, there are some indications that the religious revival may have leveled off from the mid-1990s. According to various data sources (reviewed by Elliott 1997c), it seems that by 1996 almost 90 percent of the Russian population had a positive attitude toward religion, with about half considering themselves believers in God. However, for believers, church attendance monthly or more often is found among fewer than 10 percent of the population, and other religious practice is similarly infrequent. Thus, we continue to ponder how much of the increase is in committed believers, as opposed to those driven to the church more by national-patriotic motives or simply by the desire to join the crowd rushing in that direction.

Whatever their motives, for a population that was the object of an antireligion campaign for seventy years, the evidence of extensive religious interest and the flowering of the Russian Orthodox Church is impressive. Churches have been restored and opened everywhere, and they are carrying a full schedule of services. Many people who sidestepped formal religion during the Communist period have now been baptized into church membership. Moreover, there is a host of new options besides Orthodoxy.

OBSERVATIONS ON GROWING RELIGIOUS DIVERSITY

Increased Protestant Diversity

I clearly remember how strange it seemed in 1992 to see a group publicly singing evangelical hymns and exhorting the crowd to come to Jesus for salvation, during a prayer meeting held by a local Protestant group on the steps of Kazan Cathedral in St. Petersburg. The irony was inescapable: This cathedral had been confiscated by the Soviets in the 1930s and transformed into the Museum of the History of Religion and Atheism, one of the most important outlets for antireligious propaganda for the ensuing half century. It has now been renamed the Museum of the History of Religion and has made significant efforts to restore church valuables that it possessed and to stress the positive. The Russian Orthodox Church now holds services inside the cathedral.

Protestant groups mounted an enormous campaign of expansion as the Soviet Union fell. Evangelical and pentecostal groups, including Baptists, Seventh-day Adventists, Church of Christ, Assemblies of God, and the Salvation Army, as well as nonevangelical Christian churches such as the Methodists, tried to help develop the faith in the countries of the former Soviet Union. The recent development of Protestantism has been substantial. There are very few reliable data on the extent of indigenous missionary activity, though its broad growth is evident from numerous sources. However, Elliott (1997a) has provided stunning data on the foreign missionary presence in the region. Statistics for Russia alone are not presently available, but for the FSU, by 1997, approximately 561 foreign ministry organizations were active, thirty-six of them based in Korea and the rest from Western nations. Ninety percent of these organizations are Protestant, with a total of 5,606 Protestant missionaries working in the FSU. Overall, during the six years leading up to mid-1997, Protestants established some 112 Bible schools and seminaries in Russia, and twenty-eight to thirty denominations are present in the country.[3]

The public activization of Protestants in Russia is both an indigenous and a foreign movement. While native Baptists, evangelical Lutherans, Seventh-day Adventists, and others have been broadly engaged and have used their own resources, many of these groups have also received support from abroad in building their educational programs for adherents, their clergy training programs, and the like. In 1992 Billy Graham held a massive crusade in the Olympic Stadium in Moscow, which was marked by attempts to secure cooperative support from all Christian faiths. However, there have been many attempts by groups not grounded in Russia to enter the religious market and secure some "market share" there. Often backed by considerable funds from abroad, they have raised the hackles not only of the Russian Orthodox but sometimes of indigenous Protestants as well.

There has also been a fair share of what might be called minor entrepreneurial activities carried out by foreigners in the newly open Russian religious market, and these, in particular, have offended the leaders of the Russian Orthodox Church and some other religious groups. Sometimes, foreign street evangelists appeared who did not speak Russian beyond a few words of greeting, "thank you," or "goodbye." Usually, their reason for being there was to pass out portions of the Scriptures or to invite passersby to come to a meeting where the faith would be explained to them.

The Appearance of New Religious Movements

From my perspective as a frequent visitor to the FSU, even more astonishing than the efflorescence of Protestantism in Russia was the appearance of the adherents of Hare Krishna on the streets of the big cities at the beginning of the 1990s, selling the *Bhagavad Gita* and chanting. Eastern religions had attracted a following among a small group of the urban intelligentsia since the 1960s. However, such public activities as the Krishnas demonstrated would have led directly to the police precincts in the Communist past.

Among other new religious movements (NRMs) that have been active in Russia is the Unification Church of the Reverend Sun Myung Moon ("Moonies"), Scientologists, and Aum Shrinrikyo. Foreign NRMs have aroused the fear and ire of many Russians, and an active anticult movement has arisen to counteract them and indigenous movements, as well. In 1993, when Jeffrey Hadden and I carried out interviewing in Russia, we saw evidence everywhere of native new religions, especially of the White Brotherhood led by "Mariya Devi Khristos." The latter claimed to be the reincarnation of Jesus, and she gained a significant following among young people in the larger urban centers. The White Brotherhood predicted that the world would end in November 1993, but when the group gathered in Kiev to experience the event, they were arrested (Morvant 1996). The Russian Orthodox Church and the anticult movement have condemned the White Brotherhood and many other NRMs, both indigenous and foreign in origin.

In addition to Protestant evangelical activists, advocates of Eastern religions, and NRMs, the Roman Catholic Church has also made its presence felt in many Russian cities. The Russian Orthodox Church (ROC), which identifies itself with the destiny of Russia itself, has found all these movements annoying and has taken strong action to limit their impact. This is consistent with the desire of the ROC to maintain its historical monopoly in the religious economy of Russia.

Schisms

Threats to that monopoly position have not come only from non-Orthodox sources. Alternative movements within the general faith of Eastern Orthodoxy (that is, schisms) have emerged to undermine the monopoly held by the Moscow Patriarchate, which is the overall administration of the Russian Orthodox Church. The Patriarch of Moscow and All Russia, currently Aleksi II, is the head bishop of the church and its representative within the broader Eastern Orthodox communion. Within Russia itself, at least three significant challenges to the central Moscow Patriarchate have arisen (Broun 1997). The first came from people calling themselves the True Russian Orthodox Church. They rejected the authority of the Moscow Patriarchate during the Soviet period, believing that it was compromised by its relations with the Communist state. The True Orthodox also reject all forms of citizen participation in government-related matters, such as carrying internal passports, paying taxes, and voting.

The second challenge to the authority of the Patriarchal Church has come from the Russian Orthodox Church Abroad (ROCA), which was founded in Yugoslavia by Russian émigrés in 1923. It now has three bishops based in Russia (Broun 1997) and rejects the authority of the Patriarchal Church, because of its past ties to the Soviet state. A third breakaway group is the Russian Orthodox Free Church, which has ninety-eight parishes (Broun 1997). All of these challenge the Russian Orthodox monopoly.

RUSSIA'S RELIGIOUS ECONOMY IN PERSPECTIVE

In the last phase of Communist Party rule in Russia under Gorbachev, the Soviet Union reformed all sectors of the society and culture to make them more adapted to global forces. Under the influence of international development and financial organizations that were backed by the United States and other Western powers, the Soviets initiated moves to transform the economy toward a free market structure. As the Communist regime collapsed in 1990–1991, marketizing forces increased their influence on Russia, and the new government leaders committed themselves to opening up the economy. At the same time, cultural forces were working to make other institutional sectors in Russian society more open as well.

Together with encouraging market reform in the economy, several international organizations with which the Soviet Union, and then Russia, had entered into relationships also demanded greater openness in the areas of freedom of speech, press, association, and belief or conscience. Activated by a multifaceted international human rights campaign, these organizations included the Organization for Security and Cooperation in Europe (OSCE), the European Union (EU), and the North Atlantic Treaty Organization (NATO). As with the economic and political processes, the international movement was backed by the power of Western states. These groups, in essence, were demanding the marketization of a variety of areas of culture, including religion.

What does a free market in religion entail? An open religious market involves provisions for freedom of all sorts of religious practices and freedom of the members of the population to hear the appeals of the various groups and to choose that group that is most satisfying to them, without significant limitations.

In Russia, the 1990s have been an era of religious freedom. Law codes passed in 1990 and 1991 provided sweeping guarantees of freedom of religious belief and practice (Pankhurst and Welch 1993), and the Constitution of 1993 explicitly gave religious freedom to all citizens of the Russian Federation.[4] Ironically, this era of freedom was brought on at the end of the 1980s and beginning of the 1990s by Communists and former Communists who had earlier commanded the struggle against this alleged cultural vestige of exploitative capitalism, what Karl Marx had called the "opium of the people." More ironically, this religious freedom is now endangered through restrictive legislation by democratically elected leaders.

FOR THE FUTURE: AN OPEN RELIGIOUS MARKET
OR MORE MONOPOLY?

Why is the structure of the religious market in Russia important? Many sociologists of religion claim that a diverse market structure stimulates religious activity among the population. That is, the more religious groups there are that are active in seeking members and thus competing for the adherents of other religious groups or seeking to convert the nonaffiliated, the more vigorous will be all sorts of indicators of religiousness.[5] From this point of view, the more diverse the religious market in Russia becomes, the more generally active the population will become in the areas of religious behavior.

Though available data do not permit very subtle analysis, there is clear evidence that religious interest and claims of being believers have increased a great deal since the market became open in Russia. As general church attendance levels remain low, we will have to wait to see whether or not the ultimate consequence for the Russian religious market is the full energization predicted by the economic model.

One major issue when applying the model to Russia is that of what Iannaccone (1997) has called "human capital," or religious knowledge and experience gathered during the life course. Choice of faith by individuals and the characteristics of their religious behavior are strongly shaped by the amount and type of religious human capital that they bring to religion. In Russia, the general level of religious human capital coming out of the atheist period was very low, and it will presumably take a long time for the members of the population to gather the personal religious capital to make faith choices autonomously and actively. Thus, even if the increased diversity in the religious market is tending to stimulate a growth in individual religious belief and practice, its concrete consequences may not be clearly visible for some time. In this regard, the nature of the decision to affiliate with a religious group or to become more active in religion is heavily dependent upon the sociocultural context.[6]

In these and other ways, the Russian situation provides an important laboratory for testing the religious economy model.[7] Above all, for the Russian religious market, it seems most important to keep in mind Stark's extension of the original theory to take account of the influence of the state. He says that "the most decisive factor involved [in religious economies] is whether they are free markets or whether the government regulates the economy in the direction of monopoly." He further states that "to the degree that a religious economy is monopolized by one or two state-supported firms [churches or faiths], overall levels of participation will tend to be low" (Stark 1997:17,18). The domination of the Russian market by the Russian Orthodox Church so far seems to be confirming this expectation of low participation. However, how long this consequence of monopoly can hold, given the other conditions influencing the market, only time will tell.

In this sense, the recent attempts by the government of Russia, in cooperation with the Russian Orthodox Church, to constrain the activity of diverse non-Orthodox groups and of Orthodox groups that do not accept subordination to the Moscow Patriarchate should tend to slow the religious revival there. Starting in 1992, there have been significant moves by the Russian parliament to pass legislation that would do just that by creating a registration system for religious organizations that places obstacles in the way of foreign groups and groups not registered in the Soviet Union before the period of perestroika. Though President Yeltsin vetoed such legislation in July 1997, citing major legal problems with the law, he signed a slightly revised version in September. Despite numerous remaining questions about the constitutionality of the law and its consistency with treaty obligations that bind Russia, as of this writing the law is being implemented. How severe the restrictions will be in practice is still to be seen, but the clear thrust is to strengthen the position of the Russian Orthodox Church and to return to it a semblance of monopolistic privilege.[8] If the religious economy theory is correct, this bodes ill, in general, for the vigor of religion in Russia in the future.

I conclude by noting, however, that religious monopoly is difficult to maintain under current global circumstances. Short of sealing the borders and reinstituting a police state—neither of which would be consistent with the general goals of social and economic development espoused by all but the most rabid patriotic-nationalist leaders in Russia—global religious and political forces seem inevitably to be working toward fostering religious pluralism in Russia. Thus, the evolution of the Russian religious market is far from ended.

NOTES

1. This model has been developed most fully by Stark and Bainbridge (1987) and has been extensively applied in the elaborate examination of American religious history by Finke and Stark (1992).

2.There were small populations of Protestants and Roman Catholics in various regions, but these had always tended to be ethnically separated and often persecuted, as were native Russian sectarian groups (Old Believers, Molokans, Khlysty and others).

3. Interview with Peter Deyneka of Russian Ministries, November 9, 1997.

4. Radugin (1997), in a new Russian textbook on religious studies, ably reviews the long-term changes in the legal status of religion in tsarist Russia, the Soviet Union and post-Soviet Russia. It is noteworthy that from a post-Soviet perspective, one needs to take special account not only of the rights of religious believers, but of the rights of the large portion of the population made up of nonbelievers and atheists as well.

5. See Finke and Stark (1992), Stark and Iannaconne (1994), and Young (1997).

6. See Sherkat (1997) and Ellison (1995).

7. See Hadden and Pankhurst (1993) for a first attempt in this direction.

8. Elliott (1997b) provides a concise review of the new legislation and several points of view on its impact.

REFERENCES

Broun, Janice. 1997. "Jurisdictional Conflict among Orthodox and Eastern-Rite Catholics in Russia and Ukraine." *East-West Church and Ministry Report* 5(3): Part II. Unpaginated Internet publication from the Center for East-West Christian Studies, Wheaton College, Wheaton, IL.

Davis, Nathaniel. 1995. *A Long Walk to Church: A Contemporary History of Russian Orthodoxy*. Boulder, CO: Westview Press.

Dunlop, John B. 1996. "Orthodoxy and National Identity in Russia." In Victoria E. Bonnell (ed.), *Identities in Transition: Eastern Europe and Russia after the Collapse of Communism*. International and Area Studies Research Series, Number 93. Berkeley: Center for Slavic and East European Studies, University of California at Berkeley.

Elliott, Mark. 1997a. "Updated Statistics on the Protestant Missionary Presence in the Former Soviet Union." *East-West Church and Ministry Report* 5(2): Part IV. Unpaginated Internet publication.

———. 1997b. "New Restrictive Law on Religion Passed in Russia" and following supplements. *East-West Church and Ministry Report* 5(3): Part I. Unpaginated Internet publication.

———. 1997c. "What Percentage of Russians Are Practicing Christians?" *East-West Church and Ministry Report* 5(3): Part II. Unpaginated Internet publication.

Ellison, Christopher. 1995. "Rational Choice Explanations of Individual Religious Behavior: Notes on the Problem of Social Embeddedness." *Journal for the Scientific Study of Religion* 34(1):89–97.

Finke, Roger, and Rodney Stark. 1992. *The Churching of America, 1776–1990*. New Brunswick, NJ: Rutgers University Press.

Hadden, Jeffrey K., and Jerry G. Pankhurst. 1993. "On Spitting with the Wind: Religious Organizational Vivaciousness in the Former Evil Empire." Unpublished paper prepared for the Seminar on Religious Institutions of the Program on Nonprofit Organizations at Yale University, June 3–4.

Iannaccone, Laurence R. 1997. "Rational Choice: Framework for the Scientific Study of Religion." Pp. 25–45 in Lawrence A. Young (ed.), *Rational Choice Theory and Religion: Summary and Assessment*. New York: Routledge.

Laba, Roman. 1996. "How Yeltsin's Exploitation of Ethnic Nationalism Brought Down an Empire." *Transition* 2(1). Unpaginated Internet publication of the Open Media Research Institute.

Morvant, Penny. 1996. "Cults Arouse Concern in Russia." *Transition* 2(7):20–23.

Pankhurst, Jerry G. 1996. "Religious Culture." Pp. 127–156 in Dmitri N. Shalin (ed.), *Russian Culture at the Crossroads: Paradoxes of Post-Communist Consciousness*. Boulder, CO: Westview Press.

Pankhurst, Jerry G., and Carolyn Welch. 1993. "Religion under Gorbachev." Pp. 323–336 in J. Wieczynski (ed.), *The Gorbachev Encyclopedia*. Los Angeles: Charles Schlacks, Jr., Publishing.

Radugin, A. A. 1997. *Vvedenie v religiovedenie* (Introduction to Religious Studies). Moscow: izd. "Tsentr."

Sherkat, Darren E. 1997. "Embedding Religious Choices: Integrating Preferences and Social Constraints into Rational Choice Theories of Religious Behavior." Pp. 65–86 in Lawrence A. Young (ed.), *Rational Choice Theory and Religion: Summary and Assessment*. New York: Routledge.

Stark, Rodney. 1997. "Bringing Theory Back In." Pp. 3–23 in Lawrence A. Young (ed.), *Rational Choice Theory and Religion: Summary and Assessment*. New York: Routledge.

Stark, Rodney, and William Sims Bainbridge. [1987] 1996. *A Theory of Religion*. New Brunswick, NJ: Rutgers University Press.

Stark, Rodney, and Laurence R. Iannaccone. 1994. "A Supply-Side Reinterpretation of the 'Secularization' of Europe." *Journal for the Scientific Study of Religion* 33(3):230–252.

Young, Lawrence, ed. 1997. *Rational Choice Theory and Religion: Summary and Assessment*. New York: Routledge.

15

The Raelians Are Coming!: The Future of a UFO Religion

Susan Palmer

The largest UFO religion in the world may well be the Raelian Movement International, which claims a following of some 30,000 members distributed throughout sixty-seven countries, but mostly in French-speaking Europe and in Quebec.[1] My research was based in Quebec, which has become a dynamic center for the international Raelian community and where Rael, the prophet-founder, has chosen to live.

This study is based on the participant observation method of research, conducted over eight years during intermittent attendance at Raelian meetings, where my Dawson College students and I conducted interviews and distributed question-naires. I have interviewed Rael on three occasions, and most of the local Guides, as well as some of the international leaders.

The movement was founded in 1973 by a French racing car driver and journalist, "Rael" (born Claude Vorilhon in 1946), as the result of his alleged encounter with space aliens during a walking tour of the Clermont-Ferrand volcanic mountain range in France. These aliens, whom Rael describes as small, anthropomorphic beings with pale green skin and almond eyes, entrusted him with a "message for mankind." This message concerned the true identity of the human race: The first humans were "implanted" on earth by superior extraterrestrial scientists, the "Elohim," who created humanity from their own DNA in laboratories. Rael's mission, as "the last of forty prophets" (crossbred between Elohim and mortal women), is to warn humankind that since 1945 and Hiroshima, we have entered the "Age of Apocalypse." We now have the choice of destroying ourselves with nuclear weapons or making the leap into planetary consciousness that will qualify us to inherit the scientific knowledge of our space forefathers. Science will enable 4 percent of our species in the future to clone themselves and travel through space, populating virgin planets "in our own image" (Rael 1978). Raelians are neither sectarian nor communal, but may be identified by their wearing large medallions of the swastika inside the star of David, which they explain is an ancient symbol of the eternity of time and infinity of space.

The Raelian Movement endeavors through its books and lectures to unite Christians, Jews, and Muslims in a "demythologized" interpretation of Scripture as the true history of a space colonization. Members can choose between two basic levels of commitment. At the lower level are the "Raelians"—those who have acknowledged the Elohim as their forefathers by undergoing initiation and making funeral arrangements. The "Structure" work at the higher level and are committed to active service by furthering the two goals of the movement: spreading the Message and building the Embassy in Jerusalem by the year 2025 to receive the Elohim. Members are encouraged to give 3 percent of their net income to the national Raelian Movement, 7 percent to the international movement, and 1 percent to Rael.

What are the reasons for this UFO religion's success? In attempting to account for the rapid growth and cultural influence of this movement, I will refer to Stark's theoretical model outlined in "How New Religions Succeed . . . ," as well as to some additional insights from Bozeman (1994) and Wright (1994). Stark (1987) proposes eight variables for determining success, including cultural continuity, medium tension with society, effective mobilization, normal age/sex distribution, a favorable religious "ecology," close network ties, resistance to secularization, and the socialization of children. Let us now examine the Raelian modus operandi in its struggle for survival in the light of these eight variables.

CULTURAL CONTINUITY

New religious movements (NRMs) do not ask people to discard their traditional religious culture; rather, they claim to complete and update it. Raelian beliefs retain the outward shape of Christianity, for this movement seems to try self-consciously to replicate the Catholic Church. It ordains its own priests and bishops, who perform a kind of baptismal ritual called the "transmission of the cellular code." Their beliefs are based on the Bible. *Genesis* is interpreted as a literal account of space colonization program. Miracles attest to the existence of a superior alien technology, and *Revelations* delivers a warning of the nuclear threat. Rael claims Jesus Christ as his half brother, for their mutual father, "Yahweh," is an extraterrestrial who beamed their mothers (hand-picked for their "virgin DNA") aboard a UFO for insemination.

The Raelian message also resonates with *secular* ideologies—with nuclear theology, the peace movement, the gay movement, feminism, the sexual revolution, the Human Potential Movement, and Greenpeace. Rael incorporates mystical approaches to physics into his theology and addresses the ethical issues of genetic engineering. Thus I would argue that a large part of the Raelian "success story" is related to its *cultural continuity* with both the Christian and the scientific worldview, appearing to reconcile conflicts between science and religion.

MEDIUM TENSION

A high level of tension between an NRM and society tends to invite repression and stigmatization, whereas low tension may result in attrition or secularization. The Raelian Movement manages to maintain a delicate balance between conformity and deviance.

Some of the Raelians' actions seem calculated to provoke or shock, but others appear designed to appease. Every April, the Guides plan demonstrations and a publicity campaign for their Planetary Week, and their activities seem intended to "gross out" the Catholic Church but to court the approval of secular humanists.

The barbs directed at Catholicism are numerous. All initiates send a "Letter of Apostasy" to the church in which they were baptized. This means that the Catholic Church in Quebec has received over 4,000 such letters. On October 7, 1994, the Raelians entered St. Peter's Cathedral in Rome and a Guide began to perform the transmission of the cellular plan, in front of a baptismal font, until the Vatican guards escorted them away.

Operation Condom was a well-publicized protest against the Montreal Catholic School Commission's decision to veto the proposal to install condom machines in their high schools. In late 1992, a "condom-mobile" financed and staffed by the Raelians toured the provinces of Quebec and Ontario and parked outside Catholic high schools where they distributed 10,000 condoms to the students during their recess, as well as large pink buttons that read "Oui aux Condoms à l'École."

Certain actions, on the other hand, seem calculated to court the public's goodwill. Raelians are conspicuously "politically correct." They denounce racism and sexism and joined in the Montreal Gay Parade in March 1993 to protest discrimination against sexual minorities. Shortly after Rael appeared on the Geraldo show in late 1991 and received angry letters from Jewish viewers reacting to the swastika, the medallion was altered to exhibit the curving petals of a flower.[2] It has been a long-term Raelian policy not to admit children to the Sensual Meditation rooms or camp areas, so as to avoid allegations of indecent exposure or child molestation. Rael consistently urges members to obey the local laws concerning sex of the country they live in—while adding, "but we must strive to *change* the law!"

A study of their literature suggests a gradual movement towards social respectability. Their magazine *Apocalypse* has become increasingly "slick" and no longer features nudity or the incongruous mixture of homoerotic and Playboy-style photographs it sported in the 1970s and 1980s.

Media attention in Quebec was favorable until a TV documentary aired in 1991 portrayed the Sensual Meditation camp as an unbridled sex orgy. Local rabbis were interviewed who objected to Rael's ET racialist theories, as well as to a proselytizing Raelian outside a synagogue. The playful, tongue-in-cheek media coverage of the 1980s was replaced by heavy-handed, judgmental exposés in the 1990s, as journalists adopted the pop-psychological rhetoric of the anticult movement. In October of 1992 Rael was subjected to "ambush journalism" on a French television show, "Ciel Mon Mardi," when a disgruntled apostate accused the Raelians of brainwashing his wife, stealing his children, practicing satanic rituals, and abusing children during the Sensual Meditation seminars.

Some of the Raelians' court cases have become media sensations. In 1992 the last will and testament of a former nun who joined the Raelians in her fifties and left her fortune to assist in the building of the Space Embassy was disputed in court by relatives, who claimed she had been duped by mind control techniques and the seductive attentions of a Guide. Another legal battle developed out of Bishop Guide Daniel Chabot's participation in the July 7, 1993, conference on masturbation organized by the Raelians. *The Corporation professionnelle des psychologues du Québec* launched a *deontologie* inquiry to determine whether Chabot (the head of the movement in Canada) was using his professional status to attract converts and whether his speech on the therapeutic benefits of masturbation and his involvement in an "erotique-esoterique" religion conflicted with the scientific principles generally recognized by members of his profession (*La Presse*, July 9, 1993:4). Chabot sent out a letter to psychologists in Quebec protesting the director's statements and launched a countersuit against the corporation for religious discrimination.

The Raelians appear to be steering a middle course between tension and accommodation. While they stir up controversy, they protect themselves from persecution through rational means—by deescalating conflict or by waxing litigious. They have filed defamation suits, as in the 1992 case against *les Editions Flammarion*, the 1979 case against Radio Canada journalist Paul Tounant, and a libel action against a Catholic countercult publishing company, Spiromedia. Another defensive response to negative media reports and lawsuits is through activism. In 1992 Rael requested donations for the widow of Jean Migueres, the contactee/ufologist author who was shot and killed in Paris by his father-in-law, a member of ADFI, an anticult organization. Rael then published a book denouncing the French government's support of ADFI (Rael 1992). He also founded *FIREPHIM*, an organization dedicated to protecting the rights of religious, sexual, and racial minorities.

EFFECTIVE MOBILIZATION

This key factor refers to the extent to which organizations coordinate and control individual actions to serve collective goals. The Raelian Movement exhibits a strong, dynamic leadership in its Priests and Bishops, and as members advance up the levels of the Structure, more time, energy, and discipline are demanded from them. But very little is expected from the rank-and-file "Raelians," who may drink wine, neglect to pay their tithing, and neglect to spread the Message—and even forget to do their morning sensual meditation—without fear of disciplinary reprisals. This gives the movement a broad base of associate members that constitute a recruiting field for future leaders. Many inactive Raelians attend the annual Sensual Meditation Seminar, where public promotions and demotions mark members' progress, so that apathetic Raelians can rediscover Rael's remarkable vision and take up the responsibilities of leadership.

As Bozeman (1994) notes, achieving a high level of mobilization carries with it the risk of "member burnout," or high defection rate. The Raelians do not censure Guides who temporarily retire from active service to rest on the "hockey bench" of the associate member level. This flexible arrangement provides a protective bolster of quasi-committed members encircling the dedicated core group, who would otherwise be more likely to be perceived by outsiders as deviant or threatening.

An important aspect of mobilization (not mentioned by Stark) is how an NRM achieves *upward mobility*, so as to attract members with "class." The early converts in Quebec tended to be of working-class origin. There has been a recent trend to replace some of the Guides who have blue-collar jobs with younger converts who are highly educated professionals. These are taking over as Priests and Bishops.

DEMOGRAPHIC FACTORS

A new religion needs a normal age and sex structure to produce a "population composition [capable] of sustaining its ranks" (Stark 1987:22). The Raelian Movement conspicuously fails to fulfill this condition. Men outnumber women by two to one. There are few children and a very low birthrate (a consequence of the extraterrestrials' warning of overpopulation and the faith in cloning). I would argue, however, that they have turned this situation to their advantage by designing ways to recruit teenagers. One strategy is to hold *raves* (public dances with light shows). Operation Condom might fulfill the same function, as well as the Raelian telephone hotline for suicidal teens. The Sensual Meditation camp extends permission to youth to explore their sexuality in a supervised environment where rules and precautions against STDs are clear-cut. It is not unlikely that a second generation of Raelians will emerge from these youthful candidates. These strategies more than adequately compensate for the dearth of babies.

In view of the recent persecution of child-centered NRMs, particularly in Europe, where alternative, spiritual childrearing methods have been branded as "indoctrination" and "child abuse" by ADFI, it might be argued that *childless* NRMs in the 1990s have a distinct advantage in terms of survival.

FAVORABLE RELIGIOUS ECOLOGY

In understanding how NRMs survive, Stark argues it is important to assess, first, the degree to which the religious economy is regulated or hospitable to pluralism, and, second, the condition of primary competitors, who are the conventional faiths vis-à-vis secularization and social disruptions.

Quebec is remarkably hospitable to religious pluralism. Even before the Canadian Charter of Rights, the law contained article 127, which elaborates on the rights of individuals to practice the religion of their choice. In 1851 the Upper and Lower Canada law was passed, assuring the exercise of religious freedom (Ares 1981).

Le Centre des Nouvelles Religions (CINR) in Montreal boasts entries on some 800 alternative religions. This speaks of a favorable ecology for NRMs in Quebec.

Rael praised the religious tolerance that he discovered on his first trip to Quebec. He also found the low birthrate and legalized abortion encouraging.

Concerning the condition of primary competitors, Stark (1987) postulates that if conventional faiths are weakened by secularization or by social disruptions, NRMs expressing a firm faith in supernatural beings and a strict moral code will exert a strong appeal. Moreover, social disruptions produce new market opportunities for alternative faiths. It might be argued that the Raelians' belief in godlike aliens and their strict code of alternative morality compensate for the anomie created by the decline of the Catholic Church in Quebec.

Quebec is no longer a society based upon Roman Catholic religiosity. French Canadian bishops returned from the Second Vatican Council, where they had advocated reform, and found their flocks diminishing rapidly. Active membership in church-sponsored social movements like Catholic Action dropped from 30,700 in 1961 to 3,000 in 1971. Within the same interval, the number of priests in the Montreal region declined by 50 percent, and women's religious orders declined by 22 percent (Bibby 1987).

In the same period, social welfare, hospital administration, and education were transferred from the church to secular authorities. Striking changes in cultural patterns ensued. Catholic bishops in 1974 reported to Rome that Quebec society had become "pluralistic, segmented, declericalized, secularized, permissive, industrialized, and urbanized." Considering this precipitous decline of the Catholic tradition, the appeal of the Raelians' belief in godlike aliens and their new code of ethics might be better understood.

CLOSE NETWORK TIES

Successful movements consist of dense but *open* social networks. The Raelian Movement fosters close interpersonal relationships between members, and journalists enjoy describing their "touchie-feelie" behavior. But Raelians are not particularly *sectarian* and do not sever ties to society. Some Raelians live in co-ops or inhabit the same apartment building, but many of the Guides have lovers outside the movement and live with non-Raelians. Members continue to pursue worldly goals and cultivate close ties with relatives and secular friends.

SECULARIZATION—THE RIGHT DOSE

Stark (1987) describes an accommodation process whereby the NRM maintains a delicate balance between extreme worldliness and uncompromising sectarianism. Raelians appear to be rapidly embracing the process of secularization. Initially, they defined themselves as "atheists," offering a philosophy rather than a theology, but they later found it expedient (for tax and tolerance purposes) to present themselves as a religion. In 1995 they received their charter as a bone fide religion in Canada. The invisible presence of extraterrestrials at their rites is now downplayed, and the date of the Elohims' arrival has been moved forward a decade. The emphasis today is on mental and physical health and success in career and relationships rather than on communication with transcendent alien beings. Nevertheless, Raelians retain a worldview that society regards as deviant.

SOCIALIZATION OF THE SECOND GENERATION

The Raelians make a point of *not* pressuring their children to accept the Message. If their children are curious about the Message, they lend them Rael's books, but children cannot be baptized until the age of fifteen, after passing a written test to prove their choice was an independent one. Therefore, they do not fulfill the eighth requirement. This raises the question of how Raelians will survive into the twenty-first century if the extraterrestrials fail to grace the Embassy with their presence and if cloning preparations do not work out as planned. As previously mentioned, the recruitment of teenagers may help to provide a new generation of members.

ADDITIONAL VARIABLES

Bozeman (1994) has suggested that a ninth measure of success might be the degree to which an NRM can learn to be "culturally bilingual"—that is, to translate its strictly held values and fundamentalist mythologies into a palatable form for the external society. In this way, members are able to navigate mainstream paths of civil virtue while retaining their distinctive beliefs and culture. Conflicts and deviance-labeling are avoided, and the group becomes an elite haven for seekers "secure in their won superiority, but grudgingly accepting of the good intentions and utilitarian value of other religions" (Bozeman 1994). The Raelians' strategic packaging of their workshops so as to appeal to a secular clientele while retaining their ufological lore might be interpreted as an example of "cultural bilingualism."

Wright (1994) has argued that an additional condition important for an NRM's success is *globalization*. He notes that in the moral crisis of the late twentieth century among industrial societies, we find the emergence of a "new world order" that is accompanied by an ambiguity concerning moral issues. NRMs seek to fill this void, he notes, by constructing overarching, universal ideologies. As governments fail and national boundaries dissolve, the perception of a world crisis may help to legitimate the claims of religious movements as harbingers of a new world harmony and peace.

The Raelians are nothing if not global. Although the members are still concentrated in French-speaking Europe and in Quebec, Rael traverses the planet to spread the Message. Every August Rael retreats to his power spot in the mountains of southern France to await instructions from his "eloha" father about which country to focus on next year. The Raelian message of peace is a response to the perceived world crises—international political unrest, shifts in world economy, the fragmentation of normative order with increased mobility and communications—not to mention the nuclear threat. Raelians envision a planetary future that is less culture-bound and territorial, where in group/out group differences will no longer be drawn along lines of class, ethnicity, or race. Rael has even founded a political party, the "Geniocracy," that proposes a world government based on a meritocracy—the rule of intelligent scientists and creative artists—after national boundaries, money, and the inheritance of property have been dispensed with.

CONCLUSION

This movement may well provide a model for the shape of successful NRMs in the future. In a society that produces buzzwords like "multiculturalism," "visible minorities," and "multiethnic," the Raelians' passionate assault on "religious racism" may defuse many of the popular stereotypes concerning "cults." Bristling with a militant tolerance, the Raelians almost parody political correctness.

Rael offers spiritual—or at least extraterrestrial—solutions to contemporary crises: the nuclear threat, environmental pollution, overpopulation, and the rights of women and homosexuals. He obliquely addresses the important issue of racial equality through a refreshingly "out-of-this-world" myth of seven alien races who created *homo sapiens* out of their own DNA (the blue and green ones died out).

Responding to a popular decline in science-as-faith, offering ultimate solutions to human suffering, the Raelians propose a renewed, fundamentalist faith in the omnipotence of science to disclose the mysteries of the universe. Finally, their aim is to unite the diverse cultures of postindustrial societies—with civilizations from other galaxies.

NOTES

1. The membership figures released by the National Guides state that Quebec numbers 5,000 members, Japan around 1,000, and Europe, 10,000.
2. This was announced in the October, November, and December meetings in Montreal.

REFERENCES

Ares, Richard. 1981. "Les partis politiques—les églises." P. 294 in Fernand Dumont (ed.), *Ideologies au Canada français 1940–1976*, vol. 3. Québec: Les presses de l'Université Laval.
Bibby, Reginald W. 1987. *Fragmented Gods: The Poverty and Potential of Religion in Canada*. Richmond Hill, Ont.: Irwin.
Bozeman, John. 1994. "Success and Failure within Religious Movements." Paper written for SOC-852, University of Virginia, Charlottesville, VA.
Rael. 1978. *Let's Welcome Our Fathers from Space: They Created Humanity in Their Laboratories*. Tokyo: AOM Corporation.
———. 1992. *Le racisme religieux financé par le gouvernement socialiste: halte à la violation des droits de l'homme en France*. Geneva, Switzerland: La Fondation Raelienne.
Stark, Rodney. 1987. "How New Religions Succeed: A Theoretical Model." Pp. 11–29 in David G. Bromley and Philip E. Hammond (eds.), *The Future of New Religious Movements*. Macon, GA: Mercer University.
Wright, Stuart A. 1994. "The Family: Movement Adaptation and Survival in an NRM." Paper presented at the Society for the Scientific Study of Religion, Albuquerque, NM.

PART III

RELIGION, POLITICAL ORDER, AND SOCIAL CHANGE

Beyond the meaning of religion to the individual and the internal dynamics of religious organizations is the fact that religion has a relationship with the larger society. Throughout known history, political leaders have sought to use religion to legitimate their rule. Religious leaders have often been happy to cooperate, since an alliance with powerful people could provide their groups with protection against persecution and with other benefits such as financial support for their activities. Not surprisingly, state religions were the norm for many societies in the past. However, as modern societies have become pluralistic, it has become difficult for political leaders to find any one religion with enough members to use it to gain widespread legitimacy for their government. Instead, some countries have developed civil religion (Bellah, 1967). This is a nondenominational set of beliefs that links a nation's sense of destiny as a people to a Supreme Being who is not specific to any one religion (or what one of my students called "a generic god"). The United States has such a civil religion, as is manifested, for example, in the phrase "under God" added to the pledge to the flag in the 1950s, the phrase "In God We Trust" on all the currency, the use of the Judeo-Christian Bible in the inauguration of presidents, the rallying call of "For God and Country" that has sent several generations to war, and the sense of sacredness in the temple-like structure of the Lincoln Memorial.

Nevertheless, religious values do not always lend themselves to the preservation of the existing system. Ever-increasing pluralism sets the stage for challenges to religious monopolies and for conflicts between religions, which can be disruptive to the social order. Some religious groups challenge the political-economic system by advocating alternative ways of doing things, such as promoting respect for the natural environment. In other situations churches actually provide leadership in organized efforts to bring about social change.

The chapters in Part III reflect the complexity of the relationship between religion and the large structures of societies. Graeme Lang, Mansoor Moaddel, and

Cheryl Townsend Gilkes present historical analyses. The first shows struggles between religion and governments in China, the second competing interpretations of Islam and its relationship to the modern world, and the third the emergence of African American holiness and pentecostal churches as a form of psychological survival in the face of slavery and other forms of institutional racism. Pentecostalism is also the topic of David Smilde's article, based on recent interviews with Protestants in Venezuela about their views of social change. This is followed by my own chapter on social activism among Catholics in Brazil and the chapter by Mark Rozell and Clyde Wilcox showing religion as a conservative force, in the form of the Christian Right in the United States. The final two chapters focus on new religious movements in relation to different aspects of social change. Gary Bouma examines the phenomenon of cultural diffusion in relation to new religions in Australia. Helen Berger describes the views of contemporary American Witches on ecological issues.

As societies become more secular, a greater variety of possibilities in relation to religion is likely to develop. These possibilities may be reflected in terms of both new kinds of religions and new relationships between religion and other social institutions. In the twentieth century we have seen a proliferation of ways in which religion interacts with the larger social context. The chapters in Part III offer reflections on the past and provide ideas for thinking about what may be in store for religion and for the world in the century to come.

REFERENCE

Bellah, Robert N. 1967. "Civil Religion in America." *Daedalus* 96:1–21.

16

Religions and Regimes in China

Graeme Lang

INTRODUCTION

In his classic analysis of the political consequences of Chinese religion, C. K. Yang observed that religion might "ally itself with the state," "struggle against the state ... to preserve itself or to gain political dominance," or "withdraw into seclusion" (Yang 1961:105). Seclusion was rarely achieved. Yang's other two options were more common: alliance and struggle. Religious practitioners and state officials have struggled against each other in China for three thousand years and have exploited each other for almost as long. Officials, seeking authority and control, repressed some religious activities and sponsored others. Religious practitioners, seeking security and rewards, responded with appeasement, collaboration, or revolt. This chapter will describe some of the conflicts and accommodations that developed between religions and governments in China.

THE STATE AND THE HEAVENLY BUREAUCRACY

The religions native to East, South, and Southeast Asia are polytheistic. Gods sprout like mushrooms, and every kind of object and being has been a god somewhere in the region. In China, where control by an empire was prolonged and deeply affected the whole society, the gods developed as the result of a long struggle between government officials and religious leaders. What is especially interesting is that some gods came to look like rulers and officials. At the top of the supernatural hierarchy of Chinese god-officials was the Jade Emperor. Near the bottom was the City God, who functioned like a mayor or Chinese magistrate. Statues of these gods were dressed like mandarins and carried around their territories in sedan chairs each year like magistrates. They enforced social order with harsh punishments for miscreants in the afterlife, with courts and elaborate paperwork like those of their real-life counterparts, and it required the same kinds of formal petitions and diligent gift-giving to get their attention (Yang 1961).

How did such a correspondence between gods and officials develop? Scholars have proposed various explanations of the "bureaucratic gods" phenomenon:

- Individuals may visualize gods using their experience of the holders of secular power (there is some ethnographic evidence for this effect). God-carvers also used the imagery of imperial officials to make their icons more impressive.

- Officials in China since the Tang dynasty have actively suppressed cults devoted to gods of which they disapproved, generally local nature-spirits and amoral deities. (Hansen 1993)

- Officials often tried to replace such cults with worship of respectable gods that exemplified the values of the state. For example, the state sponsored veneration, which evolved into worship, of deceased officials and military officers who had demonstrated great courage or loyalty or virtue. Living officials were required to patronize these cults and conduct the appropriate sacrifices. (Yang 1961)

In some cases, where worship of local deities was strong, the state resorted to coopting them into the pantheon (its official list of respectable gods), and transformed them in the process. For example, a goddess worshiped by fishermen in Fukien was originally a girl who died, unmarried, in 987 A.D. after miraculously saving her family at sea during a storm. She was later canonized by the imperial regime to curry favor with the coastal peoples. However, she was co-opted into the pantheon by "promoting" her, first to Celestial Concubine in the thirteenth century and finally to Empress of Heaven (Watson 1985). By the time this occurred, in the eighteenth century, she had become a patriotic deity who defended the state and its coastal communities.

Buddhist and Taoist clergy also actively promoted their own versions of godhood, sometimes copying each other or using imagery derived from the state and supporting attempts to exterminate local deities (Ebrey and Gregory 1993).

Wherever the state was weak, unconventional local gods were revived. Some were deified humans who had been extraordinary in life or in the manner of their deaths, and thereby earned power and attracted supplicants. Others were ghosts originally provided with offerings to appease their restless and dangerous spirits, and later for their power to help gamblers, speculators, and gangsters (Weller 1996). The activities and struggles among clergy, shamans, and religious entrepreneurs and the cult-sponsoring and cult-busting activities of state officials produced a complex mixture of gods and spirits which survived in China into the 20th century (Shahar and Weller 1996). These deities confronted both the secular and the Christian reformers who tried to purge the supernatural realm and its devotees in order to modernize the country.

EDITING THE PANTHEON

The revolutionaries who overthrew the Qing dynasty in 1911 included many who were hostile to Chinese "folk religion." Some were Chinese Christians, who smashed the statues of "false" gods to make room for their one God. Others were secularists who believed that imaginary gods absorbed some of the peasants' hopes and fears, diverting them from real solutions to their problems. They also believed that priests and shamans took the peasants' money for useless rituals to bribe these gods. Indeed, many of the gods dressed and behaved like officials of the regime that the revolutionaries had just overthrown. It was obvious to many of these revolutionaries that the sooner this pantheon of primitive spirits and god-officials was abolished, the better.

But practical ways of accomplishing this goal in the face of popular belief were less obvious. Some gods and temples seemed to local people to be central to their culture and local or regional history. Some gods were also deified officials or culture-heroes from the past. To destroy them was to destroy some of their heritage and to alienate potential political supporters. Between 1911 and the 1920s, innumerable temples in China were sacked or converted to secular uses. Such attacks on popular religion, along with economic and political turmoil as warlords struggled for power, propelled some religious practitioners to Hong Kong, carrying beliefs and practices that thrived in the more tolerant environment of the British colony (Lang and Ragvald 1993; Lang 1997).

In the 1920s the Chinese Nationalists (Kuomintang) set up a legislature in Nanking and enacted legislation about gods and temples. Moderates in the legislature proposed keeping the respectable gods and abolishing the primitive ones. Thus, in 1928, the Nationalist government in Chekiang province proclaimed a resolution as follows:

> The principle for recognition of temples is that we approve of retaining those dedicated to great men of the past who have contributed discoveries of arts and sciences, and those who can be held up before the people as examples of filial piety and justice for their emulation. Secondly, those dedicated to religious leaders who have founded religions on the basis of right and truth, and have been popularly believed by the people. The principle for confiscation of temples is likewise twofold: that we should do away with old pre-historic religions which can not be proved historically, or which have no contemporary meaning or value; and that we should get rid of evil religions, for example, those quasi-religious, money- making cults, or animistic worship of grass or trees, as well as legendary cults . . . which have no facts to prove their worth. (quoted in Day 1969:192)

Under "Gods to be Retained," the proclamation listed the legendary figures who founded agriculture (Shen Nung), domesticated silkworms (Huang-ti), invented writing (Ts'ang-chi), and tamed the rivers for agriculture (Yu the "water-king"), along with the philosophers Confucius and Mencius. Also allowed into the list were the high-gods or founders of Taoism, Buddhism, Islam, and Christianity. Under "Gods to be Discarded," the document listed "Stellar or Celestial Gods," "Earth Gods," "Atmospheric Gods," and "All Useless Gods," proclaiming that "all the above temples and idols should be razed to the ground so that nothing remains."

The policy of smashing god-statues, closing temples, and confiscating temple lands of "discarded" gods was not carried out everywhere in China. Indeed, some local officials and warlords in the 1930s resisted such policies or built new temples to replace those destroyed, earning the gratitude of local believers.

DESTROYING THE PANTHEON

The Communist government that took power in 1949 renewed the assault on folk religion. The Communists were not willing to recognize any gods, although they did allow a few carefully controlled religious organizations to remain open (MacInnis 1972). Religious sects were especially targeted, since the Communists believed, sometimes correctly, that leaders of these sects were often local power-holders with close connections to the ousted Nationalist regime that had fled to Taiwan in 1949. Some of these sects were apparently involved in resistance to land reform in the 1950s (Perry 1985). During the Cultural Revolution in the late 1960s, innumerable temples were sacked throughout China, and most remaining evidence of "folk religion" disappeared. By the mid-1970s, China appeared to be a secular society, although it seemed to some observers that religion had been replaced by a quasi-religious cult devoted to virtual worship of the person and writings of Mao Zedong.

The death of Mao in 1976, the rise to power of the more pragmatic Deng Xiaoping, and the new economic policies adopted after 1978 (see Vogel 1989) led to a decline in the ability and determination of the Communist Party to control all economic and social activities. Like the Nationalists in the 1920s, the Communist regime decided to tolerate certain major deities and religions, while continuing to repress most "popular" or "folk" religion. The official policy of the state distinguished between "religion," which would be permitted within the framework of state-sanctioned religious organizations, and "feudal superstition", which was to be suppressed. In 1979, *People's Daily* explained the distinction between "religion" and "superstition" to cadres and citizens as follows:

> By religion, we chiefly mean worldwide religions, such as Christianity, Islam, Buddhism, and the like. They have scriptures, creeds, religious ceremonies, organizations, and so on. These religions have histories of thousands of years. They have extensive influence among the masses. . . . By superstition we generally mean activities conducted by shamans, and sorcerers, such as magic medicine, magic water, divination, fortune telling, avoiding disasters [by supernatural means], praying for rain, praying for pregnancy, exorcizing demons, telling fortunes by physiognomy, locating house or tomb sites by geomancy, and so forth. These are all absurd and ridiculous. Anyone possessing rudimentary knowledge will not believe in them. . . . They must be suppressed. (quoted in MacInnis 1989:33–34)

The distinction between "religion" and "superstition," however, is not always clear. Exorcisms, for example, are practiced by some Christian preachers and evangelists in house-churches and rural areas.

People's Daily also recognized that some religious beliefs and activities were not covered by the above definitions and occupied an ambiguous "middle" category:

It is true, real life is much more complex than simple concepts and definitions. There still are, among the people, certain long-standing activities such as ancestor worship and belief in ghosts and deities. Although they are a kind of superstition, we generally do not prohibit them by administrative decree *as long as they do not affect collective political and economic activities*; rather, we solve the problems by patient persuasion and lasting education in science, culture, and atheism. (MacInnes 1989:34, emphasis added)

After 1979, there was a revival of these popular religious activities and beliefs, and many temples were rebuilt. Changes in economic and social policy helped to bring about this revival.

REVIVING THE PANTHEON

Many rural villages in China had much more disposable income in the 1980s than in the 1970s as a result of the increase in production due to the dismantling of the commune system. They channeled some of their new wealth into rebuilding temples and ancestral halls (Perry 1985). Temples and religious activities were also revived in the cities. The government's new openness to foreign investment contributed to the construction of temples, many of which have been rebuilt with funds from wealthy overseas Chinese. An old Buddhist temple in Chaozhou, for example, was completely rebuilt with a donation from Hong Kong billionaire Li Kashing. Christian churches have also benefitted from the willingness of some local cadres to allow donations from overseas Chinese believers (Hunter and Chan 1993). Some cadres hope that outsiders will invest in areas where they are able to visit and sponsor local churches or temples.

The central government tried for several decades to suppress religion but, like previous regimes, has only succeeded in becoming entangled with it. One of the most iconoclastic rulers in China's long history, Chairman Mao Zedong, died in 1976 after presiding over a ten-year "Cultural Revolution" in which millions of fanatical youth smashed temples and god-statues throughout China. But Chairman Mao was worshiped like a god in life, in a cult enforced by the state in every school and office. Few students of Chinese religion are surprised that pictures of Mao have been used as magical talismans after his death. In 1992, for example, thousands of peasants in Anhui bought copies of photos of the Chairman. The official explanation was that they were showing their gratitude to the Communist Party for helping them during the previous year's disastrous floods. The real reason was reportedly that they hoped the icon of a man who had been so powerful in life would protect them from a repeat of the disasters (Crothall 1992). Stories have also circulated about incidents in which a picture of the Chairman protected people from harm. In one incident, when two buses collided, only those on the bus which displayed a portrait of the Chairman were spared injury.

Mao's image was even used during the Cultural Revolution to protect religious shrines. For example, local cadres protected the god-statues in a Taoist temple in rural Guangdong in the late 1960s by building a partition in front of the statues and sealing it with a poster of Mao. When the Red Guards arrived, they did not dare to tear down Mao's image to get to the god-statues, which thus survived the general destruction of religious icons. In 1987, local government cadres responsible for this site related that in return for this act of protection, the gods had protected a regiment of soldiers from the district during the border war between China and Vietnam in 1979. (The soldiers had moved out of a camp shortly before a bombardment that killed soldiers from other regiments).

Mao tried to eliminate the gods, but he succeeded only in temporarily replacing them with his own image. Meanwhile, older gods waited patiently in the shadows, hidden by their followers to await better times. Mao is gone, and the gods have reemerged.

Officially, China now has religious freedom. But the government has reverted to the old distinction between "respectable religions," which are supposed to be permitted, and "disreputable superstitions," which are not. The latter include most folk religious practice (with some ambivalence about the worship of Mao) and unorthodox sectarian religious groups. The permissible religions include those with venerable sacred texts, well-demonstrated respect for the secular authorities, and careful avoidance of unauthorized contacts with foreign religious organizations.

The officially tolerated Protestants in China, for example, are attached to the Three-Self Patriotic Movement, which survives by advocating loyalty to the regime. While this organization is disdained by some overseas observers and by many members of Chinese house-churches for this reason, it is participating in the evolution of civil society in China. Its leader for over 30 years, K. H. Ting, has spoken out in recent years against some of the harsh actions carried out by local authorities against house-churches (Brown 1996).

A much greater threat to an imperial regime than Christian house-churches, however, are ethnic religions that carry ethnic nationalism.

STATES AND ETHNIC RELIGIONS

In large empires such as China, religion is often linked to ethnic or regional cultures and identities. Hence, religion is sometimes involved in ethnic self-assertion and occasionally in separatist movements. In China, Muslims in Xinjiang province and Buddhists in Tibet pressed for greater autonomy or separation from the empire.

Chinese state officials have responded in several ways to the political problems posed by ethnic religions: co-opting some religious leaders in return for state support and funds for seminaries, imprisoning religious activists unwilling to be coopted, and trying to control the next generation of religious leaders by approving candidates.

For example, the largest non-Chinese region in China is Tibet, which developed a distinctive form of Buddhism. Tibetan Buddhists, particularly the exiled "living Buddha," the Dalai Lama, have played a role in agitating for greater autonomy. China's strategy with regard to Tibetan Buddhism is to closely monitor and control

Tibetan religious organizations, prevent their use to foster separatism, and try to weaken the position of the Dalai Lama (Schwartz 1994). To this end, the government has cultivated cooperative or malleable Tibetan Buddhist clergy. It has also officially endorsed the selection of a six-year-old child as the reincarnation of the last Panchen Lama, who died in 1989. (The Panchen Lama had remained in China, officially supporting the regime, but had spent many years in prison for criticizing Mao's Great Leap Forward and its disastrous impact on Tibet in the early 1960s.)

Considered a "living Buddha" like the Dalai Lama, the Panchen Lama is Tibetan Buddhism's second most important figure. Beijing intended to wrest control of this important position away from the Dalai Lama, who had approved the selection of another six-year-old Tibetan child as the reincarnated Lama in 1995 (Tibet Information Network 1996). Beijing's rival candidate, also six years old, was selected several months later by drawing lots from a golden urn (first used for this purpose 200 years earlier under the Manchus). The child and his teachers were brought to Beijing to meet President Jiang Zemin, amid great publicity, and instructed by the president to accept the leadership of the Party and to cultivate patriotism toward China.

This attempt to control appointments to senior positions in religious organizations has been a common imperial response, in Asia and elsewhere, to the problem of administering provinces with ethnic religions. That an officially atheist regime has become involved in selecting a reincarnated living Buddha shows how strong is the ethnic religious culture with which the state is confronted and how great the potential threat from religious organizations that inhabit and perpetuate this culture.

There is no chance that Tibetan Buddhist leaders will ever regain the political and economic power they once possessed during centuries of feudal theocratic rule (Grunfeld 1987), nor do Tibetans want to return to such a system (Schwartz 1994). But rulers in China, who have long memories, remember the occasions when religious movements shook the foundations of the empire (Naquin 1976). The greatest of these convulsions was created by the Taiping "Heavenly Kingdom" in the 1850s.

The founder of the Taiping movement, influenced by Christian missionary writings in southern China, built a new sect around claims of divine revelation, fragments of Judaeo-Christian theology, egalitarian ideals, and communal sharing of property (Bohr 1985; Spence 1996). His movement attracted followers among the Hakka ethnic minority in Guangxi province in the 1840s, who armed themselves for protection and defeated a succession of armies sent against them. Marching north into central China, they established a kingdom based in Nanjing, which they called the "Heavenly Kingdom of Great Peace" (Taiping Tienguo); it was finally exterminated in 1864 with the loss of several million lives. The Communist Party considered the Taipings to be revolutionary "proto-socialists," though deluded by their religion. But the Party also knows the power of such ideas among determined believers.

The current regime is no less vigilant than the imperial dynasties that preceded it. Where ethnic religions present a threat to the empire, as in Tibet, imperial attempts to control them have led to extraordinary coercion and to extraordinary manipulations of religious institutions.

CONCLUSIONS

In China attempts by the state over several thousand years to control religion and bend it to state interests have led to complicated entanglements between religion and regime, each leaving its stamp on the other. Chinese gods appointed and patronized by state officials naturally reflected the imagery and politics of the imperial system and enhanced its legitimacy. However, not all gods were successfully co-opted, especially in regions such as Tibet, which developed a strong native religion in pre-imperial times.

Twentieth-century revolutionary regimes have dealt harshly with religions, seeing them as rivals with incompatible agendas. Religious organizations are no match for a hostile state in the short run, but repression is hard to sustain while the country is undergoing rapid development. Meanwhile, the loss of faith in Communism, dismay at widespread corruption, and pressing personal needs provide fertile ground for old and new religions. Ironically, because China has long repressed religious organizations, well-developed external religions such as Christianity face less competition in China from weakened native religions when state repression declines.

Chinese Buddhism and Christianity have begun to compete again at the grassroots level, offering salvation, ethical doctrines, and divine help for people with problems. But Christian house-churches and rural congregations provide a much stronger sense of community (Hunter and Chan 1993), while Christian miracles and millenarianism attract adherents in impoverished areas.

The state in the late 1990s has been preoccupied with economic development because officials know that the regime's security and legitimacy depend mainly on the material well-being of the population. Unlike previous regimes, the Party declines to claim support from the gods. As the regime's utopian visions fade, however, religious organizations offer what the state cannot provide (Stark and Bainbridge 1987) and grow cautiously stronger. The regime may not soon give up its regulation of the religious marketplace, but its right to do so will be increasingly challenged.

REFERENCES

Bohr, Richard. 1985. "The Heavenly Kingdom in China: Religion and the Taiping Revolution, 1837–1853." *Fides et Historia* 17:38–52.
Brown, Deborah. 1996. "The Role of Religion in Promoting Democracy in the People's Republic of China and Hong Kong." Pp.79–141 in Beatrice Leung (ed.), *Church and State Relations in 21st Century Asia*. Hong Kong: Center of Asian Studies, University of Hong Kong.
Crothall, Geoffrey. 1992. "Peasants Lift Mao to God Status." *South China Morning Post*, February 2.

Day, Clarence Burton. 1969. *Chinese Peasant Cults* (Second Edition). Taipei: Ch'ang Wen Publishing Company.

Ebrey, Patricia Buckley, and Peter N. Gregory (eds.). 1993. *Religion and Society in T'ang and Sung China*. Honolulu: University of Hawaii Press.

Grunfeld, Tom. 1987. *The Making of Modern Tibet*. New York: M. E. Sharpe.

Hansen, Valerie. 1993. "Gods on Walls: A Case of Indian Influence on Chinese Lay Religion." Pp. 75–114 in Patricia Buckley Ebrey and Peter N. Gregory (eds.), *Religion and Society in T'ang and Sung China*. Honolulu: University of Hawaii Press.

Hunter, Alan, and Kim-kwong Chan. 1993. *Protestantism in Contemporary China*. Cambridge: Cambridge University Press.

Lang, Graeme. 1997. "Sacred Power in the Metropolis: Shrines and Temples in Hong Kong." Pp.242–265 in Grant Evans and Maria Tam (eds.), *Hong Kong: The Anthropology of a Chinese Metropolis*. Surrey, U.K.: Curzon.

Lang, Graeme, and Lars Ragvald. 1993. *The Rise of a Refugee God: Hong Kong's Wong Tai Sin*. Hong Kong: Oxford University Press.

MacInnis, Donald E. 1972. *Religious Policy and Practice in Communist China: A Documentary History*. New York: Macmillan.

———. 1989. *Religion in China Today: Policy and Practice*. Maryknoll, N.Y.: Orbis Books. 1993.

Naquin, Susan. 1976. *Millenarian Rebellion in China: The Eight Trigrams Uprising of 1813*. New Haven: Yale University Press.

Perry, Elizabeth J. 1985. "Rural Violence in Socialist China". *The China Quarterly* 103:414–440.

Schwartz, Ronald D. 1994. *Circle of Protest: Political Ritual in the Tibetan Uprising*. New York: Columbia University Press.

Shahar, Meir, and Robert P. Weller (eds.). 1996. *Unruly Gods: Divinity and Society in China*. Honolulu: University of Hawai'i Press.

Spence, Jonathan. 1996. *God's Chinese Son: The Taiping Heavenly Kingdom of Hong Xiuquan*. London: Flamingo.

Stark, Rodney, and William Simms Bainbridge. 1987. *A Theory of Religion*. N.Y.: Peter Lang.

Tibet Information Network. 1996. *Cutting Off the Serpent's Head: Tightening Control in Tibet, 1994–1995*. N.Y.: Human Rights Watch.

Vogel, Ezra F. 1989. *One Step Ahead in China: Guangdong under Reform*. Cambridge, MA: Harvard University Press.

Watson, James L. 1985. "Standardizing the Gods: the Promotion of T'ien Hou ('Empress of Heaven') along the South China Coast, 960–1960." Pp. 292–324 in David Johnson, Andrew Nathan, and Evelyn Rawski (eds.), *Popular Culture in Late Imperial China*. Berkeley: University of California Press.

Weller, Robert P. 1996. "Matricidal Magistrates and Gambling Gods: Weak States and Strong Spirits in China." Pp. 184–211 in Meir Shahar and Robert P. Weller (eds.), *Unruly Gods: Divinity and Society in China*. Honolulu: University of Hawaii Press.

Yang, C. K. 1961. *Religion in Chinese Society: A Study of Contemporary Social Functions of Religion and Some of Their Historical Factors*. Prospect Heights, IL: Waveland Press.

17

Diversities and Discontinuities in the Islamic Response to Modernity

Mansoor Moaddel

Religion has consequences for how people live their lives in the context of a particular society at a particular point in time. How they put their beliefs into practice is a complex process sometimes characterized by conflict among those with different interpretations of their religion. Some of the present conflicts in Islamic countries result from a split between two different responses to the modern world: fundamentalism and modernism. Islamic fundamentalists reject Western ideas about science and democracy, view the West as materialistic and culturally decadent, uphold the domination of women by men, and aim to make all society Islamic. The modernists are more open to the West, accept scientific thinking, reject polygamy and male domination, and advocate democracy and the separation of religion from politics. In this chapter I will describe the tension between Islamic fundamentalism and Islamic modernism as it emerged in four countries: Egypt, Iran, India/Pakistan, and Syria.

ISLAMIC BELIEFS AND CHANGING INTERPRETATIONS

In order to understand the roots of these different positions, it is important to know something about Islamic tradition, which is a complex historical and cultural phenomenon that spans about fourteen centuries. Within that tradition are certain essential principles shared by Muslims of all ages, including the belief in the unity of God and the prophecy of Muhammad. There is also the belief that the Quran (the Muslim sacred scripture), as the word of God that was revealed to Muhammad, and the statements (called the *hadith*) attributed to the Prophet are the only authoritative sources according to which all Muslims are required to organize their lives.

The Islamic laws drawn from these basic principles were intended to build the society and regulate the everyday activities of Muslims. These laws, however, have always been subject to change according to historical conditions. The question of succession to the Prophet and the expansion of Islam into territories with civilizations that were often superior to that of the conquerors provided the first major political complications facing the Islamic movement. The Muslim jurists who were writing the laws faced practical problems about which the sacred book and the holy tradition of the Prophet had said very little or nothing at all. It took about four centuries of legal development in Sunni Islam for the laws to become crystallized into four schools (*Hanafi, Maliki, Shafi'ie*, and *Hanbali*), which would constitute the core methodology of traditional Islamic jurisprudence. Shi'ism followed Sunni Islam in most of its legal and juristic practices (Levy 1930; Momen 1985). After the eleventh century no new method of interpretation was allowed. The gate of independent reasoning by the Islamic theologians was considered closed (Levy 1930).

Islamic political theory has been differently interpreted through time. For example, the Islamic theory of *Khilafa* was supposed to resolve the problem of who would be the caliph, that is, the successor of Muhammad. Muslim theologians were unanimous about the legitimacy of the first four caliphs. However, from the seventh century onward, there were new problems facing Muslim lawmakers. For example, how was one to reconcile the Islamic notion of sovereignty with the claims of the self-made caliph among the continuously emerging military leaders and tribal chiefs in different parts of the Islamic world? Al-Mawardi (991–1031) was among the early pioneers of Islamic political theory whose *Ordinances of Government* was an attempt to legitimize the authority of the caliph vis-à-vis the challenges of other Muslim rulers who had effective power within their own territories (Gibb 1937). Al-Ghazali, a well-known theologian, religious scholar, and mystic, also made similar concessions to expediency. He recognized the political power of the sultan insofar as the latter recognized the spiritual power of the caliph. This recognition was necessary because the alternative of unseating the sultan might have resulted in chaos (Rosenthal 1958:38, 239). On the other hand, other prominent Muslim theorists were unhappy with the poor fit between the ideal Islamic theory of the state and the political reality of their time. The striking contrast between theory and reality led many of them to declare that the caliphate had ceased after the death of the fourth caliph.

With the consolidation of the Mughal, Safavid, and Ottoman empires around the fifteenth century, a set of practical guidelines and propositions were in place that had resolved some of the fundamental tensions between the existing political reality and a strict application of the early Islamic precept on sovereignty. These Islamic absolutist states were to be regulated in terms of revised Islamic laws. One important consequence of this development was the integration of the *ulama* (the Muslim theologians) into the state structure. While they provided ideological backing for the state's expansionist ambitions, the ulama in turn relied on the sword of the rulers for the propagation of their faith. They would demand, and almost always received, the support of the state in suppressing dissident views within and outside their ranks. The ulama often erected insurmountable barriers against any attempt to change Islamic beliefs.

Traditional order in the Islamic countries declined as a result of economic, political, and cultural crises that occurred from the seventeenth century on, leading to the following social transformations that would set the stage for the development of modernist beliefs: the integration of Islamic countries into the world economy, the development of capitalism, the rise of merchants and landowners, and the emergence of modern social institutions. An important factor contributing to these changes was the spread of modern ideas from Europe into the Islamic countries in the nineteenth century, generating a new awareness among Muslim intellectuals about alternative ways of organizing social and political life. Western scientific and technological achievements impressed these intellectuals and stimulated their curiosity for understanding the underlying sources of its progress. Also in the same period the Islamic belief system came under direct and persistent criticism from various groups on theological and social issues. These groups included the followers of the Enlightenment, Westernizers, think-tanks connected to the European colonial administrations, and Christian missionaries.

Westerners' criticisms of Islamic societies and the influx of diverse ideological contenders into Muslim countries led to the crystallization of a number of significant issues around which revolved the ideological questions of the late nineteenth century. Four of these issues appeared to be more salient than others: (1) the idea of civilization and the nature of Western society, (2) Western science versus Islamic methods, (3) the proper form of government and its relationship with religion, and (4) the status and role of women in society. The responses of the Muslim theologians to the challenges of the West and their positions on these issues were often diametrically opposed, as is seen in the split between Islamic modernism and Islamic fundamentalism.

ISLAMIC MODERNISM

The Islamic modernist movement is characterized by a close affinity between Islam and modern (i.e., liberal, constitutional, democratic) ideas. The central theological problem that concerns both the traditionalist and modernist Islamic thinkers revolves around the question of whether Islamic law, which shapes political institutions, should continue to reject all external sources of authority and confine itself to the four traditional orthodox sources—the Quran (sacred scripture), the statements attributed to the Prophet, the consensus of the theologians, and juristic reasoning by analogy—or whether it should reinterpret the first two sources and transform the last two to become the vehicle of modern legal and political notions (Ahmad 1967). In the course of the second half of the nineteenth century, a group of leading thinkers in various parts of the Islamic world adopted the second alternative, thus presenting a forceful challenge to traditionalism. They argued that Islam as a world religion is thoroughly capable, by reason of its inner spiritual force, of adapting to the changing conditions of every age (Adams 1933:13). One of these prominent Islamic theologians, Muhammad Abduh, went so far as to argue that the real rejection of Islam is the refusal to accept the proof of rational argument, because the hallmark of the perfect Muslim community is both law and reason. Thus Muslims could accept the result of science and rational inquiry (Turner 1974:147). Another theologian, Sayyid Ahmad Khan, attempted to reconcile Darwinian evolutionism with Islamic tenets of Creation and the Fall of Adam by arguing that the Quran affirms that the law of evolution is observable in relating one species of created beings to another (Ahmad 1967:45–46). All of the modernists rejected the claim that the only truth that could interest the community of believers is that which came from Islamic sources. These thinkers considered it appropriate to conduct their investigations by using the best available tools of the natural and social sciences, even if to do so obliged them to have recourse to books written by authors not aware of Islamic teachings (Butterworth 1982).

Although the ideas of Islamic modernism spread throughout the Middle East and the Indian subcontinent and found many interested audiences, it was in Egypt that Islamic modernism took the form of a definite movement under the leadership of Shaikh Muhammad Abduh. A leading pupil of Muhammad Abduh and his biographer, Muhammad Rashid Rida, founded the periodical *Al-Manar* in 1898. This publication became a means of propagating Abduh's doctrines and accomplishing his reforms. *Al-Manar* was dedicated to an ambitious program of promoting social, religious, and economic reforms (Adams 1933:175–181). The rise of Islamic modernism in Egypt coincided with the era of nationalist agitation and struggle against British domination. In this country the emergence and growth of nationalist and anti-British movements was facilitated by the following economic, political, and cultural factors: the growth of the bourgeois landowning class; the fiscal crisis of the state under Ismail Pasha and his successor, Tawfiq Pasha; the promotion of Arabic as the official language of the country; and the emergence of Egyptian educated elites (Sayyid-Marsot 1977). Struggles for political independence eventually culminated in 1924 in the formation of a constitutional government, when Britain officially recognized Egypt as an independent sovereign state having a hereditary form of monarchy. Under the impact of the nationalist revolution of 1919–1922, Egypt's first modern mass party, the *Wafd*, emerged, and the country experienced more than two decades of liberal politics.

Islamic modernism was not as strong in Iran. To be sure, during the Constitutional Revolution (1905–1911), a progressive faction among the theologians was deeply influenced by modern liberal thought and constitutional ideas. They began to reconcile Islamic political theory with a constitutional government (Adami'yat 1976). However, the constitutional movement eventually failed in Iran, and modernist ideas lost their influence. After a decade of turmoil, the constitutional movement ended up in the despotism of Reza Shah. Iran's first liberal nationalist experience began with the breakdown of Reza Shah's rule in 1941, and was abruptly ended by the U.S.- and British-backed coup in 1953 (Moaddel 1989). The post-coup authoritarian regime of Muhammad Reza Shah, by effectively destroying secular political organizations in society, set the stage for the rise of Islamic fundamentalism in Iran (Moaddel 1992).

Modernism was also a dominant trend among the Muslim activists of India. The first forceful challenge to traditionalism in India came in the wake of the devastating consequences of the "Mutiny" of 1857–1858. The Mutiny was a "traditionalist" response by Hindus and Muslims to resist British colonial domination of the country, and its catastrophic defeat decisively ended any hope of revitalizing the old order. However, it ushered in a new episode for culture production. The Mughal rule was formally ended. The control of India was passed from the board of directors of the East India Company to the British parliament and electorate. And major economic developments, including the construction of railroads and other infrastructures, took place after 1860.

The conservative reaction was mercilessly crushed; insofar as the Muslims were concerned, the defeats in no uncertain terms not only signified the reality of the British presence in India but also brought to the fore the striking innovativeness of its culture and dynamic institutions that were responsible for its military invincibility. The Mutiny indeed set the stage for the emergence of the modernist discourse in Muslim India.

The tumultuous days of the Mutiny affected the thinking of the Indian modernist Islamic theologian Sayyid Ahmad Khan. One thing became very clear to him, namely, that most of the Islamic doctors of law and theologians were ill equipped to deal with the intellectual problems that had besieged Islam in the modern period (Ahmad 1967). In 1864 Ahmad Khan founded a Scientific Society for the introduction of Western sciences, primarily among Muslims in India. Ten years later he founded his Anglo-Muhammadan Oriental College at Aligarh. He also began the publication of a journal, Tahzib al-akhlaq, which included articles on subjects ranging from public hygiene to rationalist speculation on religious dogma. This journal raised storms of bitter controversy. In its pages modernism emerged as a potent force and considerably changed the course and direction of Islam in India.

While Syria did not experience a strong Islamic modernist movement, it did enjoy a short period of liberal politics as a result of nationalist movements. These movements arose first against the Ottoman empire around the turn of the century, then against the French mandate between the two world wars. The complete evacuation of French troops by April 1946 brought Syrians a sequence of parliamentary democracy (1946–1949), military dictatorship (1949–1954), and again parliamentary democracy (1954–1958). After the failure of its unification with Egypt (1958–1961), the Syrian government gradually drifted to the left and developed a centralized dictatorship (Rabinovich 1972).

ISLAMIC FUNDAMENTALISM

From the 1960s on, a reaction against modernism, Islamic fundamentalism, has emerged in virtually all Middle Eastern countries. Prominent among producers of fundamentalist ideas are Hasan al-Banna and Sayyid Qutb in Egypt, Mustafa as-Siba'i in Syria, Abul Ala Maududi in Pakistan, and Ayatollah Ruhollah Khomeini in Iran. This group insists on unconditional allegiance to Islam and seeks to undermine the validity of any learning that does not have its roots in Divine Law (Butterworth 1982:87). Ayatollah Khomeini has gone so far as to argue that a truly Islamic state is the one based on the governance of jurisprudence (*velayat-i faqih*) and has identified Islam with the authority of the theologians (Moaddel 1993).

Although the spread of fundamentalist Islam throughout the Middle East occurred about forty years ago, its origins are much earlier. The first organized movement of fundamentalist Islam was the Society of the Muslim Brothers, founded in Egypt in March 1928. By the late 1930s, it had grown to become one of the most important politicoreligious organizations in the country. Although the society was courted by the British, the king of Egypt, and other conservative groups hoping to curb the influence of the Nationalists and the Communists, its alleged involvement in violence and the assassination of several prominent figures alarmed the government with the concern that the society was planning an imminent revolution. In 1948 the Egyptian government issued an order dissolving the society.

A branch of the Muslim Brothers was then established in Syria. It was organized into the Islamic Socialist Front in November 1949. Mustafa as-Siba'i, the leader of the front, declared that he would work for the realization of Islamic socialism that had been advocated by the Prophet. This flirtation with the idea of Islamic socialism, however, was short-lived, and by 1961 the Brothers had removed the term altogether from their political vocabulary (Batatu 1982:12). Since the mid-1960s, the Muslim Brothers have been involved in several bloody confrontations with the Syrian government, although none has resulted in any political change (Rabinovich 1972:109–126). In Pakistan, the *Jamma'at-i Islami* (Islamic Society) was founded in August of 1941 (Bahadur 1977). The period of its greatest influence followed the decline of Zulfagar Ali Bhutto's secular government and the military coup of 1977. It was, however, in Iran that Islam became the dominant ideology in a major revolution that brought the fundamentalists to power. The Iranian Revolutionary movement of 1977–1979 was led by Ayatolla Khomeini, one of the supreme religious leaders in Shi'i Islam. It was directed against the arbitrary rule of the Shah and his economic policies that favored modern commercial establishments and foreign companies. In addition to the Islamic opposition, many secular groups and leftist organizations participated in the Revolution. After the overthrow of the Shah, the Islamic fundamentalists monopolized power and systematically eliminated other groups whom they thought were un-Islamic.

CONCLUSION

The foregoing historical narrative reveals several important facts about Islam as a belief system and as a historical reality. First, although Islam consists of a set of essential beliefs to which all Muslims must adhere, it should not be considered a monolithic religion because Islamic norms and practices are not the same in all countries and at all times. Both the practical rule of the religion and its political theories have been subject to change according to changes in historical conditions. Even in the modern period, the Islamic movements have displayed considerable diversity. Therefore, understanding Islam in a given society not only requires a basic comprehension of its belief system but an adequate knowledge of the sociology of Islam as well—the specific social context that shapes its norms and practices. Modernism and fundamentalism are both Islamic responses to modernity. The differences in these responses, however, appear to have been a result of the differences in the sociopolitical and intellectual context in which they were produced. This is because Islamic norms and practices, like those of any other belief system, are influenced by other ideas currently dominant in the society, as well as by the sociopolitical context. Islamic modernist ideas developed around the turn of the century within the context of intellectual pluralism characterized by the presence of such diverse ideological movements as the Enlightenment, the Westernizers, and Christian missionaries, in interaction with the orthodox Islamic establishment. Islamic fundamentalism, on the other hand, emerged as a significant revolutionary movement after the 1950s. This movement emerged within a monolithic intellectual context where the society was under the control of a bureaucratic-authoritarian state. Given the market character of ideologies, the Islamic modernists were persuaded to develop moderate and eclectic interpretations of Islam because they were facing a plurality of arguments and criticisms. Islamic fundamentalism, on the other hand, was produced in reaction to the singular ideology of an intrusive state. This movement grew in such countries as Iran and Syria only after the state overthrew the existing political pluralism in society by systematically eliminating all oppositional political parties. In these societies, the state intervened not only in the economy but in cultural activities as well. With the suppression of all political parties, the state began to impose its own ideology on the society. As a result, oppositional politics were channeled through the medium of religion. Religious oppositional ideology emerged in direct reaction to the ideology of the state. Thus while the Islamic modernists were developing their ideas in relation to such diverse ideological groups as the Christian missionaries, the orthodox Islamic theologians, and the followers of the nineteenth-century Enlightenment, the Islamic oppositions from the 1960s on were facing only the all-encompassing ideology of the bureaucratic-authoritarian state. It this situation it is evident that a monolithic ideological context produced a monolithic religious movement—Islamic fundamentalism.

REFERENCES

Adami'yat, Fereydoun. 1976. *Idi'olozhi-ye Nahzat-i Mashrutiyat-i Iran* [*The Ideology of the Constitutional Movement in Iran*]. Tehran, Iran: Payam Publications.

Adams, Charles C. 1933. *Islam and Modernism in Egypt: A Study of the Modern Reform Movement Inaugurated by Muhammad 'Abduh.* New York: Russell and Russell.

Ahmad, Aziz. 1967. *Islamic Modernism in India and Pakistan, 1857–1964.* London: Oxford University Press.

Bahadur, Kalim. 1977. *The Jamma'at-i Islami of Pakistan: Political Thought and Political Action.* New Delhi: Chetana Publications.

Batatu, Hann. 1982. "Syria's Muslim Brethren." *MERIP Reports* (November–December): 12–34,36.

Butterworth, Charles E. 1982. "Prudence versus Legitimacy: The Persistent Theme in Islamic Political Thought." Pp. 84–114 in Ali E. Hillal Dessouki, *Islamic Resurgence in the Arab World.* New York: Praeger.

Gibb, Hamilton A. R. 1937. "Al-Mawardi's Theory of the Khilafah." *Islamic Culture* 11: 291–302.

Levy, Reuben. 1930. *An Introduction to the Sociology of Islam*. London: Williams and
    Norgate Limited.
Moaddel, Mansoor. 1989. "State-Centered vs. Class-Centered Perspectives in International
    Politics: The Case of U.S. and British Participation in the 1953 Coup against Premier
    Mosaddeq in Iran." *Studies in Comparative International Development* (Summer):3–22.
————. 1992. "Ideology as Episodic Discourse: The Case of the Iranian Revolution."
    American Sociological Review 57(3):353–379.
————. 1993. *Class, Politics, and Ideology in the Iranian Revolution*. New York: Columbia
    University Press.
Momen, Moojan 1985. *An Introduction to Shi'i Islam*. New Haven, CT: Yale University
    Press.
Rabinovich, Itamar. 1972. *Syria under the Ba'th, 1963–66*. Jerusalem: Israel Universities
    Press.
Rosenthal, Erwin I. J. 1958. *Political Thought in Medieval Islam: An Introductory Outline*.
    Cambridge: Cambridge University Press.
Sayyid Ahmad Khan. 1972. *Selected Essays by Sir Sayyid Ahmad Khan from the Journal
    Tahzib al-Akhlaq*. Translated by John Wilder. Unpublished M.A. thesis, Hartford Semi-
    nary, Hartford, CT.
Sayyid-Marsot, Afaf Lutfi. 1977. *Egypt's Liberal Experiment, 1922–1936*. Berkeley:
    University of California Press.
Seale, Patrick. 1965. *The Struggle for Syria: A Study of Post-War Arab Politics*. London:
    Oxford University Press.
Turner, Bryan S. 1978. *Weber and Islam: A Critical Study*. Boston: Routledge and Kegan
    Paul.

18

The Sanctified Church and the Color Line: Reorganization, Social Change, and the African American Religious Experience

Cheryl Townsend Gilkes

Religion is an important window through which to understand changes in the political economy and the social dislocations these changes create in people's lives. While change may be global in its connections and consequences, people experience change and crisis in the particularities of family, congregation, community, and society. The responses of particular peoples in particular places to the forces of dislocation and disruption can sometimes contribute to the repertoire of recovery and resistance for all of humanity. African Americans in the United States are a very small part of the world's population; they are a numerical and social minority within the United States. Yet the songs of African American religious life and political movements are sung around the world. Student activists in the People's Republic of China sang the civil rights anthem "We Shall Overcome," and mourners in Sweden sang the spiritual "Swing Low Sweet Chariot" at the site of their prime minister's assassination.

Black religion in the United States is a highly diverse phenomenon whose multiple contours have been shaped in response to and in spite of the violent dislocations of racial oppression: slavery, Reconstruction, the rise of racist legislation, migration, and ghettoization. Currently the fastest-growing segment of "the Black Church" is in that area traditionally called "the Sanctified Church" —predominantly black holiness and pentecostal denominations and congregations, exemplified according to Lincoln and Mamiya (1990:76–91) by the Church of God in Christ. Zora Neale Hurston (1981) pointed to the Sanctified Church as the locus of a revitalization and song-making movement that represented the reorganization of African and slave religions in the face of the anglicization of black America in the early twentieth century. Cheryl Sanders (1996:5) defined the Sanctified Church as "an African American Christian reform movement that seeks to bring its standards of worship, personal morality, and social concern into conformity with a biblical hermeneutic of holiness and spiritual empowerment." The Sanctified Church is all of that and more; it is the root of a complex, branching, and growing global phenomenon called "pentecostalism." According to Walter Hollenweger, a European historian of pentecostalism:

> The origins of the Pentecostal movement go back to a revival amongst the negroes [sic] of North America at the beginning of the present [twentieth] century. . . . Much more important, however, for the growth of the Pentecostal movement was its ability to make use of the North American negro's [sic] faculties of understanding and communicating by way of enthusiastic spiritual manifestations to build up a community and fellowship. These means of communications (hymns, speaking in tongues, dreams, spontaneous forms of worship) are of decisive importance in the Third World. (Hollenweger, 1972)

This chapter is about the connection between global oppression and a small community of souls, responding to the soul-shattering experiences engulfing their world. In the tradition of W. E. B. Du Bois (1975, 1989), I seek to describe and explain the Sanctified Church of the African American experience by connecting it to its historical antecedents of slavery and its aftermath. The history and importance of the Sanctified Church lies in the agency of an oppressed African American community as it reorganized its life in response to and in spite of the changing circumstances of racial oppression. Rather than viewing pentecostalism as a global social movement disconnected from the organizations, values, and sensibilities of the people who started it, this chapter seeks to reveal the ways in which the creativity and agency of a human group in defending, reorganizing, and reconfiguring its traditions shaped a central force of the late twentieth century with significant implications for the twenty-first. The Sanctified Church, the outgrowth of the "faith of the fathers" along what Du Bois called "the color line" represents a force at the foundation of the worldwide phenomenon of pentecostalism. The Sanctified Church, stereotyped as the province of the poor and the ignorant, provides, through its social witness, a model of response to injustice.

W. E. B. DU BOIS: WORLD CRISIS AND SOUL AGENCY

At the end of the nineteenth century, while looking forward to the twentieth, W. E. B. Du Bois observed, "The problem of the twentieth century is the problem of the color-line,—the relation of the darker to the lighter races of men in Asia and Africa, in America and the islands of the sea. It was a phase of this problem that caused the Civil War; . . . the question of Negro slavery was the real cause of the conflict." Du Bois recognized the interconnections between slaves in the United States and their descendants and a growing structure of international inequality. That structure of inequality was tied to the increased dependence of Europe, the homeland of "the lighter races," on the raw materials found in the lands of "the darker races." Du Bois's sociological studies had taught him that the discovery, exploration, imperialism, and colonialism that defined modernity had engendered forces in the world that connected the questions of race to the questions of world power. Not only were raw materials, such as cotton, important parts of this global inequality, but Du Bois recognized that the command of the labor of the peoples of "the darker races" was also involved. For Du Bois, the command of these peoples' labor and the violent destruction and disruption of their cultures represented a growing crisis that was only hinted at by the depth of violent struggle associated with but "a phase" of this problem, slavery in the United States.

Du Bois's observations about "the color line"—the nearly universal colonialism and labor exploitation of the modern world system—stand alongside his in-depth descriptions and analysis of its cultural, political, moral, and social consequences for black Americans in the United States. The system's assault on the humanity of African Americans fostered a duality, a "twoness," that represented not only a divided, marginalized, and alienated personage but also a double vision, a second sight, that was tantamount to the gift of ancient seers and prophets for divining and shaping the future. This global drama of the color line had soul-shattering implications. The responses of the soul represented in the sorrow songs and the religious life were the important consequences and notes of hope arising out of the travails of African Americans.

One of the most important responses to oppression devised by African Americans was their religious life, what Du Bois called "the faith of the fathers." He identified the elements of the religious life as a form of reorganized and revitalized memory that was used to assert the human presence of a dehumanized people. Black religion, with its pillars of leadership, music, and spiritual ecstasy—or "the Preacher, the Music, and the Frenzy"(Du Bois 1989:34)—represented a "gift" to the American experience that was a countervailing force to the basic inhumanity of the color line, globalized oppression, and its historical consequences.

Du Bois insisted, and rightly so, that the religious fervor and sensibilities of African Americans had shaped the religion of the United States, particularly with its distinctive emphasis on "the Spirit." Black religion was "not only a vital part of the history of the Negro in America, but no uninteresting part of American history" (Du Bois 1989:136).

THE SANCTIFIED CHURCH: DEFENDING THE SPIRIT AND THE SONG

At the time of Du Bois's observations, the Sanctified Church had not risen to prominence on the African American social landscape. According to Lincoln and Mamiya (1990:20), the prevalent religious experiences were "almost entirely Baptist and Methodist." Currently, the Baptists still dominate. The advent of the Holiness movement in African American communities occurred during the 1880s and the 1890s. The Pentecostal movement emerged in the early twentieth century. Some of the churches that emerged, especially the Church of God in Christ and the Church of Christ (Holiness), sprang from conflicts among African American Baptists over the appropriate doctrinal approaches to the Holy Spirit and the experience of sanctification. While the doctrinal histories associated with the churches in these movements point to the issues surrounding the Holy Spirit, the social histories of these churches are equally important and inextricably linked. The crises of the emancipation of the slaves, Reconstruction, and the end of Recon-struction prompted reflections upon traditional religious practices. These major social changes also necessitated a reorganization of religious life.

While emancipation was the most welcome event of the African American experience, it also precipitated a major social crisis. People sought to reconstitute their families and mend the intense disruptions of the last thirty years of slavery as this institution moved more deeply into the South and the West. Former slave masters sought to reinstitute oppressive forms of labor organization. These included tenant farming and sharecropping (Ransom and Sutch 1977) and the development of a penal system tailored to the exploitation of black labor through the use of chain gangs, portable cages, and the rental of individual farm laborers (Adamson 1983). This resulted in the separation of black communities, with families living on farms isolated from each other. As the federal presence was withdrawn from the South in the late 1870s, vigilante violence expelled African Americans from voter rolls and political offices. The elaborate legal structure known as Jim Crow followed, criminalizing intermarriage and requiring segrega-tion and separation in public accommodations, education, and other services; the Supreme Court affirmed the South's strategy in 1896. Black people adapted in order to resist and survive, and their churches were one of the spaces where they devised strategies and made choices about public and private actions.

Slave religion had emphasized the operation of the spirit in worship (Raboteau 1978; Webber 1978), and the efficacy of worship was measured by the "visible manifestation of God" called "shouting," without which "there could be no true communion with the Invisible" (Du Bois 1989: 135). It was precisely this emphasis that was soundly criticized by the black and white missionaries who descended on the South during and after the Civil War (Litwack 1979). These missionaries brought much-needed and -wanted education, but their criticisms of folk religion met with resistance. The emergence of Holiness and later pentecostal churches can be seen as cultural resistance to the pressures to "regularize" worship along more Euro-American lines.

The music of black churches also came under attack. Spirituals were considered to be slave ditties, and Baptist and Methodist churches sought to suppress this oral tradition. Bishop Daniel Payne of the African Methodist Episcopal (A.M.E.) Church tried to eliminate the traditional religion, but he found pastors who informed him that the music tradition was essential to fostering the presence of the Spirit. As some of the mainstream churches pushed education, the emergence of formally organized choirs demanded literacy from their members and further suppressed the widespread participation of "the folk." Holiness churches and mainstream churches that successfully retained their traditions, largely rural churches, continued to sing the old songs. As their members carried these rural song traditions into the North, they found themselves more welcome in the urban churches where the members were "Sanctified."

There were distinctive beliefs and practices associated with the African American religion of the Spirit that were also considered deviant within main-stream Protestantism. Black churches during slavery had nurtured a wide variety of lay leaders, including women preachers, worship leaders, and prayer warriors. Although Du Bois identified "the preacher" as an essential element of black religion, that category might be best expanded to describe indigenous or organic leadership. Sometimes these leaders were women. Activities considered the province of priests in the Anglican, Methodist, and Catholic traditions, such as leading prayers, anointing with oil, and laying on hands for healing, were activities associated with whomever God chose to endow with those gifts, a continuity of African traditional beliefs that acknowledged women as priestesses and spiritual practitioners. The churches that emerged during the Holiness and later Pentecostal movements supported the ministries of women and provided opportunities for them to preach. Baptist and Methodist churches often barred women from pulpits, allowing them roles only as teachers, missionaries, and evangelists.

Some segments of the Sanctified Church sought to challenge racist presumptions at the same time they defended those elements of spirituality that caused them to be demeaned and dismissed. Like members of the mainstream churches, men and women of the Sanctified Church, especially women, participated in what Higginbotham (1993) has identified as "the politics of respectability"—a subversion of the politics of white supremacy through public presentations of self and educational aspirations. Although they successfully defended the ecstatic dimensions of religious practice, they also sought to exercise the image of discipline that came with dress and other forms of public participation—to show that there was not "just ardor but order." Yet they consistently criticized the excesses that a politics of respectability could elicit—the elitism and the colorism that were to become the focus of criticism in E. Franklin Frazier's (1957) critiques of upper- and middle-class African Americans.

Because black churches were forced to defend their practices in language that mainstream Christians would accept, biblically based arguments emerged to defend the emphasis on the Spirit and the accompanying practices of shouting and holy dancing. The white supremacists of the South sometimes poked fun at black worship traditions in order to strengthen their arguments in favor of segregation and subordination. The Holiness movement actively challenged this racism in practice and ideas. Black preachers like Amanda Berry Smith forced white worshipers to reckon with their prejudice in order to achieve the blessings of sanctification. Camp meetings were dependent upon black participation to draw larger crowds, and black spirituality shaped this growing movement. Sometimes black and white "saints" would insist upon sharing pulpits and choirs together, eliciting violent reactions from the Ku Klux Klan.

The biblical defenses of black worship traditions opened the door for a range of questions from black people about the appropriateness of white religious ideologies that supported racism. Increasingly, the defenses of traditional spirituality among African Americans provided the foundation for challenges to the white racial hegemony of southern Christianity. Several denominations were founded by leaders whose explicit criticisms of racism and the sexual exploitation of black women made them the targets of violence. William Christian, the founder of the Church of the Living God, Christian Workers for Fellowship, was actually jailed for preaching against the exploitation of black women; he also pointed to the African origins of biblical characters in order to foster pride and self-respect. The challenge to racial supremacy sometimes led to other areas of political criticism. Church leaders like C. H. Mason were openly critical of the global politics of the early twentieth century, particularly World War I.

The growth of the Sanctified Church was quickened by the move to southern towns and cities, where African Americans went in order to escape the violence and humiliations of rural life. Many of these churches' early male leaders shared testimonies of escapes from near lynchings and other forms of violence. Women who followed urban trends in women's work often preached revivals, "dug out" churches, and then called male pastors from their home communities. Deliverance from the tragedies of rural southern life defined the spiritual biographies of church members. Overall, the new churches addressed both sufferings and aspirations for change while providing settings where the community coped with and interpreted their experiences.

AZUSA STREET AND THE GLOBALIZATION
OF BLACK SPIRITUALITY

One of the most significant developments in the history of the Sanctified Church was its role in producing and sustaining the Azusa Street Revival, the originating event in the emergence of pentecostalism. The vast majority of churches that call themselves pentecostal trace their origins to a three-year revival in Los Angeles, California. This revival, which lasted from 1906 to 1909, attracted international attention because, during the period considered to be "the nadir" of American race relations—when the forces of segregation were achieving their greatest momentum—reporters witnessed people of all colors, national origins, and races worshiping together because of the power of the Holy Spirit.

Questions about the person, office, and work of the Holy Spirit in the church were not new. The split between the Eastern and Western churches in Europe was prompted by disagreement over the Holy Spirit. The Protestant Reformation generated an atmosphere wherein numerous communities of faith were moved to question traditions through a combination of biblical insight and spiritual awakening. The Holiness movement in the United States had built on that combination. As this country moved into the twentieth century, the idea of movement and progress that was alive throughout the society was already shaping a group within churches that was seeking a more authentic and doctrinally correct relationship with the Holy Spirit. African Americans, having developed a tradition of biblically grounded apologetics for their spirituality, were poised to play a significant role in the new movements that addressed the role and importance of the Spirit in the churches.

Although white American historians of pentecostalism usually name Charles Parham as the originating leader of the pentecostal movement, the Azusa Street Revival is the event that gave rise to the movement. Led by William Seymour, a black Holiness preacher who articulated the doctrine of speaking in tongues, the

Azusa Street revival began after he was ejected from a Holiness church by the black woman pastor who disagreed with his doctrinal preaching. (Holiness people do not reject speaking in tongues, but they do not believe that it is the essential evidence of a person's sanctification.) After moving to a house on Bonnie Brae Street, Seymour's group organized a prayer meeting. Their ecstatic worship caused the house to collapse, and they subsequently moved to an abandoned A.M.E. church on Azusa Street. Since Los Angeles was a magnet for immigrants from east, west, and south, the Azusa Street Revival attracted a highly diverse following for the three years of its existence.

Members of the newly formed Church of God in Christ traveled from Memphis, Tennessee, to attend the revival. They found a space that was very familiar where the manifestations of the spirit matched that with which they were familiar in their churches of Mississippi, Tennessee, Arkansas, and the rest of the South. Although pentecostal manifestations of the spirit are doctrinally mandated as speaking in tongues, the African American perspective embraced a broader range of behaviors as evidence for being "saved and sanctified, Holy Ghost filled, and fire baptized"—from incomprehensible communication between the worshiper and God (speaking in tongues) to tears, dancing, upraised hands, and testimonies about the impact of the spirit on experience. The folk perspective accommodating this diversity was often expressed in this way:

> Some folks get happy, they run;
> Others speak in an unknown tongue;
> Some cry out in a spiritual trance;
> Others get happy and do the holy dance.

What the visitors from Memphis witnessed was a scene of highly intense African American traditional worship involving people from around the world. Not only were "the Music" and "the Frenzy" present, but so was the indigenous, organic leadership of the African American preacher. The sources of disagreements among the delegation from the Church of God in Christ were purely doctrinal. They had attended a religious meeting where language and other behaviors mirrored the language and behaviors back home. For whites, the revival represented a doctrinal, theological, and behavioral departure, and they reported it as such. Charles Parham, the purported hero of the movement, came to Azusa Street and rejected it as "a darkies' camp meeting." The Africanist presence was eventually masked, silenced, and denigrated; white ministers who had turned to C. H. Mason, the presiding bishop of a reorganized and *pentecostal* Church of God in Christ, seeking ordination and recognition eventually formed their own churches. White pentecostals divorced themselves from their African American origins and in so doing accommodated to racism. The Pentecostal movement in the United States had begun as a multiracial religious movement with the potential for embracing a radical Christian interracialism, thus challenging the most critical and enduring moral challenge to American society, its racism. Ironically, pentecostalism's Africanist roots are precisely the defining power that pentecostal historians outside of the United States recognize and embrace as its enduring strength and global appeal.

CONCLUSION

Walter Hollenweger's earlier-quoted observation that the global Pentecostal movement depended upon the Africanist roots of pentecostalism points to the importance of "the faith of the fathers [and mothers]" that Du Bois observed to be the creative reorganization and elaboration of African religious foundations. The religion that black people in the United States had devised, this manifestation of the "souls of black folk," was a religion that had enabled a people to resist the material and psychic destruction aimed at their lives. The true gift of pentecostalism is the production of a religion that has enabled people simply to resist being crushed. The discovery of pentecostalism and charismatic religion by the bourgeois mainstream in America and the rest of the First World masks the importance of this gift in an obsession with doctrine, theology, and dogma. The peoples of the Third World understand and affirm what Africans encountering Christianity in North America understood and affirmed so long ago—the power of the spirit to strengthen, restore, heal, and empower in all of the diverse and sundry ways that the oppressed may need.

W. E. B. Du Bois understood profoundly, in a way that we can only begin to appreciate at the turn of the twenty-first century, that the peoples on the underside of an oppressive global economy represent the most important hope for subverting forces of destruction. The religion of the Spirit is the locus of cultural agency. Marx talked about the role of religion in a spiritless situation, but the social, ecological, political, economic, and cultural consequences of colonialism, conquest, and enslavement have been aggressively soul-*shattering* throughout the world. pentecostalism's global appeal is the power of the Spirit to re-gather and re-member that which has been shattered and trampled. Aime Cesaire (1955), describing the horrific power of colonialism in the Third World, spoke passionately of the nations, cultures, and gods trampled underfoot and destroyed by the forces of Europe and America. The Sanctified Church's gift to the world—this diverse, maligned, and ignored institution that grew up in the midst of "a phase" of an inequitous world system, "the color line"—was and remains the constant affirmation of the resurrecting, healing, bracing, and empowering role of the Spirit and its ability to enable resistance to the destructiveness of global inequality.

REFERENCES

Adamson, Christopher R. 1983. "Punishment After Slavery: Southern State Penal Systems, 1865–1890." *Social Problems* 30(5):555–569.
Cesaire, Aime. 1972 [1955]. *Discourse on Colonialism*. New York: Monthly Review Press.
Du Bois, W. E. B. 1989 [1903]. *The Souls of Black Folk*. New York: Bantam Doubleday Dell.
———. 1975 [1924]. *The Gift of Black Folk*. Millwood, NY: Kraus-Thomson Organization Limited.

Jones, C. E. 1988. "Holiness Movement." Pp. 406–409 in Stanley M. Burgess and Gary B. McGee (eds.), *Dictionary of Pentecostal and Charismatic Movements*. Grand Rapids, MI: Zondervan Publishing House.

Frazier, E. Franklin. 1957. *The Black Bourgeoisie: The Rise of a New Middle Class*. Glencoe, IL: Free Press.

Higginbotham, Evelyn Brooks. 1993. *Righteous Discontent: The Women's Movement in the Black Baptist Church, 1880–1920*. Cambridge: Harvard University Press.

Hollenweger, Walter J. 1972. *The Pentecostals*. Minneapolis: Augsburg Publishing House.

Hurston, Zorah Neale. 1981. *The Sanctified Church*. Berkeley, CA: Turtle Island Press.

Lincoln, C. Eric, and Lawrence H. Mamiya. 1990. *The Black Church in the African American Experience*. Durham, NC: Duke University Press.

Litwack, Leon F. 1979. *Been in the Storm So Long: The Aftermath of Slavery*. New York: Vintage Books.

Lovett, Leonard. 1988. "Black Holiness-Pentecostalism." Pp. 76–84 in Stanley M. Burgess and Gary B. McGee (eds.), *Dictionary of Pentecostal and Charismatic Movements*. Grand Rapids, MI: Zondervan Publishing House.

Raboteau, Albert J. 1978. *Slave Religion: The Invisible Institution in the Antebellum South*. New York: Oxford University Press.

Ransom, Roger, and Richard Sutch. 1977. *One Kind of Freedom*. New York: Cambridge University Press.

Sanders, Cheryl J. 1996. *Saints in Exile: The Holiness-Pentecostal Experience in African American Religion and Culture*. New York: Oxford University Press.

Webber, Thomas L. 1978. *Deep Like the Rivers: Education in the Slave Quarter Community, 1831-1865*. New York: W. W. Norton and Company.

19

Beating Back the Enemy: How Venezuelan Pentecostals Think about Social Change

David A. Smilde

INTRODUCTION

Since the 1960s, Latin America has been the site of dramatic growth of Protestant pentecostalism. A common view of this religion is that it is an "opiate of the masses" that provides refuge for people who are poor and alienated from society. However, social scientists have recently been criticizing this view. While these researchers concede that pentecostals do not usually participate in what is normally considered "politics," they argue that pentecostalism has political consequences insofar as it creates new cultural expectations, social spaces, and forms of community (Levine 1995; Smith 1994; Martin 1990; Lancaster 1986; Stoll 1990; Burdick 1993; Levine and Stoll 1997). But given that pentecostalism emphasizes individual morality and salvation, how are we to understand these "political" consequences? Is this simply a case of unintended consequences? Or do Latin American pentecostals themselves think about the larger social[1] world and their role in social change?

To answer this question, I will present data from in-depth interviews with Venezuelan pentecostals, regarding their view of social problems and of their own engagement in social change. Before doing so, however, I will briefly introduce pentecostalism in its Venezuelan context and review the methodology of the study.

PENTECOSTALISM IN THE VENEZUELAN CONTEXT

Since the early to middle 1980s, Venezuela, one of the leading exporters of oil to the United States, has been besieged by economic and political problems. Low oil prices have resulted in a serious economic crisis, high-level corruption has come to dominate media reports, poverty has more than doubled, and crime rates have greatly increased. These problems are felt not only in their concrete material effects but also as challenges to patterns of cultural understanding and social behavior. Pentecostalism is one of a variety of responses to these problems.

In the pentecostal meaning system, the supernatural order of existence contains good and evil beings: on the one hand, the Holy Trinity in the form of the Father, the Son, and the Holy Spirit and the angels under their command, and on the other, the Devil and his supporting cast of demons. These "supernatural agents" have the ability to act within the present, observable universe, and life here on Earth corresponds to this division. One is either "in the way of the Lord" or "in the world." If one is "in the world," one lives "in the flesh," freely engaging in sin and pursuing "worldly concerns," that is, material and status interests rather than spiritual concerns. In the Venezuelan pentecostal view, this results in alienation from God. It creates a spiritual void that is promptly filled by Satan. "The Enemy" takes control of one's life and uses one to do evil, leading to conflict, suffering, and pain for others and (usually) for oneself. In addition, those outside of God's path may be directly harmed by Satan, or subjected to God's wrath if He decides to "claim His proper place."

If one is "in the way of the Lord," on the other hand, one lives "in the spirit," avoiding "sins" such as marital infidelity, smoking, gambling, conflict, cheating, and, most important, consumption of alcohol. One must congregate with other Christians to praise the Lord, read the Bible, bring the word to those who "don't know the Lord," and engage in activities that continually renew and maintain the connection to God, such as prayer, vigil,[2] and fasting. When the Christian does these things, pentecostals believe that God protects him or her from the Devil, controls his or her life either directly or by communicating His will to the individual, and blesses him or her directly, resulting in well-being, peace, and happiness.

METHOD

The data used in this article come from ethnographic interviews I carried out as part of fieldwork with Venezuelan pentecostals in 1994. I designed the questions to get respondents to express their view of their own involvement in social change, after listening to and participating in many informal conversations on these issues. Thus the questions employ terms and concepts from the respondents' own sociocultural context.

In total, I carried out thirty in-depth interviews in two different cities of Venezuela: La Lajita,[3] a fishing city of around 100,000 on the Caribbean coast in one of the poorest regions of Venezuela, and Montilla, a commercial center of around 120,000 in an agricultural region of the heavily Catholic Andes. I attempted to interview a variety of active pentecostal members from seven different churches. Seventeen of the interviews were conducted in La Lajita and thirteen in Montilla, fifteen with men and fifteen with women. Members from all different age groups and from recent convert to long-time pastor were interviewed. All but a couple of the respondents were inhabitants of the *barrios*, that is, the informal neighborhoods that surround Latin American cities and provide the majority of pentecostals throughout the region.

Before looking at the data it is important to reflect on what it can and cannot tell us. First, no data are presented regarding what pentecostals actually *do*. The questions used merely draw out the way respondents *think* about social problems and social change. Nevertheless, understanding the inner logic of the pentecostal meaning system can help us interpret existing research on pentecostals' engagement in social change. Second, the questions explicitly aim to draw out the *this-worldly* aspects of the pentecostal meaning system. They cannot, therefore, be used to determine the relative importance of this-worldly goals versus *other-worldly* goals (such as salvation in the afterlife). Nevertheless, the articulate and lucid manner in which these pentecostals present their ideas should demonstrate that, at minimum, these issues are frequently considered. Finally, the data are not comparative. They provide insight *only* on pentecostals. While the results easily lend themselves to comparison with other religious manifestations in Latin America, adequately doing so would require further empirical research.

THE VENEZUELAN PENTECOSTAL VIEW OF SOCIAL CHANGE

The Source of Social Problems and the Role of the Believer

The perception of the current social situation among Venezuelans of the poorer classes is that the rewards one receives have little to do with how hard one works (Briceño-Leon 1990) and that the principal cause of the current crisis is the misadministration and pilfering of Venezuelan oil and mineral resources by corrupt politicians (Briceño-Leon 1990; Levine 1994). Venezuelan pentecostals share this view, and the following question takes it as given in order to get at respondents' framing of the *source* of these problems. "We know that there is a lot of injustice in the world. There are rich people that never work and poor people who work all day long. And there are politicians that do nothing more than rob the people of their money. Why is the world this way?"

The respondents generally attributed the current condition to the separation from God. "There is a lot of injustice in the world because there is a people without Christ," said Carlos, a traveling evangelist who has been a pentecostal for seven years. Carmen, a wife and mother of two children who has been pentecostal for almost twenty years, said "He [Man] has deviated from His [God's] path and his [man's] heart has grown hard and he has grown indifferent to others. It doesn't matter to him whether others are or are not needy." Alba, a seventeen-year-old woman asserted that the world is the way it is "because men have tried to do it themselves. We should let God govern." Mariela, a twenty-eight-year-old wife and mother of two, explained exactly what happens when one is separated from God.

I would say that it is because of man's disobedience, because he hasn't wanted to follow God. . . . He has separated from the Way of God. He hasn't listened. So, since the devil goes around looking for who to devour, since he came to destroy and kill, that's what happens. He takes control of these persons that have separated from God and uses them. Then come injustice and sin, then comes robbery, then come all those things. Because if the world followed God, it would change from its wrong path, there wouldn't be injustice and corruption.

Venezuelan pentecostalism, then, contains a theory of how social problems occur—because people do not follow the Way of God. This theory, in turn, frames pentecostals' sense of how *they* can change current conditions. I asked each respondent: "What should the Christian do about injustice?" Mireya, a twenty-three-year-old woman who has dedicated her life to church work, responded as follows:

[Christ] says, "You are the light of the world. A city on a hill cannot hide, nor does one put a lamp underneath the bed. Rather you put it high so that it lights all those who are in darkness." With this He wants to say that we should preach the Gospel, that we should preach the Word to beat back the Enemy. We preach in order to get people out of the injustice they are in. Because it is a job God has given us.

Fernando, a pentecostal for eight months, said:

God has given us a powerful weapon to work against injustice, it is the Word of God, preaching the news. We, as knowers of the Word know that these things are happening because of the dominion of the Enemy, because of disobedience to God, because of Sin. . . . We should preach that God does not like the things that they [non-Christians] do, that they are disobedient before God. We should take them the message of God, to put them on the right path, which is Jesus Christ.

Such a course of action is a logical derivative of the view of the source of social problems. Insofar as the problems that beset the contemporary world have to do with wrong relations between the unconverted and supernatural agents, the most logical response is to attempt to correct these relations. Within this view, by "preaching the Word" one can make the unconverted aware of the behavior that is putting them into the hands of "the Enemy" and raising God's ire, and get them to engage in the action that will place them under the agency of God and thereby remove them from the injustice they are suffering or causing others to suffer.

Reina explained in concrete terms how this could happen. She had been telling me how she often wondered how there could be so much poverty in the world amid so much wealth.

I say to God, "Why don't you touch these people? Touch their hearts so that they can help the poor." But then we see that behind this who is plotting is Satan. He has made man's heart like it is. And that's why sin has increased and the world is like it is. God doesn't want this anymore. The true idea of God is unity, peace, love, that we all love each other. And that is the function of all of us as the people, the Church of God, to spread the Gospel, the Word of salvation, the Word of love. So that people come to the way of God. And he who is bad, let God renew him and make him a good creature, beautiful and full of love.

Involvement in Secular Social Action

While Latin American pentecostals have often been viewed as apolitical, recent research has shown that this view is exaggerated (Garrard-Burnett and Stoll 1993; Cleary and Stewart-Gambino 1997). I asked the respondents, Can a Christian form part of the government, as a senator, judge, or mayor? A couple of them indeed answered in the negative. "I don't agree with that [pentecostals participating in politics], in my personal opinion. Maybe it is because in this country there is so much corruption that it makes me fear that an *hermano*[4] is going to become contaminated," said Dalia, a twenty-two-year-old woman who has been a pentecostal for almost two years and teaches Sunday school. Flor, a thirty-five-year-old mother of two and pentecostal for three years, responded, "It's not good for a Christian to be involved in politics because then he would be more dedicated to politics. . . . He would apply himself to solving the problems of others, and he would forget about God." Thus the primary concerns are that such activity would involve an hermano in corruption or lead him or her away from concentrating on what is really relevant, his or her dedication to the Lord. Such concern is perfectly logical if the world's problems derive from separation from God. Becoming involved in politics only to lose focus on God or be swept into corruption would be like cutting off one's head to stop a bloody nose.

Most respondents, however, acknowledged the danger while supporting, with varying degrees of enthusiasm, pentecostal involvement in politics. Fernando said: "I am totally for this idea. The Christian can [engage in politics] as long as he doesn't participate in acts of corruption." María acknowledges the danger of politics but says it can be done by those who are mature in their faith. "[Participating in politics], if the person is not well with God, corrupts. You have to be really firm with God."

The same religious priorities guide the potential political activities these pentecostals imagine. Beyond generally looking for political patronage for fellow hermanos, they either would try to evangelize politicians and the public sphere or work politically to facilitate their evangelistic goals. Elena, a pastor's wife, said, "Why not form part, we as the people of God, of the Mayoralty, the State government, [or be a] Deputy in the Legislative Assembly or in the Senate? This is our purpose now, to become involved with them [those in politics] in one way or another to preach them the Gospel."

Mariela points out that a Christian might be able to remedy the corruption of the political system. "Why not? Yes he can, because that Christian is illuminating within the darkness, where there is so much corruption. Since this person is driven by God, he can see to it that, despite the corruption, there can be change." Fabio, who works as an office assistant in the state government, argues that involvement in politics could be useful for pentecostals:

> Yes, the Christian should participate in the things of government. Not in corruption; the government is always full of corruption, but rather to do good for the people, above all for Christians who are forgotten by the government. It would be good for

hermanos, Christians, to become advisors, become mayors, governors, the head of neighborhood associations. Because tomorrow [for example], we might arrive to ask for a permit and we would have open doors.

The permit he mentions refers to the permission pentecostals must obtain, often with difficulty, from municipal governments to hold their outdoor campaigns. Having political power and connections would be useful, in his view, not only to do good for the people (especially hermanos) but also because it could facilitate what is really relevant, the task of evangelization.

To further examine the Venezuelan pentecostal meaning system, I tried to portray as against God's will an event to which I knew these pentecostals would be largely opposed: the government's kicking people out of their self-constructed shacks (*ranchos*) and destroying them. The intention was to see if the pentecostal meaning system contained resources for religiously motivated, radical social action against something they define as sinful. I asked the following question: What should a Christian do if the government is acting clearly against the will of God, for example if the National Guard came and started knocking down ranchos? Could a Christian go out and join a demonstration?

Several respondents referred to Romans 13 in the Bible to point out that pentecostals can defend their rights (see Burdick 1993; Stoll 1990). Carlos, the traveling evangelist, said, "Some people think that they can do whatever they please with pentecostals, that we aren't going to look for problems. But if it goes against what the law says we protect ourselves because it is the Bible that imposes the law." However, there was a general reticence towards joining a demonstration. Reina recalled how this had happened near where she lived and explained how she just prayed.

What I did was pray, pray and plead with God: 'God have mercy.'

A Christian shouldn't do these things, like demonstrate?

I believe not, because we would be giving a bad testimony. People wouldn't see this as an act of justice, that we are trying to defend these people being thrown out of their ranchos, but rather they are going to see it like "look, she is disorderly, and she thinks she's an evangelical."

She explained further, saying, "We Christians shouldn't participate in certain things that would then bring us difficulties in our spiritual lives."

The predominant answer was that a pentecostal should defend his or her rights not through demonstration or violence but rather by appealing to the proper authorities in an "appropriate" fashion. The metaphor of "orderliness" is often used. Fernando answered, "The Bible says no, because we have to act decently and with order because we are light within the darkness and we are different from those who are outside. . . . If this happened the ideal would be for us to form a group and go and protest as a help to those people, but in an orderly way, not disorderly. We are called to this, to be orderly before the eyes of others." Carmen more explicitly explains why pentecostals should not participate in demonstrations:

There are other means, such as going to an authority who has power, making a change that could be beneficial. But going out to demonstrate and fight doesn't accomplish anything.

But sometimes it works. If the government is afraid of a demonstration they might say, "Okay we're not going to knock down those ranchos because the people are demonstrating." In that sense it might work. So I'm asking if, in your opinion, Christians couldn't demonstrate in such a way.

I don't think so, because those are the weapons of darkness, and I don't have any reason to share in violence, because then I fall away from my mandate in which one would think that I would want to share the kingdom of peace; and God is peace, joy, and love. Violence, destruction, and death is of the Enemy, the kingdom of darkness. Thus I cannot participate in violence.

As can be seen, even when I tried to present how the ends might justify the means, Carmen did not agree. As in the case of having a political position, within the pentecostal view, participation is permissible as long as it does not mean falling away from one's mandate and into the "kingdom of darkness."

CONCLUSION

In conclusion, we can see that pentecostals do care about social problems. They explain them as a result of people having turned their backs on God, and they try to resolve these problems by converting non-Christians. They are willing to participate in politics, as long as they can avoid corruption. However, the political participation pentecostals themselves imagine usually amounts to evangelizing "those in power," moralizing the political sphere, or politically facilitating the advancement of the Gospel. This makes sense given their view that the best way to change society is to bring individuals into proper relationship with God. Furthermore, they can defend their rights through legitimate channels, but shy away from raucous demonstrations that could become violent or "disorderly."

Thus Venezuelan pentecostals want to change the problematic social conditions that surround them but attempt to do so *indirectly*, by "beating back the Enemy" and facilitating the agency of God in "this world." The attempt to *directly* change the social structures of this world in accordance with spiritual and ethical values, another possibility within Christian social ethics (represented in Latin America by progressive Catholic movements), receives little consideration.

NOTES

A longer, slightly different version of this chapter will appear in *Sociology of Religion* (Vol. 59, No. 3), Copyright © 1998, Association for the Sociology of Religion, Inc.; used with permission. The research on which it was based was conducted while the author was on an International Pre-dissertation Fellowship from the Social Science Research Council with funds from the Ford Foundation and the American Council of Learned Societies.

1. To avoid confusion, I will use the term "social" and its derivatives rather than the expanded sense of the term "political." I will confine the term "political" and its derivatives to the more conventional sense of "relating to government."

2. Vigil is the practice of staying awake through the night, either alone or in groups, to pray and share testimonies.

3. Out of respect for the confidentiality of the respondents, pseudonyms are used for all people and places.

4. *Hermano* means brother in Spanish. It is the most common term used by Venezuelan pentecostals to refer to fellow believers.

REFERENCES

Briceño-Leon, Roberto. 1990. *Los Efectos Perversos del Petróleo*. Caracas: Editorial Acta Científica y Conscio de Ediciones Capriles.

Burdick, John. 1993. *Looking for God in Brazil*. Berkeley and Los Angeles: University of California Press.

Cleary, Edward L., and Hannah W. Stewart-Gambino (eds.). 1997. *Power, Politics, and Pentecostals in Latin America*. Boulder, CO: Westview Press.

Garrard-Burnett, Virginia, and David Stoll (eds.). 1993. *Rethinking Protestantism in Latin America*. Philadelphia: Temple University Press.

Lancaster, Roger. 1986. *Thanks to God and the Revolution*. New York: Columbia University Press.

Levine, Daniel. 1994. "Good-bye to Venezuelan Exceptionalism." *Journal of Interamerican Studies and World Affairs* 36:145–182.

———. 1995. "Protestants and Catholics in Latin America: A Family Portrait." In Martin Marty and Scott Appleby (eds.), *Fundamentalisms Comprehended*. Chicago: University of Chicago Press.

Levine, Daniel, and David Stoll. 1997. "Bridging the Gap between Empowerment and Power in Latin America." Pp. 63–103 in Susanne Hoeber Rudolph and James Piscatori (eds.), *Fading States and Transnational Religious Regimes*. Boulder, CO: Westview Press.

Martin, David. 1990. *Tongues of Fire: The Explosion of Protestantism in Latin America*. Oxford: Basil Blackwell.

Smith, Christian. 1994. "The Spirit and Democracy: Base Communities, Protestantism, and Democratization in Latin America." *Sociology of Religion* 55(2):119–143.

Stoll, David. 1990. *Is Latin America Turning Protestant?* Berkeley: University of California Press.

20

Religion and Social Activism: The Grassroots Catholic Church in Brazil

Madeleine Cousineau

Religion is the sigh of the oppressed creature, the heart of a heartless world, just as it is the spirit of a spiritless situation. It is the opium of the people.

—Karl Marx
Contribution to the Critique of Hegel's
Philosophy of Right, Introduction

With these words, written in 1844, Karl Marx dismissed the possibility that religion could serve as a force for social change. The oppressed may sigh at their misfortune, but religion will produce in them a druglike state that will remove the desire to become involved in any kind of activism.

This was not, however, the end of the sociological discussion on this matter. About seventy years later Max Weber pointed out that religion has a prophetic aspect. He noted that the Biblical prophets issued challenges to the authorities of their times, demanding social justice (Weber 1963:50). According to a recent interpretation of Weber's theory, religious movements may also be considered prophetic, if these movements are critical of the established order (Maduro 1982: 106–107).

While Marx may not have been entirely wrong in his assessment of religion, since in many situations it does encourage conformity to the existing order, there are other situations that lend support to Weber's view. In my research on the Roman Catholic Church in Brazil, I have found evidence of a prophetic movement in the form of base communities (in Portuguese *comunidades eclesiais de base*, or CEBs). These are groups of lay people who organize their own religious practices in the absence of priests. Lay leaders direct Sunday worship and provide instruction for people preparing for sacraments, such as baptism and marriage. They organize Bible groups whose members interpret Scripture in a way that leads them to take a critical look at the situations in which they live. Since the majority of people in Latin America live in poverty, this critical look often leads CEB members to engage in activism around such issues as housing, sanitation, health care, child care, labor, and land reform.

Before describing how the base communities developed and what forces are now challenging their continued role as sources of social activism, I would like to point out that social change is never the main purpose of religion. Its purpose is to help people relate to the transcendent, which in the Western world we call "God." The question of whether religion promotes change or persuades people to support the status quo is secondary from the point of view of religious people, although it is important to sociologists. In other words, change or conformity is what *also* happens when people are going about their religious business.

Specific sociological circumstances determine whether religion will encourage believers to be quiet or to shake up their society. Meredith McGuire (1997:248–256) has outlined four factors: the quality of belief and practices, the cognitive framework of the culture, the social location of religion, and the internal structure of religious organizations. I will describe each of these factors as it relates to the Catholic Church in Brazil.

The quality of belief and practices. For religion to serve as a catalyst for social change, it is helpful if the belief system provides a critical standard against which the existing society can be measured. Members of base communities find that critical standard in the prophetic passages of the Bible. Their belief system defines the existing society as unjust, as something that Christians should work to change.

The cognitive framework of the culture. In order to influence people to work for change, religion has to be central to the way people think. Otherwise, they will find some other stimulus for their activism. Catholicism has definitely influenced Brazilian culture. This influence is seen in customs such as church feasts, processions, devotion to saints, and religious references in everyday language.

The social location of religion. There need to be ties between religion and other social institutions. Historically the Catholic Church in Brazil was thoroughly involved in politics, education, health care, and the system of land holding. Although this relationship has changed with modernization, the ties between religion and other social institutions have not been completely dissolved.

The internal structure of religious organizations. Ordinary church members must have access to religious power. A key characteristic of CEBs is that they are led by lay people. This experience gives the laity the sense that they are important in the church. They transfer their sense of religious power to political participation.

My field research leads me to add a fifth factor to McGuire's list. This factor has been suggested by the Latin American sociologist Otto Maduro (1982:136), who combines Marx's theory of revolution with Weber's insights about the social role of religion. Maduro points out that for religion to serve a revolutionary role, there need to be objective conditions in the larger society that make it possible for people of the poorer classes to become organized. We may refer to these conditions as a *revolutionary situation.* This does not necessarily mean that there must be a violent uprising, but rather that a large number of poor people become conscious of the need to transform social structures. There are places in Brazil where CEBs are having a visible impact on social activism. There are others where they continue their religious activities but do not show evidence of trying to change society. The difference is in the political context of the region in which the CEBs are located.

I have conducted research both in rural areas of the Amazon and in an urban area near Rio de Janeiro and I did find important differences in the political context, as will be shown later. In the Amazon I interviewed 107 people, including members of CEBs, priests, religious sisters, and nonreligious activists. My research in urban communities is still in progress, with twenty-seven interviews conducted so far. Before discussing the present situation I will briefly describe the process by which the church in Brazil developed the potential for encouraging social activism. Then I will draw on my research in the Amazon as an illustration of a revolutionary situation and contrast it with my findings in urban communities.

THE PREFERENTIAL OPTION FOR THE POOR

About thirty years ago the Brazilian bishops took an official position on the side of social justice, calling this position "the preferential option for the poor." The bishops did not begin by encouraging social change. In fact, their position could be defined as a defensive one, a reaction against change. They were trying to preserve the influence of the church over society in the face of new developments. At that time the Cuban revolution was recent, and past experience had shown that Communist regimes tended to oppose religion. In the Northeast region of Brazil there was a growing peasant movement that had been organized by a socialist lawyer with strong sympathies toward Cuba. The bishops, concerned that peasants who joined this movement would leave the church, organized their own rural movement. They encouraged the formation of Catholic peasant unions, literacy projects, and other programs to improve the lives of the poor, in a way attempting to beat the Communists at their own game. Around this same time the bishops were becoming worried about the missionary efforts of Protestant pentecostals, who were converting large numbers of people. The shortage of Catholic priests was making it difficult to respond to this challenge. So the bishops began to encourage lay people to organize their own religious activities. They subdivided large parishes, building chapels where lay leaders could conduct Sunday worship without priests. These two measures—social programs and village chapels—came together in the formation of base communities. By 1970 religious writers were beginning to express the church's new position in the form of liberation theology (see Gutierrez 1973). This theology made a connection between spiritual salvation and social justice. It encouraged poor people to struggle to change society and challenged people of more privileged classes to join in solidarity with their struggle.

As the preferential option for the poor became established as church policy, it moved the church beyond the original defensive motives of some of the bishops. Nevertheless, the new view was not shared by all Catholics. There were clergy and lay people who believed that the church should concern itself only with religious matters and that advocating social justice was "too political." In the 1980s the more conservative forces within Brazilian Catholicism began to gain the upper hand.

FORCES OF CHANGE AND RESISTANCE

The main policy-making body for the Roman Catholic Church in Brazil is the National Conference of the Brazilian Bishops (CNBB). Most of its members are neither conservative nor progressive, but "moderate"—that is, open to limited changes within the church but not actively pushing for change. They tend to follow the lead of the bishops they elect to govern the CNBB. During the 1960s, 1970s, and 1980s, a small group of progressive bishops was influential because they often held the highest elected positions. However, by the 1990s there was a shift in the church. The Vatican, led by Pope John Paul II, silenced some of the liberation theologians, accusing them of expressing ideas contrary to Catholic teachings. The Vatican also began to appoint more conservative bishops to replace progressives as they retired or died. This began to have an effect on church leadership, as it became increasingly difficult for change-oriented bishops to get elected to office in the CNBB.

The decrease in the number of progressives has also produced consequences for the individual dioceses headed by the new bishops. There have been conflicts between conservative bishops and progressive priests and sisters. Members of base communities have sometimes become demoralized when trying to deal with a bishop who does not support lay leadership. Many of the new bishops downplay the importance of CEBs and give encouragement to organizations such as Opus Dei and the Charismatic Renewal Movement, whose members emphasize individual holiness, often to the exclusion of social activism.[1]

It would be a mistake, however, to assume that the conservative forces within the church have put an end to liberation theology and base communities. First of all, this theology is not merely an academic exercise, which could be weakened by dismissing the professors who teach it and blocking publication of their books. It is a set of beliefs that has permeated the church at the grassroots level, influencing the thinking of the poor and of the priests, sisters, and middle-class lay people who work with them. These people are not about to abandon the idea of a connection between faith and social justice. Second, the CEBs already exist. They have a history of more than thirty years and a lived experience that their members are not likely to unlearn. In some parts of Brazil participation in CEBs is linked to people's very survival, as they struggle to defend their right to land. This ties in with Maduro's factor of a revolutionary situation. Let us now look more closely at the relationship between CEBs and the movement of landless farmers.[2]

THE CHURCH AND THE LAND STRUGGLE

In recent years most of my research has focused on the relationship between rural base communities and the struggle for land reform in the Amazon (see Adriance 1995), although I have done some interviews and observations in urban communities in order to compare the CEB experience in different settings. The land movement provides a clear example of a revolutionary situation. It stands in sharp contrast to urban social movements, which have recently been losing strength.

In Brazil at the present time there is a crisis in social movements, brought about by political and economic changes. Between 1964 and 1985 the nation was under a military government, during which time social activists were imprisoned. Many were tortured. Some were killed or exiled. In the late 1970s, the government announced a "political opening" and began restoring some human rights. But problems of extreme poverty remained. The combination of the existence of these problems and the new freedom to speak out on political issues provided fertile ground for the rapid growth of poor people's organizations, which in Latin America are called "popular movements." Because the base communities had already been organized within the church, which during the years of military rule had been the only space where people could gather and discuss social issues, they provided a source of support for these movements. As a result, the 1980s saw both a flourishing of popular movements and a great deal of vitality in the base communities. In this context the Brazilian people demanded a return to democracy. In 1989 there was the first direct national election since before the military coup, leading to the presidency of Fernando Collor de Melo (later impeached on charges of corruption). However, Collor's neo-liberal policies failed to improve economic conditions. In fact, they became worse, as runaway inflation reduced the real income of the average citizen and increased starvation among the poor. After the optimism of the 1980s, when it had appeared that popular movements were producing results, people who had participated in those movements faced increasingly dismal prospects. The currency reform under the finance ministry of Fernando Henrique Cardoso (who was elected president in 1995) slowed the rate of inflation, but at the cost of increased unemployment. By the mid-1990s activists had become discouraged, and most of the popular movements had lost their energy. The one exception was the movement for land reform.

Brazil has one of the worst systems of land distribution in the world, with 5 percent of the landowners holding about 70 percent of the farmable land. Millions of acres are idle, while millions of people go hungry. For the movement of landless farmers the important issue is clear-cut: Unused land must be distributed among the poor, so that they can grow food and survive. Specific provisions in Brazilian law enable poor farmers to obtain land: (1) people who farm a plot of land for more than one year have the right to apply for title to that land and (2) landowners who do not use their land productively may have it taken away by the government. However, the reality is not as simple as the law. When landless farmers try to occupy unused areas, even public land to which no one holds title, they are often evicted by the police or by gunmen hired by wealthy ranchers who are also trying to claim the land. Gaining access to land involves a struggle in which poor people frequently become victims of violence.

The issue of land reform is a natural one for the involvement of church groups. Members of base communities in rural areas frequently come to believe, through their Biblical reflections, that it is the will of God that they have access to land. This belief, combined with the support of their fellow CEB members and the encouragement of sympathetic priests and sisters, leads them to participate in the movement of landless farmers. In this movement, they seek not only land for themselves but massive change in the whole system of landowning in Brazil. Land reform is also the goal of the Pastoral Land Commission, an organization begun by the church to advocate for the rights of small farmers. In addition to gathering data on rural problems, advising farmers on organizing unions, collecting food to help people survive long land occupations, and providing lawyers to help people through the process of applying for land titles, this organization helps the farmers to form CEBs, since these have been found to be an effective way of keeping the land struggle organized.

Thus, the land reform movement and the base communities support each other. The potential of CEBs to mobilize people around social issues leads them to support the land movement, since most members of rural base communities are themselves poor farmers, many without land. At the same time, the land movement helps to preserve the vitality of the CEBs by supplying them with a tangible issue around which to organize.

Practically all of the rural CEB members whom I interviewed spoke about their base communities as sources of strength, in terms of both religious faith and practical support in the land movement. Most of them were members of unions that had organized farmers to struggle for land, and many of them were leaders of these unions. They talked about how their faith had helped them to take part in land occupations, to persist despite hardship and death threats, and to have courage when facing the military police or gunmen hired by the big ranchers. Some quotes from interviews illustrate their experiences: "Those who read the Bible speak of the liberation of land. That helps us in a land occupation. The first things we remember are the Bible and faith." "I believe that God is close to me at every moment. Many times I met gunmen who were armed with revolvers, shotguns, or knives, and I walked only with faith." They also talked about the help they had received from the Pastoral Land Commission. "The Pastoral Land Commission was the first organization that gave us support." "The Pastoral Land Commission helps a lot . . . [showing] how to work with others . . . how to get organized."

In addition, rural activists who were not part of the Catholic Church, such as a local Communist Party president, volunteered the information that church groups were the most important factor in the land movement. It is clear from my research in rural areas that the church is supporting activism for social change.

URBAN BASE COMMUNITIES

More recently I have begun studying base communities in the urban diocese of Duque de Caxias, near Rio de Janeiro. There I discovered a situation very different from that in the Amazon. It is evident that there has been a loss of strength in these urban CEBs, but not because of the shift in the church away from the option for the poor. The bishop of Duque de Caxias, Dom Mauro Morelli, is one of the most progressive bishops in Brazil. He is committed to advocating the rights of the poor, does not hesitate to speak out on social issues, and encourages the development of lay leadership. Since he became bishop in 1981, the number of base communities in the diocese has more than doubled. Nevertheless, when I interviewed members of those CEBs, many of them said that their membership had decreased in recent years. Some people thought that this decrease was caused by the aggressive conversion efforts of Protestant pentecostals, but it was also clear that there was a growing sense of discouragement in relation to the social problems with which members of the CEBs had struggled. This discouragement may itself be a cause of the departure of some members for pentecostal churches, since the latter offer a spirituality that tends to comfort people in their afflictions rather than to encourage political activism. When the larger society seems resistant to change, this type of religion can be appealing.

Many of my interviewees did speak with enthusiasm about the popular movements, mentioning tangible results of their efforts, such as health centers, nursery schools, and other community projects. However, most of these projects had developed in the 1980s. For example, when I asked about a neighborhood association, people would reply, "We had one." "It has stopped now. We have to get it going again. But the people who are most involved [in the base community] are overworked." "There was much more enthusiasm in the past."

Some of the base communities that I visited had activities that were exclusively religious. Members expressed concern about local social problems, but did not seem to know what to do about them. Those who were still activists acknowledged that they were few in number and that others had become discouraged.

CONCLUSION

The contrast between the urban and rural experiences provides support for Maduro's idea of the need for a revolutionary situation if religion is to support social change. Some social scientists (Bruneau 1980; Hewitt 1991; Levine and Mainwaring 1989) have suggested that base communities flourish only in those places where bishops encourage them. This would seem to indicate that the lack of church support explains the weakening of some CEBs in recent years. However, my research shows that this is not necessarily the case. Only about one-third of the CEBs I studied in the Amazon were located in dioceses headed by bishops who were considered by the lay people to be progressive. In fact, two were in dioceses with bishops who opposed their activities. Yet in all of these places CEBs were numerous and strong. It is important to note that these base communities were located in areas of severe land conflict. In contrast, in the diocese of Duque de Caxias, which is mainly an urban area, CEBs are suffering a loss of strength, despite the efforts of a bishop who encourages them. This suggests that it is the social context, even more than direct institutional support, that accounts for the strength of the CEBs. The strong rural base communities are interacting with a revolutionary context, in the form of the land movement. Urban CEBs have been losing their political sense of direction despite institutional support.

In conclusion, the case of Brazil demonstrates that, in order to understand the impact of religion on activism for social change, we need to look not only at the beliefs of a particular religion and at its internal power dynamics but also at the broader political-economic context in which that religion finds itself. Base commu-

nities remain strong in places where their members participate in the land movement. This suggests that when people perceive the need to change their society and
feel hopeful that change will happen, religion can serve as a powerful force, providing beliefs to legitimate people's struggles as well as the practical support of
organizational structures.

NOTES

I am grateful to Helen Berger and Debra Kaufman for their helpful comments on this
chapter.
1. For explanations of how conservative religious forces have controlled or opposed
progressive initiatives in the church in other Latin American countries see Crahan (1990),
Levine (1992), and Peña (1995).
2. Although there is a specific organization in Brazil known as the Movement of the
Landless (*Movimento dos Sem Terra*, or MST), I am using lower-case letters in referring to
the movement of landless farmers in order to include *all* organizations that are working for
land reform. The MST is strongest in the South of Brazil, but in the Amazon the land
movement has been organized mainly by the Unions of Rural Workers with the support of
the Catholic Church.

REFERENCES

Adriance, Madeleine Cousineau. 1995. *Promised Land: Base Christian Communities and
    the Struggle for the Amazon.* Albany: State University of New York Press.
Bruneau, Thomas C. 1980. "Basic Christian Communities in Latin America: Their Nature
    and Significance." Pp. 225–237 in Daniel H. Levine (ed.), *Churches and Politics in Latin
    America.* Beverly Hills, CA: Sage.
Crahan, Margaret. 1990. *Religion, Revolution and Counterrevolution: the Role of the
    Religious Right in Central America.* New York: Columbia University–New York
    University Consortium.
Gutierrez, Gustavo. 1973. *A Theology of Liberation.* Maryknoll, NY: Orbis Books.
Hewitt, W. E. 1991. *Base Christian Communities and Social Change in Brazil.* Lincoln:
    University of Nebraska Press.
Levine, Daniel H. 1992. *Popular Voices in Latin American Catholicism.* Princeton, NJ:
    Princeton University Press.
Levine, Daniel H., and Scott Mainwaring. 1989. "Religion and Popular Protest in Latin
    America: Contrasting Experiences." Pp. 203–240 in Susan Eckstein (ed.), *Power and
    Popular Protest: Latin American Social Movements.* Berkeley, CA: University of
    California Press.
Maduro, Otto. 1982. *Religion and Social Conflicts.* Maryknoll, NY: Orbis.
Marx, Karl. 1964. "Contribution to the Critique of Hegel's *Philosophy of Right,* Introduc-
    tion." Pp. 41–58 in Karl Marx and Friedrich Engels, *On Religion.* New York: Schocken
    Books.
McGuire, Meredith. 1997. *Religion: The Social Context* (Fourth Edition). Belmont, CA:
    Wadsworth.
Peña, Milagros. 1995. *Liberation and Theologies in Peru: The Role of Ideas in Social
    Movements.* Philadelphia: Temple University Press.
Weber, Max. 1963. *The Sociology of Religion.* Boston: Beacon Press.

21

Pragmatism and Its Discontents: The Evolution of the Christian Right in the United States

Mark J. Rozell and Clyde Wilcox

On April 23, 1997, Ralph Reed, the executive director of the Christian Coalition, announced that he was stepping down from his post to begin a new career as an independent political consultant. Reed argued that he could accomplish his goals more effectively as a consultant than as the head of a "nonpartisan" organization and promised to become a "Christian Lee Atwater."[1] His departure forced leaders of the Christian Right to take another look at their strategies for influencing the American political process.

The modern Christian Right is a movement composed mainly of evangelical Protestant groups that seek to influence American politics in a conservative direction. In choosing strategies for achieving this goal, leaders of the movement have to decide between confrontation and accommodation. If they choose confrontation, they will maintain the strict positions on such issues as abortion, gay rights, and prayer in the public schools that their members favor. However, this approach may fail to persuade elected political leaders, who favor compromises to maintain a broad base of voter support. On the other hand, if Christian Right leaders opt for accommodation, "softening" their positions and being more pragmatic and open to compromise, they may lose the support of many of their members.

In recent years, Ralph Reed had been the leading Christian Right proponent of a pragmatic approach to politics. Under his leadership, the Christian Coalition moderated its rhetoric and altered its policy agenda. The organization backed Republicans of all ideological stripes, and Reed worked behind the scenes to win support for a more moderate GOP platform plank on abortion. Such pragmatism allowed the Christian Coalition and other movement organizations to grow, and to become important players in GOP politics, winning control of many state and local party organizations (Rozell and Wilcox 1995, 1996, 1997). Yet his pragmatism angered some leaders and many movement activists and created a deep division in the Christian Right. The future of the Christian Right—whether it expands, consolidates, or contracts—depends critically on this internal debate about strategy and tactics.

THE FIRST WAVE OF THE NEW CHRISTIAN RIGHT

The modern Christian Right[2] first mobilized in the United States in the middle to late 1970s, inspired in part by local and state activity—a parents' uprising about textbooks in the schools in Kanawha County, West Virginia, a gay rights referendum in Dade County, Florida, and a gambling referendum in Virginia (Wald 1997; Rozell and Wilcox 1996). Entrepreneurs built political organizations out of the enthusiasms of this activity: Robert Grant helped merge several antigay, antipornography, and pro-family groups in California into the Christian Voice, and Jerry Falwell launched his Moral Majority soon after the defeat of the 1978 gambling referendum in Virginia.

Matthew Moen (1992, 1994, 1997) describes the first phase of the Christian Right as one characterized by the use of moralistic language, emphasis on a narrow range of social issues, and adoption of extreme issue positions with no chance of policy success. Regarding *language*, Christian Right leaders mobilized support through such phrases as "put God back into government" and "ending the murder of the unborn." Such rhetoric may have helped to mobilize the activist base of the Christian Right, but it also made the movement appear threatening to those on the outside. Movement leaders kept the focus of their efforts on a narrow range of *social issues*, primarily abortion, gay rights, and prayer in schools (Moen 1989). They adopted such *extreme issue positions* as banning all gays from teaching, quarantining people with AIDS, and eliminating abortion rights in all cases, including rape and incest (and in some cases, even threat to the life of the mother).

Although earlier incarnations of the Christian Right had been active in the Democratic party, in the 1980s the Christian Right politically mobilized in the Republican party. Falwell became a leading figure on the national political scene after Ronald Reagan's 1980 election to the presidency. Falwell claimed to have mobilized several million conservative Christian voters, and his claim seemed to some to have credibility given the size of the Republican landslide that year.

Yet although Reagan courted the Christian Right during his presidency, he did not push to advance the movement's policy agenda. Indeed, the Christian Right achieved an important goal during the Reagan years when the president gave the movement legitimacy by rhetorically addressing socially conservative issue positions. But Reagan viewed this as a sufficient payoff to the movement that helped elect him. In public appearances Reagan would generally include some reference to a position of the Christian Right, for example, make a plea for "putting God back into the classroom," and then his administration would do little or nothing to advance such a goal through policy. Reagan understood that the Christian Right agenda was too controversial and that to focus on social issues would undermine support for his presidency and ultimately for his economic agenda and defense buildup.

It is telling that the most conservative president of the post–New Deal era would purposefully avoid pushing the policy agenda of social conservatives. The Christian Right delivered votes and campaign energy to Republican candidates in the 1980s, but got very little in return. This was due in large part, no doubt, not only to the controversial issue positions of the movement but also to the extreme and uncompromising rhetoric of its leaders.

Virginia politics during this period provides an excellent example of the uncompromising nature of the Christian Right. Virginia held its off-year state elections (for governor, lieutenant governor, and attorney general) in 1981, 1985, and 1989. In each campaign the GOP nominated a gubernatorial candidate with close ties to the Christian Right. It is also telling that in a conservative state during the Reagan-Bush era, the GOP lost all nine statewide races, primarily because Democratic nominees successfully characterized their opponents as extremists on social issues. The Democrats were aided by Republican gubernatorial nominees in two of the campaigns, promising that, if elected, they would push for an outright ban on abortions in the state, even in cases of rape and incest. In one case, just days before the election a GOP gubernatorial nominee said that he would push to mandate the teaching of creationism in the public schools. Open endorsements of the GOP candidates by the nation's two best known Christian Right leaders and state residents Jerry Falwell and Pat Robertson further helped the Democrats make the case that the GOP had been taken over by the extreme right. Christian Right leaders in these campaigns also made uncompromising demands on the Virginia GOP candidates. The message to the candidates in effect was, "you openly commit to our positions 100 percent or we walk on election day."

The Christian Right organizations of the early 1980s were ultimately limited by their particularistic religious appeal. The Moral Majority, the best-known organization of the time, had a membership almost entirely confined to Baptist Bible Fellowship churches—Falwell's home denomination. The preachers who headed the state and county organizations invited their congregations, but made Catholics and pentecostals feel less welcome.

The Christian Right of this period did not build successful grassroots organizations. The Moral Majority had at best a handful of active state chapters and very few county or other local organizations, and the other movement organizations of this period were even less focused on organizing. The Moral Majority was primarily a national organization that lived and died by direct mail fundraising. By the late 1980s, the organization was in deep financial trouble as Reagan's reelection and then Bush's election, coupled with a series of televangelist scandals, combined to dry up potential funds.

As the Moral Majority faced bankruptcy, Pat Robertson launched a bid for the presidency. Robertson lost badly, winning only 35 pledged delegates despite spending more than 36 million dollars and losing to George Bush in states where Robertson outspent Bush by three to one. By spring of 1989, the Moral Majority was disbanded, the Christian Voice had closed its PAC and was subsidized by the Reverend Moon, and Robertson was back on television hosting the Christian broadcast *700 Club*.

Scholars listed several credible reasons for the failure of the first wave of the Christian Right: the extreme rhetoric and uncompromising stands on issues; the emphasis on mass mail and leader personality-driven national organizations rather than an effective grassroots network of supporters through local and state organizations; and the religious prejudice within Christian Right organizations that made it impossible to build a broadly ecumenical movement (see, for example, Bruce 1988). Indeed, scholars and journalists alike proclaimed the death of the Christian Right. Yet ultimately the failure of the Robertson campaign provided the seeds for the second coming of the Christian Right in the 1990s.

THE RESURRECTION OF THE CHRISTIAN RIGHT

Although in some respects Robertson's campaign can be seen as an expensive failure, it sparked the beginning of a "second coming" of the Christian Right in the 1990s. Robertson's campaign had mobilized a number of young, previously apolitical pentecostal and charismatic Christians into politics, and many of them held influential positions in state and local political parties at the end of the 1988 elections. More important, Robertson converted the large contributor list from his failed presidential campaign into the beginnings of a national grassroots organization, the Christian Coalition, and hired the savvy young political tactician Ralph Reed as its executive director. In so doing, Robertson had acknowledged learning important lessons from his past activities: To succeed in the political environment required a strong grassroots presence and a visible political leader who could speak the secular language of politics and work effectively with the media. Furthermore, the controversial religious broadcaster himself had to take a more low-key role in politics.

The Christian Coalition made a major effort to build state, county, and local organizations across the country. Reed recruited state and local leaders whose background was business, interest group politics, or civic activity instead of local pastors. This enabled the Christian Coalition to build a truly ecumenical organization. The national lobbying office at various times has included mainline Protestants, evangelicals, Catholics, and even a Jew, and our research suggests that state and local chapters were similarly diverse (Wilcox, Rozell, and Gunn 1996). The Catholics and fundamentalist Baptists in the Christian Coalition may not agree on religious doctrine or even on who will get to heaven, but they can agree to support a pro-life, conservative Republican candidate.

The second coming of the new Christian Right evidences a politically maturing movement that has learned from the mistakes of the past. Reed, who himself had once compared his political tactics to guerilla warfare and bragged that he ambushed opponents and left them in body bags, more recently has written to supporters that "phrases like 'religious war' and 'take over' play to a stereotype of evangelicals as intolerant." He urged followers to avoid threatening-sounding language: "We must adopt strategies of persuasion, not domination" (Taylor 1992). Hence, for the Christian Right of the 1990s the rhetorical appeals have a more moderate sound; the issue appeals are more broad-based; movement leaders and organizations express a desire to reach out to as broad an ecumenical base as possible; and new organizations have built impressive grassroots networks (Moen 1997; Rozell 1997; Rozell and Wilcox 1996; Wilcox 1996).

For example, our interviews with a large number of leaders and activists evidence a growing awareness that it is essential to make rhetorical appeals that will generate as wide a base of support as possible, even if that means avoiding moralistic language altogether. One interesting tack has been to promote the overturning of *Roe v. Wade* on the grounds that the decision legalizing abortion was bad constitutional law, rather than on the grounds that abortion is immoral. Reed himself has argued that he merely wants the issue of abortion remanded to the states, in keeping with the Constitution's framers' notion of federalism, rather than to have the Supreme Court mandate a one-size-fits-all approach (Reed 1993).

In addition to more moderate rhetoric, Christian Right leaders increasingly emphasize the necessity of compromise. In our interviews, two prominent movement leaders in Virginia described their strategy as one of "incrementalism"; in football language, that is, they said that they believed that it was important to advance the ball down the field even as slowly as a few yards at a time, knowing that this would ultimately lead to more progress than trying to make a touchdown with a "Hail Mary" pass.[3]

A good example is the recognition by many in the movement that abortion rights are not likely to be stricken down anytime soon, nor will there be a consensus in favor of eliminating abortion. Consequently, the Christian Right more recently has largely abandoned the use of moralistic language to work on behalf of abortion restrictions—parental notification, mandatory waiting periods and counseling for those seeking abortions, no taxpayer funding for the procedure, and most recently, elimination of the practice of "partial birth" abortions. Such policies may somewhat reduce the number of abortions performed and have the advantage of being politically possible.

The second coming of the new Christian Right also is characterized by the adoption of issue appeals beyond the social agenda. To become a part of the conservative mainstream, Christian Right organizations have taken formal positions on a wide variety of issues such as the balanced budget and tax rates. The movement has worked hard to form coalitions with other conservative groups to share membership lists, co-sponsor candidate fundraisers, and join forces to back each others' candidates and issue stands. Our survey of GOP state convention delegates, for example, showed that gun owners and religious conservatives had formed a powerful coalition to back certain candidates for nomination, even though members of those two groups had very different views on social issues (Rozell and Wilcox 1996).

Without a doubt, the most difficult goal for the Christian Right to achieve has been to accept the necessity of compromise. To many in the movement, to compromise on the issue of abortion, or indeed on any issue that is associated with religious doctrine, is to enter into a deal with the devil. More than a third of Christian Right activists in the Virginia GOP indicated on our survey that they thought that compromise was not necessary for politics, and nearly half reported that there was only one true Christian position on most policy issues. Although many of the best-known and most successful leaders of the movement have learned that there can be no advancement of the agenda without compromise, the most ideological activists clearly reject the proposition that there can be any kind of compromise on moral issues (Rozell and Wilcox 1996, 1997).

The Christian Right is therefore faced with a crucial dilemma: If it continues to pursue the pragmatic course of compromise and bargaining, it is likely that many of the most ideological members will leave the movement—some to become less active in politics, others perhaps to form alternative organizations and modes of politics. On the other hand, if the movement chooses to revert to its more ideological roots, then it risks engendering countermobilization among moderates and liberals and will perhaps ultimately achieve few of its policy objectives.

PRAGMATISM AND ITS DISCONTENTS

In the 1990s, the Christian Coalition pursued a strategy of almost purely partisan politics, endorsing Republican candidates regardless of their enthusiasm for, or indeed even of their positions on, key movement issues. The coalition backed U.S. Senate candidates Paul Coverdell (GA) and Kay Bailey Hutchison (TX), although neither supported a ban on abortions, and threw their support behind the presidential campaign of Bob Dole in the 1996 GOP nomination contest, despite the presence of movement favorites such as Patrick Buchanan, Alan Keyes, and Bob Dornan in the race. Reed worked to soften the pro-life plank in the GOP platform, arguing that it cost the Republicans votes.

Reed's tactics were applauded by the media and by some moderate Republicans, who welcomed the electoral support of the Christian Coalition and who were pleased to find the group lobbying on behalf of tax cuts and welfare reform. Yet within the Christian Right, Reed's tactics were not always popular. A number of movement leaders criticized the new moderation of the movement and proclaimed that Ralph Reed did not speak for their issues or concerns. Former Moral Majority leader Cal Thomas wrote eloquently of his dismay that presidential candidate Bob Dole would spend a week of the presidential campaign defending tobacco but would not make a speech denouncing abortion. Thomas wondered if it was time to abandon the GOP, and other activists echoed his concern (Thomas 1996).

The Christian Right has labored for the Republican party constantly since 1978, and it is not clear that it has gotten much for its labors. Although Reagan rewarded his economic constituency by slashing the top income tax rate and rewarded the defense hawks by doubling the defense budget, he gave the Christian Right only rhetoric. The Republican Congress has given the Christian Right some symbolic policy victories, but once again other constituency groups have been rewarded far more richly.

The Republican Congress gave the Christian Right a ban on Internet pornography (likely to be overturned in the Supreme Court) and the Defense of Marriage Act, and then passed a ban on "partial birth" abortions (vetoed by President Clinton). Yet ideological activists in the Christian Right are quite aware of the substantial relief from environmental and worker protection regulations won by business interests and believe that the social issues once again are being shortchanged.

The Christian Right must in all likelihood choose between two futures: one in which it supports Republican candidates and bargains for incremental policy changes or one in which it insists on more fundamental policy changes, perhaps achieving no policy victories but maintaining its ability to serve as prophetic critic of the culture and government. It seems most likely that the Christian Right will continue its course of pragmatism and in the process lose a core of its activists, some of whom will leave politics altogether, others of whom will support third parties and more radical organizations. If the movement does lose some of its activist base, it will still comprise a sizable and well-organized interest group in American politics—perhaps as influential as feminists, African Americans, or environmentalists. This is the normal fate of many social movements.

Ultimately, the Christian Right's fate is constrained by its policy goals. Although the labor, civil rights, and women's movements radically transformed the American social and political landscape, they did so by demanding fair and equal treatment for their members. The labor movement asked that workers be paid a decent wage and be provided a decent and safe working environment, the civil rights movement asked that blacks be allowed into colleges and voting booths, and the women's movement asked that women have equal opportunity to enter boardrooms and other positions of power. Where the Christian Right has made similar claims—that society allow Christian students to read their Bible in study hall, for example—the movement has mostly been successful. But the core agenda of the Christian Right is not about fair treatment of Christians, but about the moral codes that Americans choose to live by. The Christian Right does not ask that their members not be forced to have abortions, they demand that other women be banned from obtaining them, for example. That kind of policy demand can only be achieved by convincing citizens that the Christian Right's moral vision is the correct one—in short, it cannot be won by politics, but only by changing the culture.

In the nineteen years since this wave of Christian Right activity started, the public has become more liberal on abortion, and especially on gay rights and women's issues. Despite the movement's efforts to change U.S. policy by electing more Republicans, GOP presidential candidate Bob Dole responded to Christian Right victories on the abortion plank in the platform by denying that he had read the document. But the most telling example of the limitations of pragmatism came in the third presidential debate, when Dole and Clinton were asked whether they supported laws banning discrimination against gays and lesbians by employers and landlords. Clinton answered in uncharacteristically direct language, endorsing such laws. Dole first stated his opposition to any "special rights" for homosexuals, but then quickly noted that his office had never discriminated against gays and lesbians and that his administration would not do so either. Pragmatists argue that their strategy is best because a President Dole would have signed the "partial birth" abortion ban, but purists retort that the campaign showed that Dole was no different from many other GOP politicians in that he lacked strong commitment to the social agenda and yet expected enthusiastic Christian Right support at the polls.

So long as the Christian Right fails to convince the public of its moral claims, most GOP candidates will continue to emphasize mainstream issue appeals or else be defeated at the polls. So long as Republican candidates distance themselves from the more controversial social issues associated with the Christian Right, movement purists will find little reason to be enthusiastic in supporting the GOP. The struggle between movement pragmatists and purists may go on for a long time.

NOTES

1. Ironically, Atwater became a Christian before his death and repented of his political tactics.

2. There had been two earlier waves of Christian Right activity in the United States, one in the 1920s focused on ending the teaching of evolution and one in the 1950s that sought to mobilize fundamentalists to fight domestic communism. For details, see Wilcox (1992).

3. The two leaders are Ann Kincaid, lobbyist for the Family Foundation, and Michael E. Thomas, former director of the Virginia Society for Human Life. As evidence of the wisdom of this strategy, after backing GOP candidate George Allen's successful campaign for governor, Kincaid became the administration's head of constituent services (the chief liaison to interest groups) and Thomas became the Secretary of Administration. Allen ran as a mainstream conservative who supported limited abortion rights and was exactly the kind of candidate the first-wave Christian Right would have rejected as not sufficiently pure on the issues.

REFERENCES

Bruce, Steve. 1988. *The Rise and Fall of the New Christian Right*. Oxford: Oxford University Press.
Moen, Matthew. 1989. *The Christian Right and Congress*. Tuscaloosca: University of Alabama Press.
———. 1992. *The Transformation of the Christian Right*. Tuscaloosca: University of Alabama Press.
———. 1994. "From Revolution to Evolution: The Changing Nature of the Christian Right." *Sociology of Religion* 55(3):345–357.
———. 1997. "The First Generation of Christian-Right Activism." In James Penning and Corwin Smidt (eds.), *The Christian Right in Comparative Perspective*. Lanham, MD.: Rowman and Littlefield.
Reed, Ralph. 1993. "What Do Christian Conservatives Really Want?" Paper presented at the Colloquium on the Religious New Right and the 1992 Campaign, Ethics and Public Policy Center, Washington, DC.
Rozell, Mark J. 1997. "Growing Up Politically: The New Politics of the New Christian Right." In James Penning and Corwin Smidt (eds.), *The Christian Right in Comparative Perspective*. Lanham, MD: Rowman and Littlefield.
Rozell, Mark J., and Clyde Wilcox. 1996. *Second Coming: The New Christian Right in Virginia Politics*. Baltimore: Johns Hopkins University Press.
——— (eds.). 1995. *God at the Grassroots: The Christian Right in the 1994 Elections*. Lanham, MD: Rowman and Littlefield.

—— (eds.). 1997. *God at the Grass Roots 1996: The Christian Right in American Elections*. Lanham, Md.: Rowman and Littlefield.

Taylor, Joe. 1992. "Christian Coalition Revamping Image." *Richmond Times-Dispatch*, December 7:B4.

Thomas, Cal. 1996. "Which Way for the Religious Right and the GOP?" *Washington Times*, October 23:A14.

Wald, Kenneth D. 1997. *Religion and Politics in the United States* (Third Edition). Washington, DC: Congressional Quarterly.

Wilcox, Clyde. 1992. *God's Warriors: The Christian Right in Twentieth Century America*. Baltimore: The Johns Hopkins University Press.

——. 1996. *Onward Christian Soldiers: The Religious Right in American Politics*. Boulder, CO: Westview Press.

Wilcox, Clyde, Mark J. Rozell, and Roland Gunn. 1996. "Religious Coalitions in the New Christian Right." *Social Science Quarterly* 77:543–558.

22

New Religions in Australia: Cultural Diffusion in Action

Gary D. Bouma

Australia is one of the most culturally and religiously diverse nations in the world. While historically dominated by Anglicans (40% of the population until the 1950s) and Irish Catholics, it now has large Italian Catholic and Greek Orthodox groups, Muslims from sixty different nations, Buddhists from more than ten nations, and rapidly growing numbers professing "earth-based, nature and goddess religions" (Bouma 1997b; Hughes 1998). There are presently two kinds of "new religions" in Australia: those which have settled here having arrived with migrants and those brought in as cultural elements in a manner similar to literary styles, culinary fads, or sports interests. Australia is not known to have developed or exported a significant religious innovation. Since, aside from Aboriginal religions, all Australian religious groups originated in other countries, both types of "new religions" present examples of cultural diffusion.

After discussing the processes of cultural diffusion and religious settlement, this chapter describes Australia's religious profile, using census data comparing Australia with similar countries. Several minority religions are presented as examples of cultural diffusion, showing how religious groups take on distinctive forms as they settle into their new host societies and raising issues concerning the management of religious diversity.

CULTURAL DIFFUSION AND RELIGION

Cultural diffusion is the process whereby beliefs, values, and practices that emerged in one place and time are adopted in other places and times. Sometimes cultural diffusion takes the form of movements like the Oxford Movement, which was a revitalization effort within Anglicanism from the 1830s and which spread very unevenly around the British Empire, or like the revitalization movement current among many Muslims. In other cases cultural diffusion occurs as people from different cultures or subcultures interact. For example, members of conservative Presbyterian groups in Australia might adopt new practices after contact with a vigorously growing pentecostal assembly.

Sometimes the path from innovation to adoption is quite clear, and sometimes it is not. For example, is the current interest among Christians in contemplative spirituality a resurgence of earlier Christian practices or a response to the growth of Transcendental Meditation or Zen Buddhism? Or are all of these responses to changes in the spiritual needs of people in postmodernity? Similarly, it is quite possible for similar cultural innovations to emerge in different places. For example, Pentecostal forms of Christianity appear to have emerged in widely dispersed places. It is an open question whether this was due to migration, itinerant messengers, spontaneous reactions to similar social conditions, or all three.

Religion provides good examples of cultural diffusion through the work of missionaries and propagandists, through the migration of people with different religious backgrounds, or through other forms of intercultural contact. As globalization increases contact between religious cultures, the likelihood of cultural elements being diffused is increased. Many smaller religious groups actively seek adherents through the Internet, making distinct religious beliefs and practices available to small numbers of widely dispersed people. The same Internet is used to find spouses for some Australian Jews who live in communities too small to facilitate local matchmaking. Various forms of Christianity are available via satellite television transmission. Meanwhile, some forms of Islam dominant in the Middle East seek to bring into conformity variant forms of Islam found around the world.

RELIGIOUS SETTLEMENT: BECOMING AUSTRALIAN RELIGIONS

Cultural diffusion does not merely result in carbon copies of religious groups replicated around the world. There is also a related process of religious settlement in which the religious group takes on features peculiar to its new host society (Bouma 1997c). For example Zen Buddhism in Australia is very different from Zen Buddhism in Japan. In Japan Zen is focused very much on providing funeral arrangements for followers who do not otherwise engage in Zen practices. The opposite is the case in Australia, where the focus is on meditation techniques. Muslims in Australia are seeking to develop a way of following Islam that is tuned to the Australian context. Richardson (1994) describes similar processes of religious settlement when missionaries seek followers for new religious movements.

AUSTRALIA'S RELIGIOUS PROFILE

Understanding new religions in a particularly country is greatly helped by a general picture of its religious profile. Such a profile is possible in Australia because a "religion question" is included in the census every five years. Table 22.1 presents the results of the 1996 census, with comparison to 1947 and 1991. Census data are useful for drawing pictures of the relative strength of religious groups in

Table 22.1
The Standing of Selected Religious Groups in the 1947, 1991, and 1996 Censuses

Religious Identification	1947 (000s)	%	1991 (000s)	%	1996 (000s)	%	Growth Rate 1991–1996	Rank in 1996
CHRISTIAN								
Anglican	2957	39.0	4019	23.86	3903	21.99	−2.89	2
Baptist	114	1.5	280	1.66	295	1.66	+5.36	6
Brethren	13	0.2	24	0.14	22	0.12	−8.33	19
Catholic	1570	20.7	4607	27.34	4799	27.03	+4.17	1
Churches of Christ	72	1.0	78	0.46	75	0.42	−3.85	13
Congregational	63	0.8	—		—			
Jehovah's Witnesses	—		75	0.45	83	0.47	+10.67	11
Latter-day Saints	3		38	0.23	45	0.25	+18.42	17
Lutheran	67	0.9	251	1.49	250	1.41	0.00	7
Methodist	871	11.5	—		—			
Oriental Christian	—		23	0.14	31	0.18	+3.48	18
Orthodox	17	0.2	475	2.82	497	2.80	+4.63	5
Pentecostal	—		151	0.90	175	0.98	+15.89	10
Presbyterian/Reformed	744	9.8	732	4.34	676	3.81	−7.65	4
Salvation Army	38	0.5	72	0.43	74	0.42	+2.78	14
Seventh-day Adventist	18	0.2	48	0.29	53	0.30	+10.42	16
Uniting	—		1388	8.24	1335	7.52	−3.82	3
Other Christian	127	1.7	206	1.23	224	1.52	+8.74	
Total	6,673	88.0	12,466	73.98	12,583	70.55	+0.94	
BUDDHISTS	—		140	0.83	200	1.13	+42.86	9
HINDUS	—		44	0.26	67	0.38	+52.27	15
JEWS	32	0.4	74	0.44	80	0.45	+8.11	12
MUSLIMS	—		148	0.88	201	1.13	+35.81	8
OTHER	4	0.1	40	0.24	69	0.39	+72.50	
Total	36	0.5	445	2.64	816	3.47	83.37	
Inadequately Described	19	0.2	49	0.31	54	0.30	+10.20	
No Religion	26	0.3	2177	12.92	2949	16.48	+35.46	
Not Stated	825	10.9	1712	10.16	1551	8.67	−9.40	
National Population	7,579		16,850		17,753		+6.18	

* In 1947 the category "Presbyterian" did not include the Reformed, who had not yet been established in Australia; the category "Uniting" from 1986 includes Methodists.

Source: Australian Bureau of Statistics

a society. They present a good picture of religious identification but do not indicate attendance, belief, or practice. Some groups have high proportions of "nominals"—those who identify with a religion but do not attend.

First of all, Table 22.1 shows that Australia is predominantly Christian (71%) with significant (more than 1%) Buddhist and Muslim groups, sizable groups of Hindus and Jews, and a small clutch of "other" religions comprising less than 0.4% of Australians. It should be noted that while nearly three million Australians (16.5%) said that they had no religion, only 7,500 called themselves atheists. At the level of individual identification, Australia is not a secular society.

Second, Table 22.1 shows that there has been a growing diversity of religious groups in Australia, including Buddhist, Hindus, Muslims, Orthodox (mostly Greek), Pentecostals, Jehovah's Witnesses, and Mormons. This increased diversity can be seen in the attention given to the Chinese new year, the publication of Muslim prayer times in the press and provision for them in the workplace, an increasing sensitivity to the holy days of the various groups, and the addition to the skyline of minarets, onion-shaped domes, Buddhist and Hindu temples, and Sikh shrines.

Finally, the table indicates that the "other" group has recently grown. This last category is where many of Australia's new or alternative religions are to be found. Fortunately, more detailed figures are available from the census to provide some insight into these smaller but growing groups. Nature, earth-based, spiritualist, and goddess religions experienced the greatest growth, 150 percent, between 1991 and 1996, attracting nearly 0.2 percent of Australians, making this group half of the "other" category in Table 22.1. These groups include Druids, Animists, Pagans (who tripled in numbers), Pantheists, Spiritualists, and Wicca/witchcraft (Hume 1997). Satanism doubled in numbers. These have been the fastest-growing groups during the 1990s. While most Australian religious groups other than Pentecostals have grown primarily because of migration, these groups have grown by conversion (Bouma 1997b).

Other minority religious groups large enough to be separately enumerated in census reports include Scientology (grew by 42% to 1,489), Eckankar (doubled to 826), Theosophy (tripled to 1,423), Tenrikyo (no change at 50), Sukyo Mahikari (unchanged at 668), and Shinto (no change at 524). In 1991, the last year for which extremely detailed census reports are available, 76 Australians identified themselves as Children of God, 165 as Unification Church ("Moonies"), 66 as Meher Baba, 434 as Anada Marga, 1,256 as Hare Krishna, 59 as Orange People, 24 as Transcendental Meditation, 1,488 as Zen Buddhists, 67 as Rosicrucians, and 25 with the White Eagle Lodge. Although these groups involve very small numbers, they attract a great deal of attention because they present a challenge to established cultures and often engage in activities on the edge of acceptability (Beckford 1985).

These census data give some idea of the size of the new or minor religions in Australia. They comprise about 0.2 percent of the population and have been enjoying exceptional growth rates, albeit from low numbers. These groups are unlikely to become significant players in Australia's religious market but do provide considerable diversity in the range of religious services available. In addition many people participate in more than one type of religious activity. This ranges from going to a pentecostal assembly but continuing to identify their religion as "Presbyterian" to engaging in spiritualist activities while also attending an Anglican Church. Many Australians wear New Age crystals or frequent the many bookshops featuring the increasing range of spiritual offerings from tarot to witchcraft.

SOME NEW RELIGIONS IN AUSTRALIA

There are no notable new religions of Australian origin. Most of those that have emerged here are either direct imports or very minor variations on themes clearly emergent earlier elsewhere, although it is possible that some neo-pagan movements will include elements from Australian Aboriginal religions. This lack of religious inventiveness reflects Australia's position as a colonial society and "branch-plant" economy until very recently and the fact that Australians are comparatively relaxed (Australians say "laid back") about religion. Rates of attendance, belief, and practice for Australians tend to be considerably lower than those in the United States and a little lower than those in Canada, but higher than those in Britain and Europe (Bouma 1992:92–108).

The typical story of all non-Aboriginal religious groups in Australia tells of how someone or a group of people came to Australia, usually for nonreligious reasons, but who had from their place of origin a distinctive belief or practice that upon arrival they set about practicing and to which they tried to attract others (Carey 1996; Ward and Humphreys 1995). This story is true of most Christian groups, as well as Muslims, Hindus, Baha'is, and Buddhists. A common but less frequent story centers on the work of an itinerant missionary or propagandist who visits Australia with the message of a "new" religious group. Such stories characterize religious groups like The Family (Children of God), the Orange People, followers of Transcendental Meditation, and many smaller Christian groups. These groups, however, are immediately affected by internal and external processes that modify them and normalize their message, causing them to appear not so different as they might have liked (Richardson 1994).

Japanese New Religions

Several Japanese new religions have attracted a substantial following in Australia—Tenrikyo, Sukyo Mahikari, Zen Buddhism, and Nichiren Shoshu Sokagakkai (Ward and Humphreys 1995; Bouma et al. 1998). These groups have come to Australia through the work of missionaries or converts who then worked to attract a following. For example, Mahikari was first established in Australia in 1974 as a result of interactions with three Japanese women. Its spread in Australia is largely due to the tireless work of Dr. Andris Tebecis. Mahikari offers techniques of healing that attract adherents from a wide range of ethnic backgrounds. It claims 2,000 members in Australia; 668 Australians identified themselves with

Mahikari in the census. Since this religion does not require the rejection of other religious affiliations and the census only permits one religion per person, this is not a serious contradiction. One of the interesting variations in societies' religious institutions is whether people are permitted to have more than one religion. Western Christian societies tend to insist on one, whereas there is no such requirement in other societies such as Japan, Vietnam, or China.

Similarly, Zen in Australia was established by missionaries coming from Japan and the United States. Nearly 10 percent of Australia's 200,000 Buddhists are Zen Buddhists. Most Australian Zen Buddhists are of Anglo-Celtic background, have at least some university education, and are employed in white-collar jobs. These features distinguish Zen from the many other strands of Buddhism found in Australia. Other forms of Buddhism have come to Australia with immigrants from Asia, beginning in the middle of the nineteenth century (Bouma et al. 1998).

Japanese religions in Australia are examples of cultural diffusion through missionaries and the promotion of these groups by converts. They are highly organized groups with carefully maintained links back to international headquarters in Japan.

Witchcraft/Goddess Religions

Neo-pagan groups are growing rapidly in Australia, because of the availability of literature on them and the word of mouth of enthusiastic followers rather than by conversion through contact with practitioners or missionaries. Unlike Japanese religions these groups are much less formally organized and unlikely to maintain membership lists or to have international headquarters. Neo-paganism represents a reaction against the sterile rationality and patriarchal culture of some forms of Christianity.

Hume (1997) and Wynack (1996) have described in great detail the beliefs and practices of neo-pagan religions in Australia such as Goddess religions and Wicca/Witchcraft and how they appeal to women seeking to find a way to give voice to their spirituality, which is genuinely feminine. They thrive on loosely structured ritual that provides an environment within which the individual can be creative. These religious groups are mainly imported from the United States or Britain and have spread mostly through the literature available in a growing number of specialist book shops rather than through propagandists. New followers are attracted by word of mouth among those who have experienced the rites offered and by invitation to join in special ceremonies usually linked to lunar cycles. Here religious cultural diffusion takes a more personal form.

MANAGING RELIGIOUS DIVERSITY

All societies have mechanisms to regulate the religious life of their members. These norms form part of a society's religious institution, which is distinct from religious organizations like churches, synagogues, mosques, temples, and denominations. These norms have to do with acceptable levels of religious practice, forms of religious belief, and acceptable levels and forms of religious conflict and competition. Recent stories coming from Europe about attempts to suppress Scientology in Germany and Denmark and the efforts of the Russian Orthodox church to limit competition by making it difficult for other groups to practice at all are examples of attempts at managing religious diversity.

Australia has had a long history of religious tolerance and of diversity, although all religions new to Australia have encountered difficulty, including the substantial harassment of some (New South Wales Anti-Discrimination Board 1984). However, since 1947 the arrival of many religions new to Australia has raised issues of the management of religious diversity. These issues confronted policy makers both within existing religious groups and within government agencies. Many within the former thought that new migrants should become members of existing groups associated with their backgrounds. This posed little problem for Anglican migrants from England or Presbyterians from Scotland. However, Reformed migrants from the Netherlands were directed to the Presbyterian Church, which is very Scottish. While many Presbyterians were very welcoming and many Reformed Dutch found a religious home there, most did not; a few years after arriving they formed their own denomination, the Reformed Churches of Australia.

Most policy makers assumed that migrants would become secular as they saw Australia becoming a secular society. This meant that no policies were needed to manage religious diversity as this would take care of itself as religion declined. Meanwhile, as more and more migrants came from increasingly diverse backgrounds, Australia's cultural life was greatly enriched by contributions in the areas of the arts, cuisine, languages, and architecture. As this happened a policy of multiculturalism was introduced that encouraged migrants to maintain aspects of the cultures they had brought with them. Rather than insisting on assimilation, cultural difference was valued and seen as contributing to the well-being and quality of life of all Australians.

Although not an intentional feature of multicultural policies, religious diversity and the maintenance of the religions brought by migrants was seen to be encouraged. Moreover, during the 1960s, 1970s, and 1980s many migrants who came to Australia took their religion very seriously. The general trend to secularization among existing religious groups was slowed, if not stopped. In this context many religious groups began to establish primary and secondary schools to foster the transmission of their religious and national cultures. Australia had had a long tradition of religious private schools and had enacted arrangements to support these schools from public funds, unlike Canada, France, the United Kingdom, and the United States. As a result, when the Orthodox wanted to establish their schools, there were no problems finding state support. The same has been so for the Jews, Muslims, conservative Christian groups, Hare Krishna, Seventh-day Adventists, or any other group that wishes to establish separate schools. In this, Australia manages religious diversity very differently from other countries and unintentionally promotes religious cultural diffusion.

Because new religious movements are different, some attract media attention and occasionally government intervention. From time to time Australian agencies try to suppress a religious group or to "rescue" children from them (Kohn 1997). Australia's Federal Police maintain a register of dangerous or suspect religious groups, and occasionally social workers will try to remove children from religious groups considered to be dangerous. These matters are usually settled through appeal to the courts, which have been increasingly open to religious diversity, particularly since decisions handed down earlier that saw the removal of prohibitions against Scientology based not on religious grounds but under the Psychological Practices Act (Richardson 1998).

NEW RELIGIONS AND THE MEDIA

Among other things, the media are an instrument of social control, a means of managing religious diversity in a society. The media construct and convey the collective conscience about various phenomena including religion. Richardson (1996:295) suggests that Australian media are "at a stage in their relationship to NRMs that American media were a decade or so ago." The Australian media tend to treat all religion with suspicion, taking the view that all nonrational activity is superstitious and if taken seriously an indication of loss of rational balance. This attitude becomes more pronounced as the beliefs and practices of the group in question deviate further from a bland rationalist liberal Protestant norm.

Australian media are quick to seize on overseas reports of the excesses of religious groups and to take the view that Australians should be wary of such groups and their local representatives if any. Groups so disparaged once included Catholics, but the zone of toleration now includes Catholics, most other Christian groups, Jews, Buddhists (who hardly ever attract negative press), and increasingly Muslims. The Gulf War was the occasion for Australian journalists to learn that Muslims in Australia needed to be understood on their own terms.

THE FUTURE: MORE GROWTH IN DIVERSITY
AND CULTURAL DIFFUSION

Since 1947 Australia's religious life has increased dramatically in diversity of style, type, origin, and degree of practice of religion. Durkheim would of course predict that this would occur with an increase in numbers. However, not only has Australia's population increased, but it has also become much more diverse through accepting a large number of immigrants (nearly 25% of Australians were not born in Australia). This population diversity has increased intercultural contact and with this the likelihood of cultural diffusion. A greater acceptance of those who are different includes an openness at least to listen to their beliefs.

A second major source of religious diversity stems from an increased desire to take charge of one's spiritual life free of organizational constraints. This desire is most evident among followers of New Age religions but also features in the way Christians are seeking ways of developing and expressing their spirituality. This seeking for new and different ways of being spiritual will encourage more cultural diffusion among religious groups. This is particularly the case among women who seek to find places and ways to express their spirituality free of male domination (Wynack 1996). These efforts are greatly facilitated by increased global travel and communication. Pilgrims have long been the agents of cultural diffusion as they go to the sacred places of their religion and encounter others who do things differently, who have variant beliefs, or who wish to learn. Moreover, on their way these pilgrims encounter other cultures whether they go to Mecca, the Ganges, St. James de Compostella, the Vatican, Lourdes, Sedona, Uluru, or just to the next city. Given this it is very likely that Australia's religious life will continue to increase in diversity through cultural diffusion. It may even make a novel contribution.

NOTE

I wish to thank James T. Richardson for carefully reading and commenting on this chapter and for his suggested inclusions.

REFERENCES

Beckford, James. 1985. *Cult Controversies: The Social Response to New Religious Movements*. London: Tavistock.

Bouma, Gary D. 1992. *Religion: Meaning, Transcendence and Community in Australia*. Melbourne: Longman Cheshire.

———. 1997a. "The Religious Settlement of Islam in Australia." *Social Compass* 44(1):71–82.

———. 1997b. "Increasing Diversity in Religious Identification in Australia: Comparing 1947, 1991 and 1996 Census Reports." *People and Place* 5(3):12–18.

——— (ed.). 1997c. *Many Religions, All Australian: Religious Settlement, Identity and Cultural Diversity*. Melbourne: Christian Research Association.

Bouma, Gary D., Wendy Smith, and Shiva Vasi. 1998. "Japanese Religions in Australia: Mahikari and Zen in a Multicultural Society." In Peter Clarke (ed.), *Japanese New Religions in the World*. London: Curzon Press.

Carey, Hilary M. 1996. *Believing in Australia: A Cultural History of Religions*. Sydney: Allen and Unwin.

Hughes, Philip. 1998. *Religion in Australia: Facts and Figures*. Melbourne: Christian Research Association.

Hume, Lynne. 1997. *Witchcraft and Paganism in Australia*. Melbourne: Melbourne University Press.

Kohn, Rachael. 1997. "Cults and the New Age in Australia." Pp. 149–162 in Gary D. Bouma (ed.), *Many Religions, All Australian: Religious Settlement, Identity and Cultural Diversity*. Melbourne: Christian Research Association.

New South Wales Anti-Discrimination Board. 1984. *Discrimination and Religious Conviction*. Sydney: NSW Anti-Discrimination Board.

Richardson, James T. 1994. "Update on 'The Family': Organizational Change and Development in a Controversial New Religious Group." Pp. 27–40 in James R. Lewis and J. Gordon Melton (eds.), *Sex, Slander, and Salvation: Investigating The Family/Children of God*. Stanford, CA: Center for Academic Publication.

———. 1996. "Journalistic Bias toward New Religious Movements in Australia." *Journal of Contemporary Religion* 11:289–302.

————. 1998. "The Evolution of Social Control of New Religions From 'Brainwashing' Claims to Child Abuse Accusations." In S. Palmer and C. Harman (eds.), *Children in New Religions*. New Brunswick, NJ: Rutgers University Press.

Ward, Rowland, and Robert Humphreys. 1995. *Religious Bodies in Australia: A Comprehensive Guide*. Melbourne: New Melbourne Press.

Wynack, Bernadette. 1996. *The Return of the Triple Goddess and the Discovery of "a Feminine Spirituality": An Examination of the Increasing Appeal of Neo-Pagan Belief Systems to Contemporary Australian Women*. M.A. thesis, Center for Women's Studies, Faculty of Arts, Monash University, Melbourne, Australia.

23

The Earth Is Sacred: Ecological Concerns in American Wicca

Helen A. Berger

Dusk was about to settle in Philadelphia as a group of twelve people gathered at the home of the high priest of MoonTide coven to celebrate the Wiccan sabbat of Yule—the winter solstice.[1] As participants entered the house, they placed the brightly wrapped gifts they had brought under the unadorned evergreen tree that stood in the corner of the living room. They handed the food they had prepared for the feast following the ritual to anyone willing to take it and then ran upstairs to put their coats on the hosts' bed. The last people to arrive were the high priestess, her husband, and her adult son.

The high priest strung the tree with lights and placed a pentagram—a five-sided star—on top of it. Some of the participants decorated the tree, while others prepared for the ritual by moving furniture out of the living room so that it could be made into a sacred space. A small round table covered with a green silken cloth was placed in the center of the room as an altar. Candles, matches, incense, images of the goddess, and symbols of the four elements—earth, air, fire, and water—that had been brought by the high priestess were placed on the altar. The room was illuminated by candles.

As the ritual was about to begin, eight members of the coven changed into red robes. One member—a woman—was robed in white. Non-Wiccan guests remained in their street clothes, although everyone removed their shoes to signify that they would be standing on sacred ground. The group, with the exception of the one woman dressed in white, gathered in the living room and sat quietly with their eyes closed as the high priest led a guided meditation about the meaning of the winter season—to people, animals, plants, and the earth. The participants were asked by the high priest to find the darkness that is winter inside themselves, to see it as a place of comfort, rest, and renewal.

He noted that this time of year had brought uncertainty to our ancestors, who lived without electricity or heat. He suggested that they might have asked: Do we have enough food stored to survive the winter? Will the sun return as it has in other years? Will life continue? He asserted that our present-day ecological concerns are not that different from those of our ancestors—concern about our own and the earth's survival.

After the guided meditation, Abby, a member of the coven, went around the circle asking people if they had come in peace and if they were joining the circle of their own free will. As each person assented, she anointed him or her with scented oil on the third eye—a spot in the middle of the forehead that is believed to be the center of intuition. The circle was then cast in the name of the three aspects of the goddess—the maiden, the mother, and the crone. The four elements—the powers of the east, south, west, and north—were called into the circle. Symbols of the four directions—incense, a lighted candle, water, and a stone—were in turn carried around the circle. By casting the circle and calling in the powers of the four directions, they had converted the secular living room into sacred space.

As the ritual proceeded, the high priestess read a short passage about the meaning of Yule. The woman dressed in white joined the circle and enacted the words read by the high priestess. Each participant was asked to place an ornament on the tree, as a gift to Mother Nature and a symbol of the group's commitment to her care. When the ritual ended, the powers of the four elements were released and the circle was unwound. The participants shared a meal and exchanged presents.[2]

Wicca, Witchcraft, or the Craft, as this religion is alternatively called, defines itself as an earth-based religion, in which the natural world is perceived as part of the divine and human beings are viewed as a component of the great web of being. In MoonTide's ritual participants were asked to focus on the seasonal changes and their meanings for themselves, all living things, and the earth. In other words, they were asked to meditate about and enjoy what was happening that day in their immediate environment—outside their heated and well-lit homes—to feel immersed in the winter and in the natural world.

The high priest drew a parallel between contemporary fears of ecological disaster and those of our ancestors. He contended that our ancestors knew that they must take care of the Great Mother—earth—if they were to survive. He requested that everyone follow the example of these ancient people and take responsibility for the earth's well-being. In the ritual participants symbolically acknowledged their obligation to the earth by presenting her with a gift—an ornament for the tree.

Ecological concerns are not unique to Wicca. Responses to the environmental crisis are also evident, for example, in Christianity and Judaism (Kerns 1996; Shibley and Wiggins 1997). However, I will show in this chapter that Witchcraft, as it has developed in the United States, has integrated ecological issues, along with a feminist perspective, into the basic fiber of the religion—its rituals, rites, and coven structure.

METHOD

My research is based on eleven years of participant observation among Witches and Neo-Pagans in the northeastern United States. The focus of this research is on groups that include both men and women, although I have attended the rituals of three all-women's groups. I was also invited to participate as a researcher in the formation of the Circle of Light coven. For two years I attended this coven's weekly meetings, sabbats (celebrations of the seasons), esabats (commemorations of the cycles of the moon), and general gatherings. Later I continued to attend occasionally until the coven disbanded in 1996. I have also attended rituals at seven other inclusive covens, that is, groups composed of men and women. I was invited to these covens after meeting members at festivals or through mutual friends or acquaintances within the Witchcraft community.

I have formally and informally interviewed more than a hundred Witches and Neo-Pagans. The forty-four formal interviews were taped. Informal interviews were not taped but were recorded in my field notes. I have relied on a snowball sample—interviewing participants to whom I was introduced through my contacts among Neo-Pagans. It was not possible to do a random sample because many groups and individuals do not openly identify themselves as Witches or Neo-Pagans as they fear they will be discriminated against at work, in housing, or child custody cases. I have also gathered information from Neo-Pagan journals and books and from the Internet.

THE ORIGINS OF CONTEMPORARY WITCHCRAFT

Gerald Gardner is credited with developing the basic components of modern Witchcraft—a reverence for the goddess of fertility and the god of the hunt, the celebration of the sabbats at the beginning and height of each season, the observance of the esabats at the new and full moons, the casting and unwinding of the circle, and the raising of energy for magical workings. He claimed to have been initiated into a coven that had remained hidden but intact since the advent of Christianity in England. The authenticity of his initiation has been questioned by both Witches and scholars (Adler 1986; Kelly 1991; Neitz 1991). However, even Witches who acknowledge that Gardner created Wicca in the 1940s view their religion as old. They contend that the worship of the primeval deities, celebration of the old agricultural calendar that follows the seasons, and reverence for the earth were all elements of the religion that existed in Europe prior to the spread of Christianity.

Wicca, which came to the United States in the 1960s, was influenced by the social movements that developed in the years that followed—including ecology, women's equality, and an interest in mysticism, self-development, and anti-authoritarianism. Because there is no central bureaucracy or leader to determine orthodoxy, or one set of ideas to which an individual must adhere, many different forms or traditions of Wicca developed (Adler 1986). People can work in groups called covens or can be solo practitioners. It is possible for an individual to create her or his own form of the religion, although there is a good deal of consistency among groups and individuals (Berger 1995).

Some members of the religion refer to themselves as Neo-Pagans or Pagans rather than Witches. The terms are often interchangeable, although on the whole

Witches are the more committed members of the religion, those who have gone through a process of initiation. All-women's groups that worship the goddess—to the exclusion of the god force—grew out of the women's movement. Many of the women who became involved in all-women's groups as a feminist form of spirituality were initially unaware of the larger Wiccan or Neo-Pagan movement (Finley 1991). However, through interaction at festivals, on the Internet, and in journals and books, a connection has developed between groups that are inclusive of men and women and all-women's groups. The growth of women-only groups, or Dianics as they are often called, has helped to foster an increased concern with feminist issues within the Witchcraft movement.

Many Neo-Pagans consider their return to the "old religion" or "old ways" as providing an alternative path or vision to the ethic of domination that they view as embedded in modern institutions. They contend that ancient religions treated nature as part of the divine and honored women, as they did the goddess. Witches argue that this view of women, nature, and the world was changed through the virtual elimination of paganism in the West and the development of mechanical philosophy (the basis of modern science), which viewed nature as an object of study to be dominated.[3] Thus there is a notion among Neo-Pagans that the "return" to the past provides an alternative vision from which to begin creating a new social order—one that integrates a respect for women with a respect for the earth. This new social order would contrast to the modernist ethos, in which science and logic are seen as superior both to nature and to the more subjective, intuitive, and caregiving qualities that have traditionally been associated with women.

THE EARTH IS OUR MOTHER

Reverence for Mother Earth, Neo-Pagans claim, results in reverence for the natural environment. Ron, who converted to Wicca from a fundamentalist Christian background in the 1960s, maintains, "We [Neo-Pagans] would like to see the earth respected and not pillaged and raped by cutting down rain forests, and stripmined, and being poisoned by acid rain and having her [the goddess's] animals become extinct. We want to stop these things."[4] This belief affects the everyday practices of Witches. For example, Iontas, a high priestess in upstate New York, asserts, "[If] you're going to view the earth as your mother—the earth being part of her [the goddess's] body—ecological issues are going to be important to you." She elaborated on this point by explaining, "So I live my life—I practice what I preach—I recycle, I treat the earth lightly—I try to live lightly on the earth, all the right things . . . as best I can."[5]

Neo-Pagans speak of the earth as sacred, the goddess, the mother, the bearer of life and death. The goddess is a central symbol within Wicca. She is sometimes spoken of as inside each of us—whether we are women or men—as a deity, or as the earth. The ambiguity of the image is not viewed as problematic within Wiccan circles. Because Wicca is a noncreedal religion, there is no one image of the goddess that all Witches are required to have. Some Witches are atheists, who view the goddess as a symbol of nature, of womanhood, or of natural forces. The image can be used in diverse ways by the same person in different rituals, meditations, or conversations. However, the image of the earth as the body of the goddess—alive and in need of care—is one that permeates the movement. As two well-known Witches suggest, "The Goddess is not an all-powerful, indestructible, non-physical being who created the world and exists apart from it, 'The All-Mother is Life. . . .' She is the very soul of the Earth and she lives or dies as all life on this planet lives or dies" (G'Zell and G'Zell 1996:29).

The concept of the earth as alive is not unique to Neo-Pagans. For example, James Lovelock (1982), a scientist, has popularized the image of the earth as Gaia. Although he uses Greek imagery, Lovelock is suggesting neither a return to Paganism nor a view that the earth is literally alive (Harvey 1997:146). Nonetheless, Lovelock's theories are popular among Neo-Pagans, who see his work as supportive of their own views of nature.

Neo-Pagans typically evoke the image of the earth as the goddess or the mother in chants, rituals, and poetry. One common chant includes these words: "She [the goddess] is waiting, she is waiting, she is waiting for her children to return. She's been waiting, she been waiting, she's been waiting for so long." Neo-Pagans view themselves as Mother Earth's "children," who are returning both to recognize her and to protect her through their rituals, meditations, lifestyle choices, and in some cases political activities.

RITUALS

As Wicca is an experiential religion, ritual rather than dogma is its central component. Sabbats, esabats, rites of passage, and personal rituals are important parts of the practice of being a Witch. These rituals are viewed as having their basis in ancient religious practices. All Wiccan rituals are interactive, requiring the participants to sing, dance, and/or meditate.

Sabbat rituals encourage participants to focus on the changes in the seasons and the meaning of those changes for themselves. For instance, in the Yule ritual described at the beginning of this paper, participants were asked to look inside themselves to find the darkness, fear, and hope of winter. On one level, the sabbat rituals usually focus on the individual and his or her problems or desires for change, as reflected in the changes of the year. On another level, the rituals encourage participants to see themselves as part of nature and as responsible for nature. In MoonTide's Yule ritual, participants placed an ornament on the tree as a symbol of their connection and obligation to the earth. Esabats, which are celebrations of the moon cycles, usually take place twice a month at the full and new moon to commemorate the mother and crone aspects of the goddess. Rites of passage honor the birth of children, puberty, marriages, and old age; they help to place the individual within the web of life. These rituals emphasize that there is in life as in nature a season of birth, youth, adulthood, death, and—many Neo-Pagans believe—rebirth.

In rituals magical energy is raised through dance, song, or meditation. This energy can be directed toward either personal goals—for instance, healing or finding an apartment for oneself or for someone else—or toward global issues—such as finding a cure for AIDS or protecting the rain forest. Most Witches believe that sending energy can help effect change. Some Witches contend that the change occurs through magic's altering the course of events. Joe, a Neo-Pagan, states, "The energy is there—it is a case of will and concentration and focusing on the desired goal. . . . It could be to heal the earth, it could be to develop your own ties with nature, it could be a very introspective thing."[6]

For Joe, as for many Witches, magic relies on using the energy that exists in thought forms—our own and those of others who join us in concentrating on a particular goal, especially if it is done in a ritual circle—the energy that has been infused into archetypes through centuries of worship, or the energy that is a natural part of the web of the universe. Other Neo-Pagans present a more psychological view of magic. Judy Harrow, the high priestess of a New York coven, suggests, "Ritual is a way of getting into an altered state of consciousness and then doing things while there. Whether it is getting ourselves through life transitions . . . [or] it is focusing our will on something which is what active magic is about."[7] Judy Harrow believes that rituals motivate people to work to transform their own lives or the larger world. Doug, a Neo-Pagan to whom I spoke after we had participated in a ritual to send energy to heal the rain forest, maintains that these rituals help to raise individuals' consciousness in a more profound manner than if they had read the same book or watched the same documentary.

ENVIRONMENTAL POLITICS AND LIFESTYLES

Every Neo-Pagan with whom I have spoken has asserted that his or her religious practice requires that he or she be ecologically concerned. Laura, the high priestess of a coven in Boston, suggests, "I think it's not that we [Neo-Pagans] don't use resources like everyone else, its just that we don't squander them. . . . When we went to Merrymeet,[8] the people running the camp were just floored that they didn't have to pick up any trash after us. To us it was like, who would throw trash on the ground?"[9]

Laura and the other Neo-Pagans with whom I have spoken claim that viewing the earth as a goddess compels them to treat the earth and women with respect. Although this view does not necessarily follow from worshiping the goddess or viewing her as immanent in nature, for many Neo-Pagans worshiping the goddess is symbolic of their commitment to gender equality as well as to environmentalism.

Andras Corban-Arthen, who with his wife founded EarthSpirit Community, the largest Neo-Pagan organization in New England, asserts, "To be a Witch, whether a woman or a man, you are a feminist. . . . Beyond that the Craft is permeated by a sense of the feminine. That is one of the things that gives it its distinct flavor, . . . the sense of kinship with the earth, which is seen as female—as the Great Mother."[10] For Andras this kinship requires not only viewing the earth as part of the divine, but returning something to her. In the last few years EarthSpirit Community has made cleaning up the local park where they conduct their outdoor rites in the Boston area part of their spring sabbat ritual. Participants come equipped with garbage bags and plastic gloves to remove trash from this small part of the Mother prior to forming into a circle to do a ritual to venerate her.

Harvey (1997) and Luhrmann (1993) state that Neo-Pagans are well represented in the ecology movement. Luhrmann notes that this is more clearly the case for British Neo-Pagans than for Americans, although she does claim that American Neo-Pagans are also involved in the environmental movement. The amount of political activity in which they are involved varies among American Neo-Pagans. Although some individuals are drawn to Wicca or Neo-Paganism for personal growth, many enter the religion because they perceive it as consistent with their social concerns and lifestyle choices (Adler 1986). In turn, being part of the Neo-Pagan community affects individuals' worldview. To participate in a Neo-Pagan gathering where several hundred people come together is to be surrounded by people who are environmentally concerned. While the gatherings last only a week or a weekend, participation in activities in the Neo-Pagan community takes place throughout the year. Ecological issues are regularly discussed. This awareness encourages some people to become politically active, even if they were not previously. However, even for those who do not join a political movement or participate in a demonstration, participation in the Neo-Pagan community results in their making decisions that directly affect how they live their lives and put pressure on their communities to provide recycling centers, on their local shops to carry environmentally friendly products, and on those around them to consider their use of resources.

CONCLUSION

Wicca, as it was developed by Gardner in Great Britain, provided a romantic "return" to the "old religion." Implicit in Wicca's practices then and now is a critique of modernity. The religion took hold in the United States during the cultural turmoil of the 1960s. Women seeking a feminist form of spirituality were drawn to the religion because of its worship of the goddess. The religion's reverence for nature was appealing to those concerned with ecological issues. For a generation that questioned authority, the religion offered a spiritual path that was nonauthoritarian and encouraged self-development through ritual and magical practices.

Because of the influx into Neo-Paganism of feminists and environmentalists these social issues have become firmly woven into the rituals, practice, and world-view of Neo-Pagans. In turn through their rituals and prolific body of literature Neo-Pagans provide a critique of contemporary gender relations and images of nature. Instead of perceiving nature as separate from the human world to be conquered and controlled, Neo-Pagans offer an image of nature as within us—and of us as part of the natural web of life. For Neo-Pagans the earth is the Great Mother to be honored and protected. Although Wicca remains a minority religion, some of its rituals and images are becoming absorbed into the larger culture—most important, the image of the divine having a feminine aspect and the earth as alive and in need of care. Wicca offers a challenge to more traditional religions and to the larger culture to reexamine their attitudes toward the earth and all of her occupants.

NOTES

1. Unless speaking of published authors or otherwise noted, pseudonyms are used throughout this chapter for the names of covens and people.
2. Excerpt from field notes, December 1992.
3. For example, see Starhawk (1982).
4. Interview with Ron, November 6, 1986, in Massachusetts.
5. Interview with Iontas, January 19, 1997, in New York City.
6. Interview with Joe, November 1988, in Boston.
7. Interview with Judy Harrow, May 1987 in western Massachusetts. This is her legal name.
8. Merrymeet is a large festival that draws hundreds of Neo-Pagans from around the United States.
9. Interview with Laura, 1997.
10. Interview with Andras Corban-Arthen, December 6, 1986 in Medford, Massachusetts. This is his legal name.

REFERENCES

Adler, Margot. 1978, 1986. *Drawing Down the Moon*. Boston: Beacon Press.
Berger, Helen A. 1995. "Routinization of Spontaneity." *Sociology of Religion* 56(1):49–62.
Finley, Nancy J. 1991. "Political Activism and Feminist Spirituality." *Sociological Analysis* 52(4):349–362.
G'Zell, Morning Glory, and Otter G'Zell. 1996. "Who on Earth Is the Goddess?" In James R. Lewis (ed.), *Magical Religion and Modern Witchcraft*. Albany: State University of New York Press.
Harvey, Graham. 1997. *Contemporary Paganism: Listening People Speaking Earth*. New York: New York University Press.
Kelly, Aidan A. 1991. *Crafting the Art of Magic: Book I*. St. Paul, MN: Llewellyn Publications.
Kerns, Laurel. 1996. "Saving the Creation: Christian Enviromentalism in the United States" *Sociology of Religion* 57(1):55–70.
Lovelock, James E. 1982. *Gaia: A New Look at Life on Earth*. Oxford: Oxford University Press.
Luhrmann, Tanya M. 1993. "The Resurgence of Romanticism: Contemporary NeoPaganism, Feminist Spirituality and the Divinity of Nature." Pp. 217–232 in Kay Milton (ed.), *Environmentalism: The View from Anthropology*. London and New York: Routledge.
Neitz, Mary-Jo. 1991. "In Goddess We Trust." Pp. 353–372 in Thomas Robbins and Dick Anthony (eds.), *In Gods We Trust*. New Brunswick, NJ: Transaction Press.
Shibley, Mark A., and Jonathon L. Wiggins 1997. "The Greening of Mainline American Religion: A Sociological Analysis of the Environmental Ethics of the National Religious Partnership for the Environment." *Social Compass* 44(3):333–348.
Starhawk. 1982. *Dreaming the Dark*. Boston: Beacon Press.

Suggestions for Further Reading

Adriance, Madeleine Cousineau. 1995. *Promised Land: Base Christian Communities and the Struggle for the Amazon*. Albany, NY: State University of New York Press.

Ammerman, Nancy T. 1991. *Baptist Battles*. New Brunswick, NJ: Rutgers University Press.

Baer, Hans A., and Merrill Singer. 1992. *African-American Religion in the Twentieth Century*. Knoxville: University of Tennessee Press.

Barker, Eileen. 1984. *The Making of a Moonie*. Oxford: Basil Blackwell.

————. 1995. "The Scientific Study of Religion? You Must Be Joking!" *Journal for the Scientific Study of Religion* 34(3):298–310.

Becker, Penny Edgell, and Nancy L. Eiesland (eds.). 1997. *Contemporary American Religion: An Ethnographic Reader*. Walnut Creek, CA: AltaMira.

Beckford, James. 1989. *Religion and Advanced Industrial Societies*. London: Unwin Hyman.

Bellah, Robert N. 1964. "Religious Evolution." *American Sociological Review* 29(3):358–374.

————. 1967. "Civil Religion in America." *Daedalus* 96:1–21.

Berger, Helen A. 1998. *A Community of Witches: Contemporary Neo-Paganism and Witchcraft in the United States*. Columbia, SC: University of South Carolina Press.

Berger, Peter L. 1967. *The Sacred Canopy*. Garden City, NY: Doubleday Anchor.

Beyer, Peter. 1994. *Religion and Globalization*. Newbury Park, CA: Sage.

Casanova, José. 1994. *Public Religions in the Modern World*. Chicago: University of Chicago Press.

Christ, Carol, and Judith Plaskow (eds.). 1979. *Womanspirit Rising: A Feminist Reader in Religion*. San Francisco: Harper and Row.

D'Antonio, William V., James D. Davidson, Dean R. Hoge, and Ruth A. Wallace. 1996. *Laity: American and Catholic*. Kansas City, MO: Sheed and Ward.

Davidman, Lynn. 1991. *Tradition in a Rootless World: Women Turn to Orthodox Judaism*. Berkeley: University of California Press.

Davidson, James D. et al. 1997. *The Search for Common Ground: What Unites and Divides Catholic Americans*. Huntington, IN: Our Sunday Visitor.

Demerath, N. J., and Rhys Williams. 1992. *A Bridging of Faiths: Religion and Politics in a New England City*. Princeton, NJ: Princeton University Press.

Dowdy, Thomas, and Patrick McNamara (eds.). 1997. *Religion: North American Style* (Third Edition). New Brunswick, NJ: Rutgers University Press.

Durkheim, Emile. [1915] 1995. *The Elementary Forms of the Religious Life*. New York: Free Press.

Finke, Roger, and Rodney Stark. 1992. *The Churching of America: Winners and Losers in Our Religious Economy, 1976–1990*. New Brunswick, NJ: Rutgers University Press.

Geertz, Clifford. 1985. "Religion as a Cultural System." Pp. 1–46 in M. Banton (ed.), *Anthropological Approaches to the Study of Religion*. London: Tavistock.

Gordis, David M., and Yav Ben-Horin (eds.). 1991. *Jewish Identity in America*. Los Angeles: Susan and David Wilstein Institute of Jewish Policy Studies, University of Judaism.

Herberg, Will. 1960. *Protestant-Catholic-Jew*. Garden City, NY: Doubleday.

Hertel, Bradley R., and Cynthia Ann Humes (eds.). 1993. *Living Banaras: Hindu Religion in Cultural Context*. Albany: State University of New York Press.

Hoge, Dean, Benton Johnson, and Donald A. Luidens. 1994. *Vanishing Boundaries: The Religion of Mainline Protestant Baby Boomers* (Third Edition). Louisville, KY: Westminster/John Knox Press.

Ireland, Rowan. 1991. *Kingdoms Come: Religion and Politics in Brazil*. Pittsburgh: University of Pittsburgh Press.

Johnstone, Ronald. 1992. *Religion in Society* (Fourth Edition). Upper Saddle River, NJ: Prentice-Hall.

Kaufman, Debra. 1991. *Rachel's Daughters: Newly Orthodox Jewish Women*. New Brunswick, NJ: Rutgers University Press.

Kelley, Dean M. 1977. *Why Conservative Churches Are Growing* (Second Edition). New York: Harper and Row.

Lawson, Ronald. 1998. " Broadening the Boundaries of Church-Sect Theory: Insights from the Evolution of the Non-schismatic Mission Churches of Seventh-day Adventism." *Journal for the Scientific Study of Religion* 37(3).

Lehman, Edward C. 1985. *Women Clergy: Breaking through Gender Barriers*. New Brunswick, NJ: Transaction Books.

———. 1993. *Gender and Work: the Case of the Clergy*. Albany, NY: State University of New York Press.

Lenski, Gerhard. 1963. *The Religious Factor*. Garden City, NY: Doubleday and Company.

Levine, Daniel H. 1992. *Popular Voices in American Catholicism*. Princeton, NJ: Princeton University Press.

Liebman, Charles S., and Eliezar Don-Yehiya. 1983. *Civil Religion in Israel*. Berkeley: University of California Press.

Martin, David. 1978. *A General Theory of Secularization*. New York: Harper and Row.

Marx, Karl, and Friedrich Engels. 1964. *On Religion*. New York: Schocken Books.

Richardson, James T., Mary Harder, and Robert B. Simmonds. 1979. *Organized Miracles: A Sociological Study of a Jesus Movement Organization*. New Brunswick, NJ: Transaction Books.

Riesebrodt, Martin. 1994. *Pious Passion: The Emergence of Modern Fundamentalism in the United States and Iran*. Berkeley: University of California Press, 1994.

Robbins, Thomas, and Dick Anthony (eds.). 1993. *In Gods We Trust* (Second Edition). New Brunswick, NJ: Transaction Books.

Robbins, Thomas, and Roland Robertson (eds.). 1987. *Church-State Relations*. New Brunswick, NJ: Transaction Books.

Robertson, Roland, and William R. Garett (eds.). 1991. *Religion and the Global Order*. New York: Paragon House.

Roof, Wade Clark. 1993. *A Generation of Seekers: The Spiritual Journeys of the Baby Boom Generation*. San Francisco, CA: Harper San Francisco.

Roof, Wade Clark, and William McKinney. 1987. *American Mainline Religion: Its Changing Shape and Future*. New Brunswick, NJ: Rutgers University Press.

Rozell, Mark J., and Clyde Wilcox (eds). 1997 *God at the Grass Roots, 1996: The Christian Right in American Elections*. Lanham, MD: Rowman and Littlefield.

Schoenherr, Richard, and Lawrence Young. 1993. *Full Pews, Empty Altars*. Durham, NC: Duke University Press.

Simmel, Georg. [1906] 1959. *Sociology of Religion*. New York: Philosophical Library.

Stark, Rodney, and William Sims Bainbridge. 1996. *A Theory of Religion*. New York: Peter Lang.

Stevens-Arroyo, Anthony M., and Gilbert R. Cadena, (eds.). 1995. Old Masks New Faces: Religion and Latino Identities. New York: Bildner Center for Western Hemisphere Studies.

Wallace, Ruth A. 1992. *They Call Her Pastor: A New Role for Catholic Women* (Albany, NY: State University of New York Press.

Warner, R. Stephen. 1988. *New Wine in Old Wineskins*. Berkeley: University of California Press.

Weber, Max. [1904] 1958. *The Protestant Ethic and the Spirit of Capitalism*. New York: Scribner.

————. [1922] 1963. *The Sociology of Religion*. Boston: Beacon Press.

Wilson, Bryan R. 1990. *The Social Dimensions of Sectarianism*. Oxford: Clarendon.

Wuthnow, Robert. 1988. *The Restructuring of American Religion*. Princeton, NJ: Princeton University Press.

TEXTBOOKS

Chalfant, H. Paul, Robert Beckley, and C. Eddie Palmer. 1994. *Religion in Contemporary Society* (Third Edition). Itasca, IL: F. E. Peacock.

Johnstone, Ronald L. 1992. *Religion in Society: A Sociology of Religion* (Fourth Edition). Upper Saddle River, NJ: Prentice-Hall.

McGuire, Meredith. 1997. *Religion: The Social Context* (Fourth Edition). Belmont, CA: Wadsworth.

Roberts, Keith. 1995. *Religion in Sociological Perspective* (Third Edition). Belmont, CA: Wadsworth.

JOURNALS

Journal of Church and State
Journal of Contemporary Religion
Journal for the Scientific Study of Religion
Review of Religious Research
Social Compass: International Review of Sociology of Religion
Sociology of Religion (formerly called *Sociological Analysis*)
Studies in Religion/Sciences Religieuses (published in Canada)

Index

About the Contributors

HELEN A. BERGER is Associate Professor of Sociology at West Chester University of Pennsylvania. She has been involved in research on the new religious movement of Witchcraft and Neo-Paganism for more than eleven years. Her book, *A Community of Witches: Contemporary Neo-Paganism and Witchcraft in the United States* will appear in the fall of 1998. She has also published several articles in this area. At the present time she is newsletter editor for the Religion Section of the American Sociological Association.

GARY D. BOUMA is Professor of Sociology at Monash University and Visiting Fellow in the Research School of Social Sciences at the Australian National University. His recent research examines the impact of immigration on Australia's religious profile, the process of religious settlement, the emergence of religious plurality in Australia as compared with other Western nations, and the management of religious diversity. He is the author of more than fifteen books and 150 articles. His most recent books include *Mosques and Muslim Settlement in Australia* (1994) and *Many Religions, All Australian* (1997).

GILBERT R. CADENA is Chair of the Ethnic and Women's Studies Department at California State Polytechnic University, Pomona. He is interested in the role of religion in social change and has written on Latino clergy, liberation theology, and Latinos and the Catholic Church. As a member of the Executive Board of the Program for the Analysis of Religion among Latinos (PARAL), he is collaborating with other social scientists and religious scholars on a national study of Latino religious identity. He is co-editor of *Old Masks, New Faces: Religion and Latino Identities* (1995), and he lives in Southern California.

MADELEINE COUSINEAU is Professor of Sociology at Mount Ida College and a Lecturer at the University of Massachusetts, Boston. She has focused her research on religion and social change in Latin America and is the author of two books and several journal articles on this topic, as well as editor of the ASA's *Syllabi and Instructional Materials for the Sociology of Religion* (1998). She has served on the executive councils of the Association for the Sociology of Religion, the Society for the Scientific Study of Religion, and the Religion Section of the American Sociological Association. Her publications prior to 1996 are under the name Madeleine Adriance.

MARY CUTHRELL CURRY is Assistant Professor of Sociology at the University of Houston. She received her M.A. in Sociology from the New School for Social Research and her Ph.D. from the City University of New York. She has focused her research on religious change and is the author of *Making the Gods in New York: The Yoruba Religion in the African American Community* (1998). At present, she is engaged in research in the department's RENIR (Religion, Ethnicity, New Immigrants Research) Project. She is also chair of the Women's Caucus of the Society for the Scientific Study of Religion.

M. HERBERT DANZGER is Professor of Sociology at Lehman College and at the Graduate Center of the City University of New York. He has written several articles on community power structure, conflict, and social movements, based on research supported by NIMH and NSF. His studies of "return" to Jewish traditionalism benefitted from two academic years in Israel, at Bar Ilan University as senior lecturer and at Hebrew University as Fulbright Professor. The chapter in this book is part of a research project on Soviet émigrés in Israel and the United States. His earlier work on this project is described in his *Returning to Tradition* (1989).

JAMES D. DAVIDSON is Professor of Sociology at Purdue University. He received his Ph.D. from the University of Notre Dame. He is senior author of *The Search for Common Ground* (1997), and has served as president of the Religious Research Association and the North Central Sociological Association, executive secretary of the Society for the Scientific Study of Religion, and editor of the *Review of Religious Research*.

N. J. DEMERATH III is Professor of Sociology at the University of Massachusetts, Amherst, and the current president of the Society for the Scientific Study of Religion. He is a long-time student of American religion and religious organizations (cf. *Sacred Companies*, 1997). His most recent interest has been in religion and politics, both locally in New England (cf. *A Bridging of Faiths*, 1992) and globally in some fourteen countries around the world (cf. *Crossing the Gods*, forthcoming).

FRANK R. DEREGO, JR., is a graduate student in the sociology of religion at Purdue University, where his research has focused on the relationships between race, ethnicity and religion. He has an M.A. in sociology from Purdue and an M.A. in religious studies from the Catholic University of Louvain, Belgium. His doctoral research involves a social history of black leadership in the Roman Catholic Church.

CHERYL TOWNSEND GILKES is MacArthur Associate Professor of African American Studies and Sociology and Director of African American Studies at Colby College, as well as an associate minister at the Union Baptist Church in Cambridge, Massachusetts. Her articles on sociology of religion, African American women, W. E. B. Du Bois, and African American religious traditions have appeared in several journals and anthologies. In addition to her ongoing research on the Sanctified Church, she is currently at work on a book exploring the importance of the Bible in the formation of African American culture, titled *That Blessed Book: The Bible and The African American Cultural Imagination*.

BRADLEY R. HERTEL is Associate Professor of Sociology at Virginia Tech. He is co-editor of *Living Banaras* (with Cynthia A. Humes) and the author of numerous book chapters and articles in such journals as the *Journal for the Scientific Study of Religion, Review of Religious Research*, and *Social Forces*. His research focuses on the relationship between religion and social structure in India and the United States. His teaching interests include the sociology of religion, social stratification, minority group relations, and statistics and research methods.

DEAN HOGE is Professor of Sociology at the Catholic University of America and a graduate of Harvard Divinity School and Harvard Graduate School (Ph.D. in sociology). His research has been mainly on American religion. His books include *Vanishing Boundaries* (co-authored with Benton Johnson and Donald A. Luidens); *Money Matters: Personal Giving in American Churches* (co-authored with C. Zech, P. McNamara, and M. Donahue); *The Future of Catholic Leadership: Responses to the Priest Shortage*; and *Laity, American and Catholic*, (co-authored with W. D'Antonio, J. Davidson, and R. Wallace).

BENTON JOHNSON is Professor Emeritus of Sociology at the University of Oregon. He has devoted most of his research to the sociological study of U.S. religion. In recent years he has explored the reasons for the decline in old-line Protestant denominations, an exploration culminating in his collaboration, with Dean Hoge and Donald Luidens, on *Vanishing Boundaries*, a study of baby boomers raised as Presbyterians. He has been president of the Society for the Scientific Study of Religion, the Association for the Sociology of Religion, and the Religious Research Association, and has served as editor of the *Journal for the Scientific Study of Religion*.

DEBRA RENEE KAUFMAN is Professor of Sociology at Northeastern University and Matthews Distinguished Professor in recognition of her outstanding scholarly achievement, professional contribution, and creative classroom activity. Her book, *Rachel's Daughters* (1991), has been nominated for three awards. She is the author of numerous articles and chapters on women, work, family, and feminist methodology and theory; a reviewer for many gender journals; and a member of the editorial board of *Contemporary Jewry*. She is currently working on identity politics and concepts of the other and completing research on Jewish identity among 20- to 30-year-olds in the United States, England, and Israel.

GRAEME LANG is Associate Professor of Sociology at the City University of Hong Kong and the author (with Lars Ragvald) of *The Rise of a Refugee God: Hong Kong's Wong Tai Sin* (1993). He serves as program leader of the East Asian Studies undergraduate program at City University, and teaches courses on science, technology, and society to students in East Asian studies and in computer science. His current research includes a survey on the impact of deindustrialization on displaced Hong Kong industrial workers and a study of the revival of the cult of Wong Tai Sin in China.

RONALD LAWSON is Professor in the Urban Studies Department at Queens College of the City University of New York. He earned his Ph.D. in history and sociology from the University of Queensland, Australia. His research career can be divided into three segments: historical urban sociology in Australia, which culminated in *Brisbane in the 1890s* (1973, 1987) and several journal articles; the politics of the tenant-landlord relationship in New York (*The Tenant Movement in New York, 1904–1984* [1986], and many articles); and his current research on Seventh-day Adventism in fifty-five countries, from which many papers have been published and a book is being prepared.

EDWARD C. LEHMAN, JR. is Distinguished Professor Emeritus, State University of New York, Brockport, and president-elect of the Religious Research Association. He has devoted most of his research to the women-in-ministry movement in mainline Protestant churches and has authored several books and numerous articles on the subject, including studies in the United States, the United Kingdom, and Australia. He has served as president of the Association for the Sociology of Religion, executive officer of the Society for the Scientific Study of Religion, and editor of the *Review of Religious Research*.

DONALD A. LUIDENS is Professor of Sociology at Hope College, Holland, Michigan. He has centered his research on mainline Protestant denominations, principally the Reformed Church in America and the Presbyterian churches. Along with publishing numerous articles in scholarly and religious journals, he has recently co-edited two books on Dutch Reformed communities in the Netherlands and in diaspora, *Rethinking Secularization* and *Reformed Vitality*. He has been a principal researcher in three nationwide surveys of the RCA, each of which has been used to build denominational policy and direction. He currently serves on the board of directors of the Religious Research Association.

MANSOOR MOADDEL is Professor of Sociology at Eastern Michigan University. He is currently doing historical and comparative research on the determinants of ideological production in the Islamic world. This project is supported by grants from the National Science Foundation, the United States Institute of Peace, the United States Information Agency, the National Endowment for the Humanities, and Eastern Michigan University. He has served on the council of the Religion Section of the American Sociological Association and is the author of several journal articles and of *Class, Politics, and Ideology in the Iranian Revolution* (1993).

NANCY NASON-CLARK is Professor of Sociology at the University of New Brunswick, Canada. She engages in research on gender, violence, and religion, and is the author of *The Battered Wife: How Christians Confront Family Violence* (1997) and numerous journal articles and chapters in edited collections. She is president-elect of the Association for the Sociology of Religion, a member of the executive council of the Society for the Scientific Study of Religion, and former book review editor for *Sociology of Religion*. She coordinates the Religion and Violence Research Team of the Muriel McQueen Fergusson Centre for Family Violence Research.

SUSAN PALMER lives in Montreal, Quebec, where she teaches in the Religion Department of Dawson College and is an adjunct professor at Concordia University. She is the author of *Moon Sisters, Krishna Mothers, Rajneesh Lovers* (1994) and *AIDS as an Apocalyptic Metaphor in North America* (1997). She has also co-edited *Millennium Messiahs and Mayhem* with Thomas Robbins (1997) and *The Rajneesh Papers* with Arvind Sharma (1993) and has written numerous articles on the Raelian Movement and other new religious movements.

JERRY G. PANKHURST is Professor of Sociology at Wittenberg University. He specializes in the sociology of religion and political sociology applied to communist and post-communist societies. His publications include two volumes on Soviet society and articles on family, ideology, and various aspects of religion in Russia and the societies of East-Central Europe. Recent research examines the influence of religious culture on democratization in post-Soviet Russia. During 1997–1998 he was a visiting scholar at the Merson Center at Ohio State University and Senior Fellow at the Center for the Study of World Religions, Harvard University.

HELEN RALSTON is Professor Emerita of Sociology at Saint Mary's University in Halifax, Nova Scotia. She has focused her research (funded by grants from the Social Sciences and Humanities Research Council of Canada, the Shastri Indo-Canadian Institute, and Saint Mary's University) on religion in India and on the interconnections of race, ethnicity, class, gender, and state policies in South Asian immigrant women's lived experience, and has published two books and several articles dealing with these related topics. She has served as Canada's representative on the councils of the International Sociological Association and the International Society for the Sociology of Religion.

MARK J. ROZELL is Associate Director of the University of Pennsylvania Washington Semester Program. He is the author of five books and co-author (with Clyde Wilcox) of *Second Coming: The New Christian Right in Virginia Politics* (1996). He is also co-editor (with Wilcox) of the books *God at the Grass Roots: The Christian Right in the 1994 Elections* (1995) and *God at the Grass Roots, 1996* (1997). His numerous essays have appeared in leading political science journals and edited compendia.

DAVID A. SMILDE is a doctoral candidate in Sociology at the University of Chicago and a research associate at the Centro de Estudios de Desarrollo of the Universidad Central de Venezuela. His research on the conversion of Venezuelan men to pentecostalism has been supported by the Social Science Research Council and by a Fulbright-Hays Dissertation Abroad Fellowship. He is author of five articles on religion in Latin America, including "The Fundamental Unity of the Conservative and Revolutionary Tendencies in Venezuelan Evangelicalism: The Case of Conjugal Relations," *Religion* Vol. 27 No. 4 (October) 1997.

DAWID VENTER is a Lecturer in the Department of Anthropology and Sociology at the University of the Western Cape. He has focused his research on multi-racial and multi-ethnic congregations in South Africa. He has written four practical workbooks on analyzing religion in urban contexts and some academic articles and contributed to the first South African edition of David Popenoe's *Sociology*. He has served as a council member of the South African Sociological Association (SASA), is currently an assistant editor of the SASA journal as well as convener of the Working Group for the Social-Scientific Study of Religion. He is a co-founder of the Institute for Urban Ministry.

CLYDE WILCOX is Professor of Government, Georgetown University and the author of several books and articles on the Christian Right, including *Second Coming: The Christian Right in Virginia Politics* and *Onward Christian Soldiers: The Christian Right in American Politics*. His other research interests are gender politics, campaign finance, and science fiction and politics.

YONGHE YANG is a statistician/methodologist for the Gallup Organization, Rockville, Maryland, who has focused his attention on survey design and statistical modeling. He has participated in numerous research projects conducted by the Government and Education Division of the Gallup Organization. He is the co-author of "What American Culture War? A View from the Trenches as Opposed to the Command Posts and the Press Corps" in *Culture Wars in American Politics: Critical Reviews of a Popular Myth*, edited by Rhys H. Williams, 1997.

ISBN 0-275-96078-1

90000>

EAN

9 780275 960780

HARDCOVER BAR CODE

AM700-MN
59